AF743393

Ambiguity in EU Law

Ambiguity – an expression or utterance giving rise to at least two mutually exclusive interpretations – has been traditionally regarded as an ever-present, and therefore trivial, feature of EU law, alongside other forms of linguistic indeterminacy. At the same time, ambiguity has been condemned as a perilous defect in the legal text, since it is commonly assumed that the Court of Justice of the EU (CJEU) would necessarily exploit it to engage in judicial activism. In contrast, more recent theories present ambiguity as a means of promoting greater acceptability and coherence, while trusting the CJEU's willingness to exert judicial restraint for the benefit of judicial co-operation.

This groundbreaking work challenges some of the theoretical assumptions about ambiguity in EU law and puts forward a more accurate and complete theory about the CJEU's strategic use of ambiguity. Ambiguity is here transformed from an underestimated or misunderstood detail of undetermined significance to a desirable systemic feature of the EU legal order with concrete properties and impact. Ambiguity as the implicit basis of the CJEU's decision-making is shown to be strategically valuable for the implementation of the authority of EU law at some of the most pivotal moments in the evolution of the EU legal order. This interdisciplinary investigation presents in-depth linguistic and legal analysis of ambiguity found in the text of key provisions of EU Treaties and in the language of some of the CJEU's leading preliminary rulings in the area of fundamental rights, freedom of movement and EU citizenship. The book suggests a categorisation of examples, basic guidance about the type of case and situation where the phenomenon is likely to emerge as well as an assessment of the advantages and disadvantages of this unusual judicial technique.

The book will be a valuable resource for researchers and academics working in the areas of Law and Language, Public International Law, EU Law, and Multilingualism.

Dr. iur. Sofiya Kartalova is a Postdoctoral Researcher at the Department of Public Law at the Max Planck Institute for the Study of Crime, Security and Law, Freiburg im Breisgau, Germany.

Law, Language and Communication

This series encourages innovative and integrated perspectives within and across the boundaries of law, language and communication, with particular emphasis on issues of communication in specialized socio-legal and professional contexts. It seeks to bring together a range of diverse yet cumulative research traditions in order to identify and encourage interdisciplinary research.

The series welcomes proposals – both edited collections as well as single-authored monographs – emphasizing critical approaches to law, language and communication, identifying and discussing issues, proposing solutions to problems, offering analyses in areas such as legal construction, interpretation, translation and de-codification.

Series Editors

Anne Wagner is Professor of Legal Semiotics and Research Professor at Centre de Recherche Droits & Perspectives du Droit, équipe René Demogue, Lille University, France. She is the Editor-in-Chief of the International Journal for the Semiotics of Law (Springer) and President of the International Roundtables for the Semiotics of Law. She has been awarded the National Research Grant for her research career. Her main research interests include semiotics, verbal and non-verbal sign system analyses, language and law, legal culture and heritage, legal translation, legal terminology, and legal discourse studies.

Vijay K. Bhatia, formerly Professor of English, City University of Hong Kong, is now Adjunct Professor at Chinese University of Hong Kong, and Visiting Professor at the Hellenic American University, Athens (Greece). He is also the founding President of the Languages for Specific Purposes and Professional Communication Association for Asia-Pacific. His research interests include Critical Genre Analysis, academic and professional discourses in legal, business, newspaper, and promotional contexts; ESP and Professional Communication; simplification of legal and other public documents; intercultural and cross-disciplinary variations in professional genres.

Titles in the series

Law, Language and the Courtroom
Legal Linguistics and the Discourse of Judges
Edited by Stanisław Goźdź-Roszkowski & Gianluca Pontrandolfo

Ambiguity in EU Law
A Linguistic and Legal Analysis
Sofiya Kartalova

Fair Trial Rights and Multilingualism in Africa
Perspectives from Comparable Jurisdictions
Catherine S. Namakula

For more information about this series, please visit: www.routledge.com/Law-Language-and-Communication/book-series/LAWLANGCOMM

Ambiguity in EU Law

A Linguistic and Legal Analysis

Sofiya Kartalova

Routledge
Taylor & Francis Group
LONDON AND NEW YORK

First published 2023
by Routledge
4 Park Square, Milton Park, Abingdon, Oxon OX14 4RN

and by Routledge
605 Third Avenue, New York, NY 10158

Routledge is an imprint of the Taylor & Francis Group, an informa business

© 2023 Sofiya Kartalova

The right of Sofiya Kartalova to be identified as author of this work has been asserted in accordance with sections 77 and 78 of the Copyright, Designs and Patents Act 1988.

All rights reserved. No part of this book may be reprinted or reproduced or utilised in any form or by any electronic, mechanical, or other means, now known or hereafter invented, including photocopying and recording, or in any information storage or retrieval system, without permission in writing from the publishers.

This book is a revised version of a dissertation accepted by the Faculty of Law of the University of Tübingen in 2020. The library number is D21.

The author acknowledges the generous support provided by the Research Training Group 1808: "Ambiguity – Production and Perception" at the University of Tübingen, which is funded by the DFG (Deutsche Forschungsgemeinschaft) under project-number: 198647426.

Trademark notice: Product or corporate names may be trademarks or registered trademarks, and are used only for identification and explanation without intent to infringe.

British Library Cataloguing-in-Publication Data
A catalogue record for this book is available from the British Library

Library of Congress Cataloging-in-Publication Data
A catalog record has been requested for this book

ISBN: 978-1-032-27990-9 (hbk)
ISBN: 978-1-032-27991-6 (pbk)
ISBN: 978-1-003-29487-0 (ebk)

DOI: 10.4324/9781003294870

Typeset in Galliard
by Deanta Global Publishing Services, Chennai, India

To my parents

Contents

Acknowledgements

This book is a revised version of my dissertation "The Strategic Value of Ambiguity for the Authority of EU Law in the Dialogue between the Court of Justice of the European Union and the National Courts", which was accepted in 2020 by the Faculty of Law at the University of Tübingen (*Eberhard Karls Universität Tübingen*), Tübingen, Germany. I would like to sincerely thank my supervisor, Prof. Dr. Wolfgang Forster, for his steadfast support and helpful advice. I am also very grateful to my other two supervisors, Prof. Dr. Martin Nettesheim and Prof. Dr. Joachim Knape, as well as to Prof. Dr. Stephan Dusil, who presided the examination committee at the defence of my doctoral dissertation, for their insightful and useful comments.

I would like to acknowledge the generous support provided by the Research Training Group 1808: "Ambiguity – Production and Perception" (*Graduiertenkolleg 1808: "Ambiguität – Produktion und Rezeption"*) at the University of Tübingen (*Eberhard Karls Universität Tübingen*), which is funded by the DFG (*Deutsche Forschungsgemeinschaft*) under project-number: 198647426. As a Research Assistant (*Wissenschaftliche Mitarbeiterin*) at Research Training Group 1808: "Ambiguity – Production and Perception", I explored the linguistic phenomenon of ambiguity alongside researchers of a wide range of academic backgrounds (Linguistics, Literary Criticism, Rhetoric, Law, Theology, Psychology, Media Studies, and Philosophy/Ethics) and levels of seniority (PhD students, PostDocs, and Professors). I thank them all for our regular stimulating discussions and enjoyable and friendly collaboration. More specifically, I would like to express my gratitude to Prof. Dr. Matthias Bauer, Prof. Dr. Angelika Zirker, and Inken Armbrust for the great kindness, unwavering support, and faith in my abilities as a researcher that they have shown me time after time.

I would also like to thank Professor Anne Lise Kjær, Prof. Dr. Ralf Poscher, Prof. Dr. Isolde Burr-Haase, Dr. Gregory Scontras, Professor Shai Dothan and Professor Jan Komárek for their expert advice and helpful comments on my research at various stages of my doctoral studies. I am also grateful to iCourts – the Danish National Research Foundation's Centre of Excellence for International Courts at the University of Copenhagen, for giving me the excellent opportunity to participate in their Visiting programme in February and March 2018 and benefit from the welcoming attitude and first-rate expertise of the researchers there.

Similarly, I am very grateful to Routledge and the series editors of "Law, Language and Communication" – Professor Anne Wagner and Professor Vijay Kumar Bhatia – for publishing my book, which is an invaluable opportunity to share my ideas with a larger audience. I would also like to thank Alison Kirk, Anna Gallagher, and Katie Stokes for their professional, timely, and informative response to all of my questions during the editorial and production process, as well as the two anonymous reviewers whose thoughtful comments helped me improve my work. I revised my dissertation and prepared this book for publication while working as a Researcher, and later as a Postdoctoral Researcher (Postdoc), at the Department of Public Law at the Max Planck Institute for the Study of Crime, Security and Law in Freiburg im Breisgau, Germany. I would like to thank Prof. Dr. Ralf Poscher for his helpful guidance and support as well as my colleagues there for their friendship and kindness.

Finally, on a personal note, I would like to thank my parents, Svetlan Kartalov and Regina Kartalova, for the unconditional love, care, and support they have always given me. I dedicate this book to them, as a sign of my gratitude for the inspiration and strength I have drawn from their own lifelong appreciation and respect for knowledge and the power of the written word.

Part 1

In Search of the Strategic Value of Ambiguity for the Authority of EU Law

1 Introduction

In M.C. Escher's well-known woodcut "Sky and Water I" (1938),[1] the impossible is perfectly poised on the edge between two worlds. The question of who has intruded into whose space lingers in the mind of the observer. Could it be that the birds are swimming in the water? Or is it, perhaps, that the fish are flying in the sky? Forever torn between two equally plausible versions of reality, the observer remains in thrall of *ambiguity*.

Ambiguity impacts the participants in verbal or written communication in a similar way. In linguistic terms, ambiguity evokes in one's mind "uncertainty or doubtfulness of the meaning of language".[2] An expression is considered ambiguous if it has two or more distinct interpretations whose corresponding truth conditions cannot be valid at the same time.[3] This means that the available readings of a sample of ambiguous language cannot be true simultaneously. This singular property sets ambiguity apart from other forms of linguistic indeterminacy, such as vagueness or generality. A lack of familiarity with these basic properties of ambiguity is a blind spot that may compromise the accuracy and exhaustiveness of any analysis of the legal text.

Ambiguity comes in many forms, such as lexical ambiguity, referential ambiguity, syntactic ambiguity, and polysemy, with the latter two being the most prominent variations of ambiguity in legal texts, especially when it comes to *hard cases*.[4] The outcome of a hard case has to be determined on the basis of principle, since "no settled rule dictates a decision either way".[5]

A polysemous expression in the law entails "two (or more) related senses of one lexical meaning".[6] For example, ambiguity in the form of polysemy could

1 On ambiguity in Escher's prints and, more specifically, on the principle of equivalence in "Sky and Water I": Teuber 1974: 94–95.

2 Lanius 2019: 123.

3 Gillon 1990a: 394; Winkler citing Wasow, Perfors, & Beaver; and Kennedy 2015: 1. Kennedy (2011: 508) defines ambiguity as follows: "[a kind of uncertainty] that manifests itself as a variation in truth conditions: one and the same utterance token can be judged true of one situation and false of another, or the other way around, depending on how it is interpreted".

4 Lanius 2019: 123, 129.

5 Dworkin 1975: 1060.

6 Lanius 2019: 126.

DOI: 10.4324/9781003294870-2

be illustrated by focusing on the dictionary definitions of the noun "a circle".[7] If one were to say, "We are not allowed into that circle", one might be referring to being banned from stepping into a circle drawn on the pavement with chalk as part of some children's game at the playground, or being ineligible to secure entry into the circle of members of a particularly exclusive and prestigious club. In the former case, "a circle" would be understood as "a shape", whereas in the latter it would be defined as "a group". The samples of polysemy (as a form of ambiguity) presented in this book are largely based on multilingual analysis of legal terminology.

Syntactic ambiguity refers to "the relationship between the words or word groups in a sentence".[8] To illustrate syntactic (or phrasal) ambiguity, one might refer to the sentence "Flying planes can be dangerous".[9] This utterance could be interpreted as "The act of flying planes can be dangerous", if "flying" is allocated the function of a verb. Conversely, it could be read as "Planes that fly can be dangerous", if "flying" is given the role of an adjective. The samples of syntactic ambiguity this book will analyse are based on the syntactic structure of utterances in the legal text in English.

At this stage, it becomes evident that the linguistic phenomenon at hand is in possession of a unique property – ambiguity guarantees the coexistence of a set number of interpretations (at least two) that are clear, concrete, knowable, and mutually exclusive. Thus, ambiguity is to be distinguished from similar categories, such as vagueness and generality.

Ambiguity in the legal text may accompany generality, or even be a consequence thereof, but it is by no means its equivalent. In a legal context, generality is responsible for the regulation of a number of situations under one generalised rule.[10] In other words, connotation of a general expression is considered "a genus of more than one species".[11] The noun "brother" in the sentence "My brother lives in the house next door" could be interpreted as indeterminate with respect to age (an older or a younger brother?), with its condition of application being predicated on familial relationships.[12] However, these possible variations in meaning do not amount to ambiguity, since the truth or falsity of the statement remains unaffected in each case.[13]

To illustrate the distinction between vagueness and ambiguity, let us consider the sentence "What is so funny about that?". The speaker may be questioning the reason why their partner in conversation laughed (if "funny" is meant in the sense

7 Similarly, Gillon (1990a: 394) illustrates ambiguity with the example of "the word 'pike': it can mean a kind of fish, or it can mean a kind of weapon".
8 Dunahoo citing Perrin 1970: 142.
9 Solan citing Chomsky 1993: 64.
10 Poscher 2012: 130.
11 Gillon 1990a: 394.
12 This example is based on Kennedy's example sentence "Julian's brother is heavy", on the distinction between ambiguity and vagueness (Kennedy 2011: 507–508).
13 Kennedy 2011: 508.

of "humorous, hilarious") at a serious remark or looked puzzled (if "funny" is meant in the sense of "bizarre, strange") at a painting from the speaker's avant-garde art collection.[14] Those are two concrete situations that are equally plausible, but mutually exclusive, which makes this an example of ambiguity.

In contrast, if one were to say, "The punchline to that joke was funnier than I expected", it is clear that "funny" is meant in the sense of humorous, which is implied in the context of a joke, and that the speaker expected the joke to be funny to begin with, which is why the comparative form of the adjective "funny" is used. Therefore, there is no ambiguity there.[15] Vagueness is concerned with the question of precisely *how funny*, on the spectrum from a polite chuckle to a delighted giggle to uproarious laughter, the speaker expected the punchline to the joke to be in the first place. To add an extra layer of complexity to the deliberation on vagueness, we also do not know *how much funnier* (on the same spectrum) the punchline ended up being compared to the speaker's initial expectation. This is how vagueness and ambiguity differ from each other. While vagueness is responsible for an "infinite number" of readings that "flow over into each other imperceptibly", ambiguity ensures that there is a demonstrable, clear-cut difference in the ways an expression could be interpreted.[16] It would then be fair to say that "[a]mbiguity ... is about multiple meanings; vagueness is about meaning in borderline cases".[17]

The EU legal order provides fertile ground for ambiguity to take root and thrive, given the plurality of legal traditions and languages coexisting within its borders. As a result, ambiguity is often perceived as inherent to EU law. This popular, yet most likely erroneous, assumption is the natural consequence of the aforementioned difficulty in distinguishing ambiguity from other forms of linguistic indeterminacy as well as the inability to envision in concrete terms what insight into the workings of the EU legal order ambiguity might be able to offer. To conclusively prove or disprove this claim, however, one must adduce reliable empirical evidence spanning the entirety of EU law, which would be a monumental task besides the point of this book. Nevertheless, even if one were to concede that EU law is rife with ambiguity, not every sample of ambiguity has strategic value for the implementation of EU law.

In fact, the discovery of such ambiguity, whether it would be situated in the EU legislative text or on the pages of the rulings of the Court of Justice of the European Union (CJEU), is a rare occurrence. This book will demonstrate that the strategic implications of a sample of ambiguity central to the ultimate resolution of a legal problem are highly revealing of the CJEU's priorities

14 This example is based on Kennedy's example sentence "Sterling's cousin is funny", on the distinction between ambiguity and vagueness (Kennedy 2011: 507–509).

15 There is no ambiguity there, unless the speaker meant the remark sarcastically, meaning that their expectation was that it was not going to be funny at all. However, this is a context-dependent assessment, which is a matter for pragmatics, and not semantics.

16 Deemter 2010: 113.

17 Poscher 2012: 129.

and motivations in decision-making as well as of the nature of the relationship between adjudicator and legislator. The examples provided in this book focus on some of the leading preliminary rulings of the CJEU in the area of freedom of movement, fundamental rights, and EU citizenship. Each case study, presented in a separate chapter in this book, deals with the *real*, and not hypothetical, impact of ambiguity on the CJEU's decision-making, which is only *implicitly* evident in the Court's reasoning. On the basis of this selection, ambiguity is shown to have laid the foundation of the Court's reasoning in some of the pivotal moments of the constitutional evolution of the EU legal order by facilitating the effective implementation of the authority of EU law.

The 'authority of EU law' is presently a concept in need of a clear and widely accepted definition in EU constitutional law, although it has been discussed as a matter of exception in a few contributions.[18] Joseph H.H. Weiler highlighted the crucial role that acceptability and compliance play in this respect: "Faithful application by domestic courts of [CJEU] rulings is the best guarantee for their authority within the EU. Take that away and that authority is called into question with a cascading and contagious effect on other branches of government".[19] Such non-compliance would also have a disastrous effect on the CJEU itself.[20] It is primarily in the dialogue between the CJEU and the national courts, which unfolds through the preliminary ruling procedure under Article 267 TFEU, that the authority of EU law is implemented in practice.[21] In this sense, the national courts and the CJEU could be seen as "the guardians of the EU legal order".[22]

For the purposes of this book, the meaning of 'the authority of EU law' could be plainly summarised as follows: *a constitutional problem of fundamental significance that pertains to the delimitation of competences of the CJEU with respect to the regulating and shaping of the national legal orders.* In this sense, the 'authority of EU law' embodies the idea, which is central to the problem of the primacy of EU law, that "the law of the European Union represents an independent legal order with an autonomous legislative power as a Union".[23] Thus, it is fair to say that "EU law originates from itself, according to its own particular fundamental rules".[24]

18 Chalmers, Davies, & Monti 2010; Walker 2005: 591–594.

19 Weiler 2019: 3. Weiler (2019: 3) also admitted that 'the authority of EU law' is "hopelessly underspecified", in that there are "no respectable social science metrics to gauge such and one is reduced to impressions, institutions and sporadic markers".

20 Weiler 2019: 3.

21 Lenaerts 2019: 21–25, 30.

22 Lenaerts 2019: 22.

23 Nettesheim 2021: 155. The original excerpt in German reads: "Entscheidend für eine „europäisch" inspirierte Lösung der Vorrangfrage ist die Anerkennung des Grundgedankens, dass das Europäische Unionsrecht eine **eigenständige Rechtsordnung mit einer autonomen Unionsgewalt** darstellt". (Translation into English done by the author of this book.)

24 Nettesheim 2021: 155. The original excerpt in German reads: „Das Unionrecht entsteht aus sich selbst heraus gemäß seiner besonderen Grundregeln". (Translation into English done by the author of this book.).

If the CJEU's ultimate goal is to ensure the implementation of the authority of EU law, how is the Court likely to strategically use ambiguity for the fulfilment of this goal? Will the CJEU invariably exploit ambiguity in the EU Treaty text to expand EU competences, risking accusations of judicial activism, as most suspect? Or will the Court exercise judicial restraint in its treatment of ambiguity, in the interest of ensuring its continued co-operation with the national courts and promoting greater acceptability and coherence, as some hope? When, how, and to what concrete strategic end will the CJEU produce ambiguity in its own preliminary rulings? It is precisely in this context that the some of the inaccuracies in our traditional understanding of ambiguity in EU law will be corrected on the basis of the provided examples, and a more accurate and complete theory of the strategic value of ambiguity for the authority of EU law will be articulated.

The primary aim of this book is to highlight the significance of ambiguity-based reasoning as a rare and unusual technique in the arsenal of the CJEU with its own concrete characteristics, which has a profound impact on its decision-making in some of its leading preliminary rulings. A selection of case studies will demonstrate how – by means of strategically producing or strategically resolving ambiguity – the CJEU ensures the effective implementation of the authority of EU law by overcoming challenges of utmost constitutional importance. The results of this investigation will present the reader with a workable analytical and methodological framework to examine the phenomenon of ambiguity in this context, which features a basic typology of examples, guidelines as to the type of case and situation where the phenomenon is likely to occur, as well as an overview of its advantages and disadvantages.

2 Ambiguity in Legal Texts

There is a common assumption that ambiguity is a defect in the legal text in need of eradication by means of correction or amendment of the legal document or, where these options are not available, by means of interpretation.[1] In the context of legal drafting, ambiguity has been listed as one of "three major curable diseases [that] infect language", the other two being vagueness and generality.[2]

This negative view of ambiguity is no surprise, given that Paul Grice's classic maxim "Avoid ambiguity" proved to be the norm in linguistics. According to Grice, ambiguity is typically described as an obstacle in the way of efficient communication, due to the need to be disambiguated and its capacity to generate misunderstandings.[3] Thomas Wasow stressed the beneficial contribution of ambiguity by retorting: "Ambiguity avoidance is overrated".[4]

In the linguistic literature, there are two main opposing views on the matter, expressed by Chomsky and Piantadosi, Tily, and Gibson.[5] Noam Chomsky understands ambiguity as having an adverse effect on the ease with which actors communicate.[6] Piantadosi et al. expressly oppose Chomsky's well-established claim with their recent assertion that:

> ambiguity is in fact a desirable property of communication systems, precisely because it allows for a communication system which is "short and simple." We argue for two beneficial properties of ambiguity: first, where context is informative about meaning, unambiguous language is partly redundant with the context and therefore inefficient; and second, ambiguity allows the re-use of words and sounds which are more easily produced or understood.[7]

Piantadosi et al. ultimately provide "strong evidence for the view that ambiguity exists for reasons of communicative efficiency" within the system.[8] Wasow

1 Kulick 2016: 266.
2 Dunahoo 1970: 139.
3 Wasow citing Grice 2015: 29–30.
4 Wasow 2015: 29.
5 Winkler 2015: 3.
6 Winkler citing Chomsky 2015: 3.
7 Piantadosi, Tily & Gibson 2012: 281.
8 Piantadosi, Tily & Gibson 2012: 288.

DOI: 10.4324/9781003294870-3

elaborates on this position by explaining that ambiguous language could lead to greater efficiency within the system, thanks to the ability of one participant in communication to draw inference about the intended meaning of another participant in communication on the basis of "incomplete information".[9]

The contrasting views, described above, drew the battle lines in the debate on the impact of ambiguity on communication, along the issue of whether ambiguity has a detrimental or beneficial effect on a communicative system. The same opposition has been transferred to the realm of legal drafting and interpretation.

For instance, Andreas Kulick provides an analytical framework and examples of UN Security Council Resolutions on the strategic use of ambiguity[10] in international law. Kulick claims that ambiguity (and vagueness) in international law could have various aspects: a problem, a solution, an opportunity, or a challenge.[11] If ambiguity is seen as a problem (as is most commonly the case), the interpreter (e.g. an adjudicator, a government official, or a counsel) seeks to resolve it for the purposes of giving advice or reaching a decision.[12] If treated as a solution, ambiguity could be used to facilitate a negotiations breakthrough between the contracting parties to an international treaty or between the drafters of a resolution for an international organisation.[13] Ambiguity could be viewed as an opportunity in cases where it opens up a wide range of possibilities of interpretation and thus allows the judge to engage in law-making and policy-making.[14] Thus, ambiguity fulfils the constructive function of *flexibility*.[15] Finally, the elusive quality that enables ambiguity to constantly shift between a problem and an opportunity defines ambiguity as a challenge.[16]

The main aim of this book is to highlight the idea of ambiguity in EU law as an *opportunity* for strategic judicial behaviour by the CJEU. For this purpose, the Court will be shown to strategically produce or strategically resolve ambiguity. In this sense, ambiguity will be shown to have a positive impact on the communicative system (the EU legal order).

9 Wasow 2015: 45.
10 Kulick (2016: 265) distinguishes between the different manifestations of ambiguity (and vagueness): between strategic and non-strategic use and between its production and perception (resolution).
11 Kulick 2016: 260–261.
12 Kulick 2016: 273.
13 Kulick 2016: 274.
14 Kulick 2016: 274.
15 Kulick 2016: 272–273, 274. Kulick (2016: 272) claims ambiguity also fulfils the function of flexibility in cases where the legislator produces ambiguity to avoid taking a stance on important issues at the drafting stage and instead implicitly delegates that to the adjudicator. This idea also falls in line with the idea of ambiguity as a solution (Kulick 2016: 274). For example, see the EU legislator's approach to drafting Article 53 CFREU in the *Melloni* Case Study in this book.
16 Kulick 2016: 275.

Ambiguity and Legal Interpretation in a Pragmatic Context

For the present purposes, a discussion on ambiguity and communication would be incomplete without attention being paid to the issue of how to construe the meaning of a legal text. As it is known, legal meaning of a given provision could be given a literal or purposive interpretation.[17] Quite apart from the remit of legal meaning,[18] however, the *communicative* meaning of a legal text encapsulates the following notion: "what an appropriate hearer would most reasonably take a speaker to be trying to convey in employing a given verbal vehicle in the given communicative-context".[19] Communicative meaning is realised in the realm of pragmatics.

Pragmatics is commonly referred to as "meaning in use" and "meaning in context".[20] The participants in the communication process move through levels of meaning by attaching a particular sense to a word, a sentence or a phrase: from *abstract meaning* ("what a word, phrase, sentence, etc. could mean [for example, the dictionary meanings of words or phrases]") to *contextual meaning* ("the sense in which the speaker/writer is using the word in context").[21] Therefore, pragmatics could also be understood as:

> *meaning in interaction*. This reflects the view that meaning is not something which is inherent in the words alone, nor is it produced by the speaker alone, nor by the hearer alone. Making meaning is a dynamic process, involving the negotiation of meaning between speaker and hearer, the context of utterance (physical, social and linguistic) and the meaning potential of an utterance.[22]

In linguistics, pragmatics is usually differentiated from *semantics*, since semantics is preoccupied with meaning as encoded in the formal elements of language such as words or syntax, whereas pragmatics is interested in the manner in which these forms full of meaning are employed in certain contexts to give expression through communication of a range of thoughts and concepts.[23] Although it still remains unclear where the boundary between the semantic meaning of a legal rule ("what is said") and its pragmatic interpretation in ("what is implied") the adjudicative process lies, the contribution of pragmatics in the context of legal interpretation must not be underestimated.[24]

The idea of pragmatics ties in neatly with one of the central discussions in legal interpretation on "whether and how much meaning is 'in the text'".[25] The

17 Slocum 2017: 119.
18 Slocum 2017: 119.
19 Slocum 2017: 120.
20 Thomas 2014: 1–2.
21 Thomas 2014: 2, 5.
22 Thomas 2014: 22.
23 Carston 2013: 9.
24 Smolka & Pirker 2016: 14.
25 Stein 2017: 338.

"pragmatic turn" in law has been typically sidelined, perhaps because it is perceived as a departure from the established mode of thinking of the law as a permanent record of unchangeable meaning and possibly because it opens the door to unpredictable factors that might have a destabilising effect on the law.[26] If the pragmatic outlook on the law is taken to its extreme, it could be argued that:

> the law has no real a priori existence independent of the history of realization, and that it does not lie dormant in some "text," and that, consequently, it is constituted, or brought into existence, only in the moment of active performance in any act of adjudication in the performance of an act of language.[27]

At the same time, the normative implications of legal interpretation, informed by the pragmatic context of a legal rule, cannot be ignored. This is even more so, when indeterminacy, and more specifically *ambiguity*, enters the picture. This is why, if the pragmatic perspective of the law is to be adopted, the starting point for assessing whether an expression is ambiguous or not would have to change. From the viewpoint of formal semantics, Paraphrase 1 of any given ambiguity *cannot be true at the same time* as Paraphrase 2.[28] The logic of true-or-false seems out of place when assessing the "truth value" of the interpretation of a legal rule, which means that it would be more appropriate to conduct this assessment on the basis of "pragmatically, i.e. extralinguistically, determined content".[29] Thus, each paraphrase yields both linguistic and communicative meaning. The same idea is echoed in Miguel Poires Maduro's maxim: "The textual ambiguity of EU law is also a function of a deeper normative ambiguity".[30] Such an approach demands a full correspondence between the linguistic and normative aspects of a relevant sample of ambiguity in the legal text, with the latter features being pragmatically realised in the communicative context of the EU legal order.

In one of the very few works on legal interpretation and pragmatics in the context of international law, Jennifer Smolka and Benedikt Pirker recommend a shift towards "an understanding of interpretation in international law as language use" on the basis of "cognitive economy [which] ensures that language is never fully explicit, and that meaning must be inferred".[31] Although such an approach to legal interpretation is aimed at ensuring greater transparency and empirical plausibility of legal interpretation in international law as well as an improved understanding of the receiver's experience in the communication process, it admittedly has its limits.[32] This analytical method would be of little assistance when it comes to moral, social, or political assessment as well as the evaluation

26 Stein 2017: 341.
27 Stein citing Jäger 2017: 343.
28 Winkler citing Kennedy 2015: 1.
29 Stein 2017: 346.
30 Maduro 2007: 143.
31 Smolka & Pirker 2016: 28.
32 Smolka & Pirker 2016: 29–30.

of arguments in the context of the authority and power issues associated with legal interpretation.[33] A more succinct iteration of the same idea goes as follows: "pragmatics cannot do everything; it cannot take the final interpretive decision itself, as it is fundamentally descriptive and not normative".[34]

Indeed, pragmatics does not *in and of itself* determine the interpretative decision, but it certainly cannot be said that a judge's decision-making process is insulated in a vacuum, away from the pragmatic context that surrounds it. On the contrary, the concrete pragmatic context of the legal system shapes the circumstances in which this decision is taken, as well as our understanding of its meaning. As operating within the *sui generis* organisation of the EU, the pragmatic context of the CJEU's decision-making is bound to be defined by the EU legal system's unique structural characteristics and other constitutional peculiarities, which results in a singular arrangement of legal rules, concepts, principles, and doctrines.

Ambiguity and Strategic Behaviour

The Perspective of the Legislator

Due to its capacity for yielding distinct, contrasting, and mutually exclusive interpretations, ambiguity in the legal text creates an opening for strategic behaviour, to be exhibited by the legislator during the drafting process and/or by the adjudicator at the interpretation stage. In this context, ambiguity follows the general logic of a broader phenomenon under which it is subsumed – 'strategic indeterminacy in the law'.[35] In such a scenario, the legislator or the adjudicator is called upon to act in a situation in need of legal resolution which is made unusually challenging due to a clash of interests of beliefs (hard cases).[36] The strategic use of ambiguity is typically a response to the necessity to strike a delicate balance between competing principles or values of the legal system in question, without interference with key constitutional tenets.[37] Ambiguity in this sense can be strategically used as a cost-effective solution that infuses the law with flexibility, which in practice could mean that the legislator or adjudicator could delegate or defer the task of decision-making.[38]

Perhaps the most relevant form of ambiguity for the legislator, especially in the context of international law, is *constructive ambiguity*. This phenomenon could be succinctly defined as follows: "Constructive ambiguity is the deliberate use of ambiguous language in order to achieve agreement during the negotiation of a legal text".[39] In international law, constructive ambiguity is particularly

33 Smolka & Pirker citing Venzke 2016: 29.
34 Smolka & Pirker 2016: 36.
35 Lanius 2019.
36 Lanius 2019: 284.
37 Lanius 2019: 284.
38 Lanius 2019: 284; Kulick 2016: 272–274.
39 Byers 2021: 93; Kulick (2016: 283) puts forwards a similar definition.

well-suited to use in constitutional treaties, since it affords the necessary flexibility to accommodate for their application in the long run with respect to a great variety of issues (which were often unforeseeable at the time of drafting).[40] Constructive ambiguity leads to diverging interpretations when the official (equally authoritative) language versions of the same UN Security Council resolution are compared.[41] Different readings of constructive ambiguity in the same resolution could also lead to competing accounts of the factual situation or to contrasting interpretative approaches.[42] In this sense, the strategic implementation of constructive ambiguity in international law closely resembles that of ambiguity in EU law.

In international law, constructive ambiguity has proven to be particularly useful when it comes to dealing with high-stakes scenarios. The strategic benefits of constructive ambiguity include the prevention or postponement of armed conflict, reconciliation in the name of pursuing a common goal, or building support or providing justification for a certain decision or course of action.[43] Where there is constructive ambiguity employed strategically, the states are free to take action without the risk of causing damage to their status or influence, but still within the limits of both legal rules and the reactions of other states.[44] In other words, constructive ambiguity is particularly beneficial to the international legal system, since it demands that states "agree to disagree" on the basis of exchanging legal arguments, and not be tempted to show wilful disregard of international law.[45]

The Perspective of the Adjudicator

Ambiguity is an extremely intriguing subject of study when situated in the legislative text, since the adjudicator has to strategically exercise their discretion to make a judicial choice of interpretation, thereby resolving ambiguity. It might also be the case that the adjudicator may choose to strategically produce ambiguity on the pages of their ruling by formulating legal principles, inventing terminology, constructing arguments, or restating the law in their own words. These creative choices will expose the actual circumstances and priorities informing the judge's decision-making and will be indicative of the nature of the relationship between the judiciary and the legislator.

Depending on whether the court chooses to openly acknowledge ambiguity as the foundation of its decision-making, it may strategically engage with ambiguity in an explicit or implicit way. To illustrate the former possibility, let us consider Lawrence M. Solan's study on how ambiguity-based analysis may be employed strategically in judicial reasoning to achieve a particular end. By examining the principles applicable to the interpretation of ambiguity in criminal

40 Kulick 2016: 284.
41 Byers 2021: 99.
42 Byers 2021: 100–101.
43 Byers 2021: 108–110.
44 Byers 2021: 113.
45 Byers 2021: 114.

statutes, contractual clauses, and insurance policies in the jurisprudence of US courts, Solan established that:

> judges regularly take advantage of these interpretative principles to justify their decisions, even when the application of them is highly suspect from a linguistic perspective. Judges try to do justice, but at times feel constrained to play games with language in order to justify the justice they do, which undermines the very legitimacy for which they strive.[46]

In contrast, the samples of ambiguity presented in this book involve no explicit reference to ambiguity in the legislative text or in the language of the court's rulings. Nevertheless, the legal and linguistic analysis of a sample of ambiguity will show that there is a strong possibility that the ambiguity found there is at the heart of the court's reasoning.

As with Solan's examples, the crux of the matter with the implicit strategic use of ambiguity lies with legitimacy. When a court is producing ambiguity, it goes without saying that the adjudicator would rather keep its methods covert, in order to uphold the illusion of legitimacy. However, consider the following with respect to the strategic resolution of ambiguity: if a court's reasoning is indeed based on ambiguity in the legislative text, would it not make more sense for the court to make its strategic resolution of ambiguity explicitly known, in order to quell any doubts as to its reasoning? After all, what better endorsement for the legitimacy of its preferred interpretation could a court hope for than the support of the legislative text itself?

Actually, a court has a number of reasons to steer clear of this seemingly neat and convenient solution. Firstly, this would be a complex and time-consuming venture, especially if the legislative or adjudicative process takes place in a multilingual environment. The court will also have to come up with a feasible and universally applicable methodology for analysing samples of ambiguity, which demands expertise in linguistics. The end result will probably be highly contestable and unpredictable. Secondly, to expressly acknowledge the presence of ambiguity in the legislative text would be tantamount to openly questioning the effectiveness of the legislator in drafting that provision. Finally, since ambiguity entails the linguistic and legal equivalence of (at least) two contrasting interpretations, a court's ultimate preference for one over the other could be easily challenged. Therefore, an explicit acknowledgement of the connection between the court's reasoning and ambiguity may be more trouble than it is worth.

Nevertheless, the CJEU has sometimes *explicitly* acknowledged that one or more language versions of an EU legislative act contain ambiguous or vague wording. Mattias Derlén[47] provides several pertinent examples. In the *EMU Tabac*

46 Solan 1993: 92.

47 Derlén 2009: 56–57. The relevant examples include: *EMU Tabac* (Case C-296/95), *Paterson* (Case 90/83).

case, ambiguity in all language versions but two was deemed inconsequential by the Court, since the context and purpose of the provision were clear.[48] In the *Paterson* case, what seems to be syntactic ambiguity, which appears in all language versions but one, was disregarded, as the Dutch language version was sufficiently clear to "exclude uncertainty".[49]

It must be noted that, in both of these examples, the issue of ambiguity was brought to the Court's attention as a key argument in the legal dispute.[50] For this reason, the CJEU had to address this issue to adjudicate effectively. Furthermore, these instances are simply part of the normal course of legal interpretation in a multilingual environment. As such, they do not amount to strategic behaviour by the Court aimed at the implementation of the authority of EU law on a systemic scale. Unlike with the Case Studies in this book, there the Court is not interested in resolving the ambiguity for any strategic purposes or formulating a legal argument with constitutional implications, based on the competing interpretations of ambiguity. Rather, the CJEU is more concerned with the issue of reconciling the different language versions in a coherent manner that falls in line with the purpose and context of the provision.[51]

The examples in this book show that the *implicit* strategic use of ambiguity in a court's reasoning could be useful behind the scenes as a source of inspiration, an intuition as to the direction in which to guide the analysis. It is a template and a starting point for constructing a strategically advantageous interpretation that is logical, cohesive, and faithful to the spirit of the legislative text. In this sense, an interpretation originating from ambiguity carries the spark of authenticity due to a perceived resemblance to the wording of the legal text and the legislator's intent. This might contribute towards a sense of familiarity and rightness associated with the outcome that a free-standing interpretation conjured up solely by the court would otherwise lack. Whether this translates into the advantage of longevity, despite challenges by subsequent case-law, remains to be seen by the end of this book.

48 *EMU Tabac*, Case C-296/95: paragraph 40. The CJEU further claimed that "the existence of possible ambiguity in a provision can only be established by reference to the context of that provision" (*EMU Tabac*, Case C-296/95: paragraph 39). See also Derlén 2009: 57.

49 *Paterson*, Case 90/83: paragraphs 10–11. See also Derlén 2009: 56–57. The CJEU does not explicitly refer to ambiguity but gives a description of the linguistic discrepancy between the language versions that fits the profile of syntactic ambiguity.

50 In the *EMU Tabac* preliminary ruling, the argument was raised by the applicants in the main proceedings (*EMU Tabac*, Case C-296/95: paragraph 38). In the *Paterson* preliminary ruling, and the preliminary reference was made by a British national court and the argument was brought up in the observations of the United Kingdom submitted to the CJEU (*Paterson*, Case 90/83: paragraph 10).

51 When faced with linguistic discrepancies between different language versions of the same legal rule, the CJEU was primarily concerned with upholding the equality between language versions and the uniform interpretation of EU law, while taking into account the context and purpose of the provision (*Cricket St. Thomas*, Case C-372/88, paragraph 19). See also: Derlén 2009: 57.

Finally, one might question the legal weight of an adjudicative decision taken under such precarious circumstances:

> According to the common assumption, the indeterminacy of the law entails that a decision made under conditions of legal indeterminacy cannot be a legal decision … If legal materials and legal methods do not determine the decision made in a given case … a decision must be made with the help of other, non-legal criteria. Adjudication in cases where the law is indeterminate is no longer considered a legal decision, but as the exercise of some kind of political, moral, economic or otherwise non-legal discretion.[52]

In response, Ralf Poscher argues that the inclusion of political argumentation into the legal analytical process would interfere with the autonomy of the law and generate internal inconsistency with respect to the legal rule created as a result.[53] Therefore, adjudication on scenarios involving indeterminacy remains in the legal domain, even in hard cases where the answer is not immediately apparent.[54]

52 Poscher 2017: 308–309.
53 Poscher 2017: 315–316.
54 Poscher 2017: 314.

3 Ambiguity in EU Law

The EU legal order constitutes an environment particularly conducive to the emergence of ambiguity. The language of EU law is notoriously abstract, convoluted, and extremely rich in linguistic indeterminacy, lending itself to a wide spectrum of interpretations. This inherent characteristic is further exacerbated by the plurality of legal traditions and multilingualism in the EU legal order as well as by the proclivity for teleological and meta-teleological interpretation consistently exhibited by the Court of Justice of the European Union (CJEU). The language used in the drafting of the EU Treaties and the CJEU's rulings certainly contributes to this impression. Thus, inter-lingual indeterminacy, which combines ambiguity, vagueness, and generality, is inherent to adjudication in the EU legal order.[1] Under these circumstances, it is no wonder that ambiguity, which seems to be traditionally treated as just one of many forms of linguistic indeterminacy, came to be widely regarded as an ever-present, and therefore trivial, feature of EU law.

Indeed, the subject of linguistic indeterminacy in EU law has been broadly discussed before in this context. For example, Trevor C. Hartley argues that uncertainty could be viewed as intrinsic to EU legislation, even more so than to legislative acts produced by a national legal system.[2] Hartley further identified five forms of uncertainty in EU law,[3] which all fall under the category of "unnecessary uncertainty": "uncertainty that is not the inevitable consequence of the objective of the legal rule".[4] Only one of these forms is directly relevant to the current

1 Paunio & Lindroos-Hovinheimo 2010: 396–397. Paunio & Lindroos-Hovinheimo are citing Cao in using the concepts of inter-lingual indeterminacy and intra-lingual indeterminacy. More information on Cao's intra- and inter-lingual uncertainty (and more specifically, inter-lingual ambiguity) will be provided in the next chapter of Part 1 (3. A Framework for Analysis). Paunio & Lindroos-Hovinheimo explain that inter-lingual indeterminacy is additional to the intra-lingual indeterminacy that can be found in a legal text written in a single language.
2 Hartley 1996. Hartley uses the English legal system as a basis for this comparison.
3 Hartley 1996. Hartley lists the five forms of uncertainty in EU law: linguistic uncertainty (1996: 266–270), drafting uncertainty (1996: 270–273), deliberate uncertainty (1996: 273–274), secret agreements (1996: 274–278), judicial uncertainty (1996: 278–281).
4 Hartley 1996: 265.

DOI: 10.4324/9781003294870-4

discussion.[5] Hartley explains that judicial uncertainty could be produced by the CJEU itself either through its preferred method of interpretation of EU legislative acts or through the uncertainty found on the pages of its rulings.[6] Although it might be informative about the overall relationship between uncertainty and EU legislation, Hartley's analysis is too broadly drafted to be realistically used in practice to produce any definitive conclusions about how the Court employs uncertainty (or ambiguity) in a deliberate and strategic manner.

Out of the many forms of indeterminacy in EU law, vagueness seems to have attracted the most scholarly attention. For her investigation on instances of vagueness in EU Directive 2011/92, Patrizia Anesa seems to have adopted the classic approach to vagueness as a form of linguistic indeterminacy that ensures the applicability of the legal text to a wide variety of situations.[7] In fact, vagueness was shown to be "the most pervasive form of indeterminacy" in the Directive in question.[8] The different varieties of vagueness identified there included: contestability, linguistic fuzziness, incoherence, generality, underspecificity, and incompleteness.[9]

To reduce vagueness, the interpreter of EU legislation need only search for "specifying definitions or intra-textual references" within the legal instrument itself.[10] When it comes to the strategic resolution of ambiguity such an option is not available to the CJEU. The Court is left to resolve ambiguity without any additional legislative guidance inside or outside of the legislative text. Anesa further argues that the legal interpretation of ambiguity is unproblematic, since the clarification of ambiguity in the legislative text simply demands that the ambiguous expression be put in context and the correct interpretation will become immediately obvious.[11] This expectation for unproblematic interpretation of ambiguity may be valid for some unintentional, non-strategic, or latent ambiguity in the legislative text that has not yet been (and is unlikely to be) subjected to judicial deliberation. However, if an ambiguity in EU legislation is strategically resolved by the CJEU (especially if there is evidence that it might have been

5 There are two forms that are indirectly relevant. Linguistic uncertainty regarded as "the inevitable consequence of the multilingual nature of the [EU]" (Hartley 1996: 269). In the *Akerberg Fransson* and *Keck* Case Studies, the relationship between multilingualism and ambiguity will be discussed. Further, deliberate uncertainty, which occurs when "terms are used in the [EU] instrument precisely because they are uncertain", is the result of the need to reach an agreement between the representatives of the Member States on the meaning of the words in the legislative act (Hartley 1996: 273). For the purposes of this book, it is irrelevant whether the EU legislator produced ambiguity strategically or non-strategically. However, as it will be seen in the *Melloni* Case Study, the possible strategic use of ambiguity by the EU legislator could serve as evidence that the ambiguity was present in the relevant provision and central to the CJEU's reasoning behind its own act of strategic resolution of ambiguity.

6 Hartley 1996: 278–281.

7 Anesa 2014: 208.

8 Anesa 2014: 208.

9 Anesa 2014: 203–206.

10 Anesa 2014: 201.

11 Anesa 2014: 202.

strategically produced by the EU legislator), it is most probably the case that the context and purpose of the provision cannot unequivocally enforce the correct interpretation. In such instances, the Court usually has to decide between (at least) two *equally plausible* interpretations that are diametrically *opposed* to each other, without any legislative guidance to tip the scales in favour of either reading. Therefore, the Court is at *full* liberty to choose one interpretation over the other, thus exposing its constitutional and strategic priorities. This is a situation quite distinct from legal interpretation of vagueness, where the Court compares and contrasts a range of options which *more or less* different from each other, on the basis of legal solutions which are supported by the legislative text to *a greater or lesser degree*.

Martina Bajčić has also analysed the vague nature of EU legal concepts, which are infused with meaning through extralinguistic knowledge, applied dynamically to a variety of legal subfields through the CJEU's teleological reasoning.[12] Using this analytical framework, she investigated the concepts of a "worker" and an "establishment" in EU labour law.[13] Bajčić claimed that "vague concepts of EU law do not represent determinate categories with clear-cut demarcation lines", but instead should be defined as "open-ended, fuzzy, and constantly 'on the move'".[14] Thus, the meaning of vague concepts of EU law is "not fixed", since "whether or not a concept as the carrier of a legal norm applies to different cases is decided by the CJEU following an assessment of the facts of a particular case".[15] Ambiguity fulfils a similar function to vagueness, in that ambiguity offers (at least) two interpretations of the same term or utterance, which opens up a range of possibilities of understanding the same legislative text. However, the difference lies in that the various interpretations of ambiguity are distinct and *mutually exclusive*. The strategic resolution of ambiguity by the Court leads to a choice of *one* interpretation over the other(s). Even in the single example of strategic production of ambiguity in this book, the CJEU strategically resolved the ambiguity it produced on the pages of the same ruling. Therefore, the ultimate result of the CJEU's adjudication in that case is that only one interpretation of ambiguity remains true (normatively valid). This is not to say that ambiguity production has no strategic value for the Court. On the contrary, the strategic production of ambiguity was a means for the Court to achieve its strategic aim by justifying its activist choice of interpretation. The ambiguity strategically produced by the CJEU "lived" on the pages of the ruling just long enough to fulfil its strategic purpose and not a moment longer.

Even though vagueness and ambiguity are both forms of linguistic indeterminacy, neither of the studies on vagueness in EU law presented above construct an analytical framework that is suitable and sufficient for the purposes of investigating the phenomenon of ambiguity in EU law, as conceptualised by this book. To

12 Bajčić 2018: 100–104.
13 Bajčić 2018: 102–105.
14 Bajčić 2018: 106.
15 Bajčić 2018: 106.

put it simply, what works for vagueness does not necessarily work for ambiguity (at least not fully).

Finally, to illustrate how the implicit presence of ambiguity in the CJEU's reasoning has been treated until now, let us consider the commentary by scholars of EU constitutional law to the Case Studies of this book. Whether it would be in a passing remark, a tangential observation or a footnote in the far corner of the page, the awareness that ambiguity was hidden somewhere in the legislative text or the CJEU's reasoning was palpable among commentators.[16] The concealed presence of ambiguity gave rise to observations on the lack of legal certainty the decision produces and on the overall increased indeterminacy as a result of extreme meta-teleological interpretation by the Court.[17] Sometimes the legal commentators made an incidental statement that hit close to home, but then led the analysis in a different direction or left that remark completely unsubstantiated by further evidence or closer examination.[18]

In any case, ambiguity was almost never given the recognition it deserves as the key to the central legal problem, however acutely felt its effects might have been. Every time, the true extent of the significance of ambiguity for the resolution of the case escaped commentators.

To sum up, ambiguity in EU law has often been overlooked and, to a certain extent, misunderstood until now. The phenomenon of ambiguity in EU law needs a framework for analysis that combines linguistic knowledge about its definition and properties and an in-depth understanding of its interaction with the constitutional peculiarities of the EU legal order. This framework for analysis must be developed specifically for ambiguity and distinct from that for other forms of indeterminacy, such as vagueness and generality. This brief overview highlighted the need for a proper, coherent, and systematic understanding of the way the presence of ambiguity in EU legal texts relates to the CJEU's decision-making. In its absence, any interest in the actual significance of ambiguity will rarely, if ever, mature beyond a mere intuition, mentioned in passing and left unexplored

16 For example, see Sarmiento (2013:1275–1277), Masing (2016: 501) and Chalmers (2010: 143) with respect to the Case Study of *Åkerberg Fransson*.

17 This was the case with *Melloni*, for example, where the CJEU's interpretation has been criticised for being "short and cursory and extremely self-referential" (Rauchegger, 2015: 114).

18 For example, see Lansbergen & Miller (2011): *Ruiz Zambrano* is indeed "an ambiguous revolution" (Lansberger & Miller, 2011: 287) in that ambiguity is central to the revolutionalisation of this branch of CJEU case-law, as the relevant Case Study will show. However, Lansbergen & Miller (2011) fail to articulate the linguistic specifications of the sample of ambiguity as well as the relationship between the Court's decision-making and the ambiguity found in the legislative text. Instead, the Court's confusing justification as to the potential (un)conditionality of the right to access to the labour market in the EU in the context of the definition of 'deprivation' is highlighted (Lansbergen & Miller, 2011: 298, 303, 306).

Moreover, consider that Gerard Conway made a correct observation about the ambiguous language of Article 34 TFEU and its effect, but failed to see the connection with the terminological distinction drawn in *Keck*, its exact location (the noun 'measures') and consequently, abandoned this line of reasoning unfinished (Conway 2012: 41).

in the relevant literature on EU constitutional law. This book will propose such a framework for analysis, which will facilitate a change in the established mode of thinking about ambiguity in EU law and reinstate ambiguity-based reasoning to its rightful place in the strategic arsenal of the CJEU.

Ambiguity and the CJEU

The CJEU's Teleological and Meta-teleological Reasoning

Ambiguity-based reasoning is a powerful judicial technique that the CJEU employs in its reasoning only very rarely. The CJEU's style of reasoning normally consists of linguistic (semiotic) arguments, systemic (contextual) arguments, and dynamic arguments.[19] Linguistic arguments are typically associated with the values of "certainty; the rule of law", systemic arguments promote "systemic values of autonomy, integrity and consistency", and dynamic arguments are representative of the values "integrity coherence; innovation; reflexivity".[20] Among these, the Court is primarily seen relying on teleological arguments in its legal interpretation.[21]

Ambiguity-based reasoning is particularly relevant to the CJEU's 'constitutional reasoning'. When the Court of Justice interprets the EU Treaties for the purposes of ruling on the validity of EU secondary legislation, the Court is engaging in *sensu stricto* constitutional reasoning.[22] In cases where the CJEU assesses the validity of national legislation and issues preliminary rulings on the interpretation of EU law, the Court is applying *sensu lato* constitutional reasoning.[23] Since the preliminary rulings presented in this book all deal with constitutional issues of great significance for the authority of EU law, it is reasonable to conclude that the Case Studies illustrate the CJEU's *sensu lato* constitutional reasoning.

To explain how ambiguity comes into play here, it would be beneficial to understand first how an argument based on constitutional reasoning in the jurisprudence of the CJEU is generally structured. To begin with, it is quite common that a judgment follows "a cumulative parallel structure, in which distinct, autonomous considerations lead to the same conclusion".[24] Similarly, the Court frequently presents "one-line conclusive arguments – a self-standing structure, in which every premise is presented as a necessary component of the argument".[25] Some judgments include "parallel, individually inconclusive, but together conclusive arguments".[26] Based on this evidence, it seems often a multitude

19 Paunio citing Bengoetxea 2013: 26.
20 Paunio 2013: 28, Figure '1.1'. Paunio points out the connection with Bentgoetxea's categorisation (Paunio 2013: 28, footnote [149]).
21 Paunio citing Bengoetxea, Lasser and McLeod 2013: 30.
22 Itzcovich 2017: 289.
23 Itzcovich 2017: 290.
24 Itzcovich 2017: 291.
25 Itzcovich 2017: 291.
26 Itzcovich 2017: 291.

of arguments come together to form the basis of the CJEU's constitutional reasoning. More importantly, there are other times when the Court puts forward a 'one-line conclusive argument' – a succinct standalone legal solution. This is where the outcome of ambiguity-based reasoning is most evident. This was the case in all of the Case Studies on the strategic resolution of ambiguity, since the Court repeated the resultant formula in its subsequent case-law. To some extent, it was also true for the single Case Study on the strategic production of ambiguity, since the Court's interchangeable use of terms was predicated on an ambiguous term of its own making.

At this stage, one begins to wonder if ambiguity alters the normal course of the CJEU's constitutional reasoning at all. What difference does it make if the CJEU has based its 'one-line conclusive argument' on the strategic resolution (or the strategic production) of ambiguity or not? By the end of this book, it will become clear that ambiguity-based reasoning has certain advantages as well as disadvantages in comparison to other more traditional methods of adjudication, with regards to both the long-term and the short-term application of the Court's legal solution. Therefore, ambiguity as the implicit foundation of the CJEU's reasoning *does* make a difference. In addition, it is important to know how, when, and under what circumstances the CJEU uses ambiguity as a template for its legal reasoning, which will give us a more accurate and complete understanding of the role, function, and strategic value of ambiguity in EU law. Such knowledge will reveal the *extent* of the difference ambiguity makes in the EU legal order.

Finally, let us consider how ambiguity-based reasoning interacts with the type of arguments the Court of Justice prefers in its constitutional reasoning. Giulio Itzcovich reports that CJEU uses a wide range of such arguments, e.g. analogies, arguments based on the applicability of the EU Treaties, harmonising arguments with respect to national law or international law, EU precedent, implicit concepts or principles of EU law, 'linguistic-logical formulae based on silence', references to scholarly works or to foreign law, and even non-legal arguments.[27] The Court rarely discusses the plain and ordinary meaning of a term, since this would require an extensive analysis of the language versions of the Treaty text.[28] Itzcovich failed to find any arguments "establishing/debating the text of the Treaties", which confirms the necessity to study the implicit, rather than explicit, presence of ambiguity in the CJEU's reasoning.[29] The CJEU only exceptionally considered "the purpose of the Treaty-maker", which is likely because "the Court does not want to tie the future developments of European law to the past intentions of the representatives of the Contracting Parties" and this is not the standard approach to the interpretation of international treaties.[30]

27 Itzcovich 2017: 292–298, 301–304.
28 Itzcovich 2017: 293–294.
29 Itzcovich 2017: 292.
30 Itzcovich 2017: 300–301.

At this stage, a few words are in order about the interpretation of international treaties. This area is governed by the principles laid out in Article 31–33 of the 1969 Vienna Convention on the Law of the Treaties (VCLT). Article 31(1) VCLT postulates that "[a] treaty shall be interpreted in good faith in accordance with the ordinary meaning to be given to the terms of the treaty in their context and in the light of its object and purpose". Furthermore, Article 31(2) VCLT clarifies the meaning of the "context" of an international treaty for the purposes of interpretation. Article 32(a) VCLT highlights the importance of consulting the preparatory materials of the treaty and the circumstances surrounding its conclusion in cases where the interpretation approaches detailed in Article 31 VCLT have left the meaning of a provision "ambiguous or obscure". Finally, Article 33 VCLT contains a set of instructions on the interpretation of treaties which have been authenticated in two or more languages.

In addition, scholars traditionally distinguish between three main approaches to treaty interpretation:

> (1) the textual approach, suggesting that treaties should be interpreted according to their language; (2) the subjective approach, suggesting that treaties should be interpreted according to the intention of the state parties that have signed them, and (3) the teleological approach, suggesting that treaties should be interpreted according to their object and purpose.[31]

These rules have been accepted and implemented in practice as a matter of customary international law.[32] Multilingualism also plays an important, albeit controversial, role in international treaty interpretation. In particular, there is tension inherent in the requirements of Article 33 VCLT, arising between the presumption of similar meaning between the different language versions and the need to compare them during routine interpretation of treaties authenticated in two or more languages.[33]

This roughly sketched framework of guidelines that normally governs international treaty interpretation also applies to the search for a correct interpretation of vagueness and ambiguity in the treaty text:

> Where the ordinary meaning of a treaty provision is vague, using the object and purpose will make the meaning of the provision more precise. Where the ordinary meaning is ambiguous, using the object and purpose will help to determine which one of two possible meanings is correct, and which one is not.[34]

In other words, the presence of ambiguity in the treaty text requires that an international court determines the object and purpose of the treaty (teleological

31 Dothan 2019: 766.
32 Dothan citing Dörr and Schmalenbach 2019: 767.
33 Kuner 1991.
34 Linderfalk 2007: 203.

interpretation).[35] This method of interpretation demands an evaluation not only of the treaty text but also of the intention of the contracting parties and the goals of the treaty regime taken in its entirety.[36]

Indeed, the CJEU already has a proclivity for engaging in a teleological and meta-teleological interpretation of EU law, with the latter term being defined as follows:

> a particular systemic understanding of the EU legal order that permeates the interpretation of all its rules. In other words, the Court was not simply been concerned with ascertaining the aim of a particular legal provision. It also interpreted that rule in the light of the broader context provided by [the EU] legal order and its "constitutional telos".[37]

There is a "clear association" between the two categories of interpretation and their vital significance for establishing the authority of EU law in the face of any challenges by the national courts.[38] The normative power of these methods of interpretation is founded on the autonomy of EU law, which entails "an independent normative claim (EU law determines its own criteria or validity)" as well as "a claim of completeness (that it can provide legal answers to all the legal questions that emerge within its jurisdiction)".[39]

However, Suvi Sankari's work makes some important adjustments to the traditional understanding of the Court's legal reasoning described above by demonstrating that in reality the CJEU is not inclined to engage in "uncritical further integration at any and every opportunity".[40] Further, the Court's reasoning is dependent primarily on systemic reasons, and not on dynamic ones.[41] Lastly, the CJEU tends to "[reason] relatively formally" and in keeping with all the well-established interpretative criteria that define its adjudication, which results in both general and local coherence of the legal system.[42] Therefore, it would be inaccurate to assume that just because the CJEU resorts to teleological and meta-teleological interpretation, the Court ordinarily reasons with a default preference for an expansion of EU competences (and in the extreme case – judicial activism), all the while exhibiting wilful and random judicial behaviour.

Although it may be that the reputation of the CJEU's teleological and meta-teleological interpretation is tainted by accusations of judicial activism, this is mainly due to the perceived *total disconnect* between the legislative text and the Court's argumentation.[43] This rigid understanding of legal certainty, as being

35 Dothan 2019: 790.
36 Dothan citing Barak 2019: 790.
37 Maduro 2007: 140.
38 Maduro 2007: 140.
39 Maduro 2007: 140.
40 Sankari 2013: 251.
41 Sankari 2013: 251.
42 Sankari 2013: 249.
43 Paunio & Lindroos-Hovinheimo 2010: 408.

indebted to the ordinary use of words, has been resisted, since the process of adjudication is innately subjective, in that a single and authoritative meaning cannot be objectively pinpointed.[44] This is so on account of the ever-changing, dynamic process of creation of meaning through language in communication, which means that any attempt by the Court to monopolise the control over the meaning of language is "unnatural" and represents a short-sighted view of its function in the legal system.[45] Therefore, it would be imprudent to base legal reasoning entirely on linguistic analysis.[46] This idea is even more pertinent in the context of EU multilingualism and Cao's "inter-lingual uncertainty", which will be discussed later in this chapter.[47] Thus, it could be concluded that teleological and meta-teleological reasoning is necessary in the EU legal order, in order to satisfy the requirements of legal certainty – acceptability and predictability – in circumstances of enhanced indeterminacy.[48]

Despite the perceived association between teleological interpretation and judicial activism, Maduro argues that the combination between teleological and meta-teleological reasoning could be beneficial to the EU legal order.[49] Maduro envisions teleological interpretation as a way to curtail the normative implications of textual ambiguity, which generally flourishes in the context of constitutional pluralism and EU multilingualism.[50] In his view, teleological interpretation is helpful in this sense, as it enriches and broadens our understanding of EU law above and beyond the concrete circumstances of the case at hand.[51] Further, Maduro insists that teleological reasoning actually boosts the accountability and transparency of the Court's decision-making process by ensuring that EU law is interpreted in a normatively consistent manner – a more stringent criterion than the wording of the text or mere intent.[52] Further, a reliance on universal legal principles in adjudication helps with reaching agreement on controversial matters and enhancing the adaptability of EU law to the ever-growing demands of the integration process.[53]

It is worth pointing out that some aspects about the nature of the relationship between ambiguity and teleological and meta-teleological reasoning have been interpreted inaccurately to date. The Court's reasoning appears to be a means of damage control, since ambiguity is seen as a disruptive force, the adverse effects of which need to be mitigated. This is a rather simplistic and one-sided appreciation of the role of ambiguity in the EU legal system. Ambiguity could also be credited

44 Paunio & Lindroos-Hovinheimo 2010: 409.
45 Paunio & Lindroos-Hovinheimo 2010: 398–399, 408–409.
46 Paunio & Lindroos-Hovinheimo 2010: 397.
47 Paunio & Lindroos-Hovinheimo, 2010: 409–410; Cao, 2007: 71.
48 Paunio & Lindroos-Hovinheimo, 2010: 397.
49 Maduro 2007: 142.
50 Maduro 2007: 142–143.
51 Maduro 2007: 143.
52 Maduro 2007: 144.
53 Maduro 2007: 144–145.

for its *positive* contribution on a systemic level, in terms of creating opportunities for the Court of Justice to exercise its teleological and meta-teleological reasoning, which helps the Court affirms its authority and develop legal doctrines. In the next section, this process will be discussed in further detail.

The Preliminary Ruling Procedure as the Main Channel of Judicial Dialogue between the CJEU and the National Courts

The main aim of the CJEU's strategic behaviour is the effective implementation of the authority of EU law. The fulfilment of this agenda is no small feat, but it has arguably transformed the CJEU into "the most powerful supranational court in world history".[54] The winning combination of factors that helped the CJEU along the way included: the horizontal and vertical fragmentation of power in the EU, which protected the CJEU from political attacks and encouraged the lawmaker to endow the Court with extended competences; the single market where the CJEU could advance its doctrines against relatively low political resistance and set in motion an alternating cycle between negative and positive integration; and finally, the Court engaging in judicial activism, in order to develop common legal norms approved by the majority Member State governments.[55]

These important milestones have been primarily achieved through the main channel of communication between the CJEU and the national courts – the preliminary ruling procedure under Article 267 TFEU.[56] The preliminary ruling procedure is a mechanism of key systemic significance for the implementation of the authority of EU law, which was designed to ensure the continuous dialogue between the CJEU and the national court. The basis of that exchange is the interpretation and validity of EU law. Although there is admittedly a recent shift towards systemic thinking in the context of pluralism or the authority of EU law,[57] the research effort concentrates mainly on 'systemic defiance' by the national constitutional courts in exceptional cases of constitutional conflict. This book investigates the strategic value of ambiguity for the implementation of the authority of EU law as it occurs *on a daily basis and over time*, which could only be reliably observed against the background of the preliminary ruling procedure.

54 Kelemen 2018: 223.

55 Kelemen 2018: 226, 229, 234.

56 Also known as the "preliminary reference procedure". See also Itzcovich (2017: 280) for the importance of the preliminary ruling procedure as a dialogue between the CJEU and the national courts: "the central instrument of the EU for judicial control [that is] vital in order to achieve the uniform application of European law over all of Europe ... By means of preliminary rulings, the Court has been able to develop a constructive and mutual relationship (a 'dialogue' ...) with the national courts, which means that the European and the national courts have collaborated in shaping the content of European law 'in action' without establishing formal hierarchical relationship between themselves; the Court of Justice has initiated a process of 'constitutionalisation' of the European Treaties, making it acceptable to the national courts".

57 Dyevre 2016; Avbelj 2017.

The national courts are the CJEU's valued partners in the preliminary ruling procedure, and thus in the implementation of the authority of EU law. The national courts have generally accepted the principles of primacy, direct effect and indirect effect, barring some resistance on account of the scope of EU law.[58] National courts have shown "limited or very limited interest" to multilingual interpretation, but have compensated for that by "loyally [allowing] the meaning of the national version to be determined by other language versions".[59] All in all, the national courts can be characterised "loyal but not very active in matters of [EU law]".[60]

A preliminary reference may be the result of a national court having trouble interpreting ambiguity found in the EU Treaty text. The legal acts of the Union must be drafted in a way that is "clear, easy to understand and unambiguous" and "precise, leaving no uncertainty in the mind of the reader".[61] This is because of the apprehension that "any over-complexity or ambiguity, however slight, could result in inaccuracies, approximations or complete mistranslations in one or more of the other Union languages".[62] Terminological consistency is also recommended, since there must be no trace left of "ambiguities, contradictions or doubts as to the meaning of a term".[63] Regardless of whether this is a deliberate (strategic) drafting choice or not, ambiguity of crucial constitutional significance still finds its way into the EU Treaty text, as this book will show.

At the same time, national courts are also exposed to the effects of ambiguity found in the wording of the CJEU's rulings. The lawyer-linguists in charge of translating the Court of Justice's rulings aim to translate the text literally to preserve ambiguity, especially when it comes to new points of law.[64] Thus, the main goal of the translation exercise often seems to be to maintain ambiguity, rather than to resolve it.

For this reason, ambiguity could be perceived as fuel for the preliminary ruling procedure,[65] as its presence induces a national court to seek clarification on the meaning of EU law from the CJEU. In a communicative context, the dialogue between the CJEU and the national courts within the preliminary ruling procedure could also be re-imagined as an interactive alignment model of dialogue,[66] in order to emphasise its systemic credentials. The participants in this dialogue aim to reach an understanding on the basis of an 'implicit common ground'

58 Derlén 2009: 312.
59 Derlén 2009: 312.
60 Derlén 2009: 312.
61 Joint Practical Guide 2015: Guideline 1.1, p. 10.
62 Joint Practical Guide 2015: Guideline 5.2, p. 16.
63 Joint Practical Guide 2015: Guideline 6.2, p. 20.
64 McAuliffe 2014: 83–84.
65 Kulick (2016: 275) uses a similar formulation to describe the interaction between the strategic use of vagueness and ambiguity (VaA) and the political dimension of international law in general terms: "VaA are the fuel on which this engine runs".
66 Pickering & Garrod 2004: 175–176, 178–179.

and resolve conflict through 'interactive repair in cases of misalignment'.[67] This concept is reminiscent of Maduro's idea of constitutional pluralism relying on the "systemic compatibility" between the EU legal system and the national legal systems, mentioned earlier.[68] It also evokes associations with the idea that the CJEU and the national courts are striving towards "a shared legal paradigm through judicial reasoning" through their dialogue, which is aimed at increasing the stability of the system.[69] Whether ambiguity is capable of promoting greater acceptability and coherence as a result of this process, as suggested above, remains to be seen by the end of this book.

For all of these reasons, the Case Studies presented in this book comprise some of CJEU's leading preliminary rulings. As the Court acts as the "motor" of EU integration,[70] it stands to reason that ambiguity found at the core of a CJEU ruling will be highly impactful for this process and, accordingly, for the development of the authority of EU law. Ambiguity is a detail of pivotal importance in hard cases where the CJEU is called upon to make a judicial choice that would shift the boundaries of EU competence, especially if the outcome of its deliberation will mark a turning point in the constitutional evolution of the EU legal order.

The CJEU's Strategic Behaviour

The bewilderment occasionally provoked by the CJEU's bold reasoning in landmark preliminary rulings, such as the Case Studies in this book, is customarily attributed to the Court's proclivity for teleological and meta-teleological interpretation. The Court is normally accused of going beyond the mandate given by the Member States as the 'masters of the treaty', thereby neglecting or misinterpreting legislative intent. This standard explanation of the CJEU's judicial behaviour could be seen as a solid basis for mounting accusations of judicial activism. The Court of Justice is often taken to task for having remained *silent*, having provided *insufficient* or otherwise *deficient* justification for its decision-making. The Court's reasoning is somehow found *lacking*. In the absence of actual knowledge of the inner workings of the CJEU's decision-making process, which seems to be locked in an impenetrable "black box of European law",[71] it is impossible to be certain about the actual thought process and the possible strategic considerations that informed the Court's reasoning and led to its ultimate decision. Nevertheless, given the scarcity of clues left behind by the Court, it would certainly make more sense to dispel the sense of puzzlement by speculating on what *is* on the page, rather than what is *not* on the page. This is where knowledge of *ambiguity* comes into play.

67 Pickering & Garrod 2004: 178–179, 173–174.
68 Maduro 2007: 149.
69 Paunio 2013: 157, 175–176, 192.
70 Horsley 2013.
71 Grimmel 2014: 68.

This book takes a step further and suggests that selected samples of ambiguity in the CJEU's preliminary rulings have strategic value for the implementation of the authority of EU law. When it comes to describing the use of ambiguity in communication, the term "strategic" is closely associated with the terms "intentional" or "purposeful".[72] The strategic use of ambiguity must be contrasted with non-strategic use, in which the speaker employs ambiguity "unintentionally or by mistake".[73]

Beyond that, in terms of the CJEU's decision-making, the idea of *strategic value* is linked to the notion of *rhetorical strategy*, which entails an orator's consideration of how to achieve success and effectiveness within a complex communicative process; at the centre of this anticipatory consideration, which ultimately leads to the planning of action for persuasion, stands an analysis of the relevant relationships between the goal, the resistance in the way of its realisation and the means to achieving said goal.[74] Thus, ambiguity gives the CJEU the opportunity to make the most strategically advantageous judicial choice with respect to the effective implementation of the authority of EU law in the particular adjudicative situation.

It is not unreasonable to suggest that the preliminary ruling procedure provides fruitful ground for the study of the CJEU's strategic behaviour, including its strategic use of ambiguity. There is evidence to suggest that the preliminary ruling procedure allows room for strategic judicial behaviour, in that it could create an opportunity for the national courts to strategically exercising their discretion to refer.[75] It is also possible that the CJEU may strategically choose to refuse to provide an answer to the preliminary reference.[76] Furthermore, the presence of indeterminacy in the preliminary ruling procedure is closely associated with strategic judicial behaviour. The CJEU could use "purposively imprecise concepts" to "avoid direct conflict".[77] Furthermore, "deliberate imprecision" within the Court of Justice's reasoning could potentially stimulate dialogue, promote the advancement of EU law and empower national courts.[78] There is

72 However, Winkler cautions against assuming universal equivalence between "strategic" and "intentional"/ "purposeful" use in an interdisciplinary context, since this may not be the case in some areas of study (e.g. literary studies). Winkler 2015: 297, footnote [25]; See also Winter-Froemel & Zirker 2015 on "strategic ambiguity".

73 Winkler 2015: 313.

74 Knape, Becker & Böhme, 2009: 153–154. The original excerpt in German reads: "Eine rhetorische [Strategie] ist das auf einen komplexen kommunikativen Prozeß bezogene Erfolgs- und Effektivitätskalkül des Orators, in dessen Mittelpunkt die Analyse der relevanten Ziel-Widerstand-Mittel-Relationen steht. Dieses rhetorisch-strategische Kalkül ist ein antizipatorisches Kalkül. Analytisch betrachtet ist es auf der Planungsebene angesiedelt, betrifft also noch nicht die kommunikativen Handlungen selbst. Als Handlungsplan für den Gesamtprozeß bewußten rhetorischen Handelns (gerichtet auf Persuasion (…)) muß es erst realisiert werden". (Translation into English done by the author of this book.)

75 Nyikos 2006: 525–537.

76 Tridimas 2011: 737–756,739–740; Tridimas 2015: 409.

77 Leczykiewicz 2008: 773–786, 781–782.

78 Tridimas 2015: 409.

reason to suggest that the CJEU might be open to using strategic means, such as ambiguity-based reasoning, to fulfil its adjudicative agenda.

Shai Dothan's study on judicial tactics relies on a game-theoretic approach to demonstrate precisely *how* international courts increase their reputation. Although the CJEU is not explicitly listed as one of the international courts under scrutiny, there is nothing to preclude its inclusion as it fits the profile of an international court.[79] The concept of "reputation" could be tremendously helpful in understanding how the authority of EU law is implemented by the CJEU in the preliminary ruling procedure, where the Court essentially engages in a dialogue with one of the national courts. The *reputation* of an international court is defined as follows:

> When two actors act in a repeated game, they observe each other's behavior and try to predict the future behavior of the actor faced. The belief each actor forms about the future behavior of the other actor can be referred to as that actor's reputation … Reputation can describe not only the predicted behavior of a specific actor, but also the predictions of a relevant community about the behavior of certain actors toward that actor. The reputation of courts … refers to the belief of the relevant community about the prospects of compliance with the future judgments of the court. Therefore, the reputation of the court is determined by predictions about the behavior of parties that are subject to the court's judgments and not the predicted behavior of the court itself. A court with a high reputation is expected by the relevant community to be complied with more often than a court with a low reputation.[80]

One relevant strategic approach through which an international court could increase its reputation is to issue a demanding judgment or one that contains discretionary reasoning.[81] Compliance with such a judgment reveals that "the complying party has signalled that it expects a high reputational sanction for non-compliance" which is an indicator of high reputation for the international court.[82] In cases where the court's reputation is diminished on account of continual non-compliance, however, the court needs to issue a less demanding judgment.[83] In all of these cases, the international court is said to be 'walking on the brink of non-compliance'.[84] This is a high risk strategy involving the international court being potentially exposed to reputational damage in case of non-compliance.[85]

79 Similarly, the European Court of Human Rights is included in Dothan's examples. Dothan 2014: 212–261.
80 Dothan 2014: 8–9.
81 Dothan 2014: 114–115.
82 Dothan 2014: 114.
83 Dothan 2014: 124.
84 Dothan 2014: 115–117.
85 Dothan 2014: 117–131.

Another relevant judicial tactic might be 'incrementalism', which refers to the gradual build-up to a demanding judgment: "[international courts] do not immediately set precedents that damage the interests of other parties, but rather shape these precedents step by step in a series of separate decisions".[86] This is especially the case when international courts generate a string of increasingly more contentious case-law, ultimately culminating in a decision that will extend the scope of their discretion or introduce a dramatic doctrinal shift in the law.[87] This is a low risk strategy designed to reduce the margin of error associated with each new step and give the court the opportunity to adjust its approach in time.[88]

Dothan does not explicitly make the connection between these strategies and the categories of 'judicial activism' and 'judicial restraint', which are customarily used to describe the fluctuations in the CJEU's adjudicative approach. It must be borne in mind that Dothan's categories merely describe existing judicial tactics (i.e. ways to go about fulfilling a court's strategic agenda). As such, they cannot be readily equated with judicial activism and judicial restraint, since the latter two categories are indicative of the dynamics of the constitutionally prescribed relationship between the legislator and the judiciary. It would be more accurate to suggest that Dothan's theory is helpful in providing a blueprint of the mechanics of how judicial activism and judicial restraint are implemented in practice. More importantly, Dothan's theory proves that international courts can (and in fact, do) enhance their reputation by means of strategic judicial behaviour. This provides a solid foundation for the claim that the CJEU could facilitate the implementation of the authority of EU law through strategic means, including through the strategic use of ambiguity.

Nevertheless, this analysis would be incomplete without establishing a connection between Dothan's judicial tactics and the categories of 'judicial activism' and 'judicial restraint', since the latter are essential to understanding the clash of existing theories on ambiguity in the EU legal order and, as such, are integrated into the typology of examples presented later in this chapter. Let us begin with a brief examination of the concept of 'judicial activism' and its relevance to this book.

It has become nearly axiomatic to equate the CJEU's acts of judicial activism to disregard for the EU legislator's intent, a proclivity for engagement on a political level or mere judicial recalcitrance, which is by no means compatible with the ideal for a legitimate judicial interpretation.[89] To this end, a number of scholars have doubted the legitimacy of the Court's decision-making on account of the Court's notorious disregard for textual evidence and legal tradition and reliance on systemic interpretation to further the EU's interests.[90] However, the

86 Dothan 2014: 131–132.
87 Dothan 2014: 132.
88 Dothan 2014: 133–136.
89 Pollicino 2004: 285–286.
90 Horsley citing Hartley, Neill, Rasmussen and Conway 2013: 938.

stark differentiation on the basis of legitimacy is the result of an out-of-date and simplistic understanding of the judge as "an inanimate, robot-like spokesman of the law".[91]

In this sense, the role of the CJEU judiciary would be more accurately described, if due attention is paid to systemic interpretation as well as *the freedom of choice in judicial decision-making* – a position that exemplifies "the revolt against formalism".[92] When it comes to the former, the Court is interested not only in historical and textual evidence, but also in the utility and purpose of systemic components, to the demands of tradition, to its case-law and academic commentary as well as to the cohesion between the developmental stages of the legal system.[93] With respect to the latter, the Court's decision-making is described in terms of the exercise of discretion and the need to balance and assess competing solutions in the light of not only logical but economic, political, social, and other considerations.[94] At some point, one must accept that the Court legitimately engages not only in 'mechanical' interpretation and analysis of the legal text, but also in 'creative' law-making through adjudication.[95] The standard to which the Court is to be held accountable should be its own concrete position and progress with respect to the integration process, and not a misleading and inaccurate comparison with the normative ideal of "what good (constitutional) courts should do".[96] To put this issue into perspective, let us consider the idea that:

> The widely shared conclusion that the ECJ had an interest in expanding the ambit of European law cannot be directly deduced from the mere fact that it has *de facto* done so. The European law itself, as a self-contained context of reasoning and action, must be seen as the intervening variable.[97]

What Grimmel is implying here is that the CJEU may be acting *in the interest of the EU legal system itself*, when deciding to engage in what is perceived as politically motivated judicial activism. Therefore, before hastily mounting accusations of judicial activism, one needs to delve deeper into the complexities of EU law.[98] In other words, to gain appreciation for the CJEU's highly abstract style of adjudication, one need simply scrutinise more closely the actual constitutional context of the CJEU's decision-making, as it would reveal the circumstances and considerations that informed the Court's decision-making.[99] By this account, the Court is simply taking the necessary steps to further integration as the primary

91 Pollicino 2004: 286.
92 Pollicino 2004: 286–287.
93 Pollicino citing Koopmans 2004: 287.
94 Pollicino citing Cappelletti 2004: 287.
95 Pollicino 2004: 286.
96 Horsley 2013: 941.
97 Grimmel 2012: 534.
98 Grimmel 2012: 534.
99 Horsley 2013: 939.

goal of the Union, as defined by the treaties and as enabled by international law.[100]Ambiguity-based analysis of the CJEU's jurisprudence is therefore a move in the right direction.

One decisive step towards severing the nexus with formalism would be to question the underlying assumption that the EU legislature has produced a precise and practicable legal norm in the form of any given provision of EU law, which the Court of Justice need only follow faithfully to guarantee the legitimacy of its decision-making. This assumption may very well be erroneous, as the discovery of samples of ambiguity at the heart of key EU Treaty provisions prove later in this book.

The Case Study of *Melloni* is the classic case of strategic resolution of ambiguity found in the legislative text. It could be argued that the Court "is not to blame for disrespecting the literal meaning of the texts, because there is no such meaning".[101] This means the CJEU is merely responding to the "nonsense", defined in linguistic terms, produced by the EU legislature in circumstances of EU multilingualism.[102] Therefore, the CJEU may be habitually resorting to extreme *meta-teleological* interpretation[103] not out of sheer wilfulness, but out of the necessity for effective adjudication. According to this theory, the Court should be absolved of blame, as it merely plays the cards dealt by the legislator. This description certainly provides a much-needed alternative to the widely accepted activist explanation for the Court's conduct. It demonstrates that the traditional criterion for judicial activism needs to be revised, in order to provide an assessment of the Court's conduct that more accurately reflects the challenges inherent in the realities of the EU legal order. Still, the shadow of judicial activism cannot be fully cast aside. There are two equally plausible interpretations of ambiguity on the table and the CJEU ends up choosing the one that would expand the remit of EU competence. In the light of this fact, it is not the accusation of judicial activism *itself*, but the grounds for the accusation, that should be reassessed. The activist Court is once again incriminated by its strategic production of ambiguity in the *Åkerberg Fransson* Case Study, where the CJEU takes the initiative to invent an ambiguous term of its own and pragmatically enforce the interchangeable use of otherwise divergent terms, thus completely disregarding legislative intent.

At this stage, it is worth exploring how precisely the CJEU goes about implementing judicial activism in practice. Judicial activism often manifests itself in

100 Horsley 2013: 939. The theoretical debate on legislative intent, and especially the intent of the EU legislator, is vast and convoluted. To attempt a summary thereof would be impracticable given the time constraints and perhaps even irrelevant for this purpose. The examples presented in this book, including the *Melloni* Case Study, will necessarily touch upon these issues, but in a very goal-oriented and efficient manner, only insofar as the needs of the concrete Case Study demand it.

101 Kjær 2010: 298.

102 Kjær 2010: 298–300, 315.

103 Maduro 2007: 140.

a court's jurisprudence in an overt fashion, i.e. as a single controversial judgment. This is the case with the *Melloni* and the *Åkerberg Fransson* Case Studies, for example. Judicial minimalism, however, allows for "the covert pursuit of an activist judicial agenda", whereby judges aim to "avoid mistakes by acknowledging the limitations of their knowledge (so they are to feel their way rather than make bold leaps)".[104] Judicial decisions in the tradition of *judicial minimalism* are said to be "shallow rather than deep" and "narrow rather than wide".[105] In choosing this strategic approach, the adjudicator is striving to minimise both the cost of decision and the cost of error.[106] It may be argued that judicial minimalism is essentially generating incompletely theorised agreements which function as hollow abstractions that need to be filled with of specification at some point down the line.[107] This approach has the advantage of flexibility, since it maintains a non-committal attitude on substantive value questions, thus leaving plenty of decision-making leeway both for the lawmaker and for the other courts.[108] In this sense, judicial minimalism is conducive to the emergence, and more importantly the strategic use, of linguistic indeterminacy. Ambiguity allows for the string of case-law necessary for the incremental advancement of a legal doctrine through judicial minimalism to unfold in time, as will be shown in the *Ruiz Zambrano/ Dereci* Case Study. Thus, it would seem that with the CJEU, judicial activism may manifest itself through both of Dothan's judicial tactics – "walking on the brink of non-compliance" and "incrementalism".

That being said, let us now focus on judicial restraint. For the purposes of this book, judicial restraint denotes a situation where the CJEU either strategically resolves or strategically produces ambiguity in a way that would limit the scope of EU competence. The latter is a significantly less likely, but still possible, scenario. 'Judicial restraint' is closely associated with formalism or the idea that "judges apply law, they don't make it".[109] In this sense, the Case Study of *Keck* is an apt illustration of that principle, since there the CJEU gave a legitimate interpretation of an ambiguous term found in the legislative text (i.e. an interpretation that was fully in line with legislative intent) which ultimately resulted in a limitation on EU competences. *Keck* is a good example of a less demanding judgment within the framework of "walking on the brink of non-compliance".

Dothan explains that when an international court encounters continuous non-compliance with its judgments and therefore a decrease in its reputation, it resorts to issuing *less* demanding judgments as an expression of "strategic restraint", in order to avoid further non-compliance and preserve its reputation.[110] This is precisely what happened with the CJEU, since the outcome in *Keck* is a reaction

104 Posner 2012: 521.
105 Sunstein 2008: 826.
106 Sunstein 2008: 825.
107 Sunstein 2008: 828–829.
108 Smith 2010: 361.
109 Posner 2012: 520.
110 Dothan 2014: 124.

to a legitimacy crisis the CJEU was facing at the time.[111] In addition, it might be possible that judicial restraint could be exercised as part of the judicial tactic of "incrementalism", if one were to accept that judicial minimalism "makes no sense, for the measure of a phenomenon in itself carries no value significance, positive or negative".[112] Unfortunately, this book is unable to offer such an example for reasons explored in the final chapter of this book, which for now leaves this possibility in the realm of speculation.

Theories on the CJEU's Relationship with Ambiguity

The nature of the CJEU's relationship with ambiguity is nowadays subject to scholarly debate. On the one hand, ambiguity could be viewed as an instrument that the Court of Justice exploits for the expansion of EU competences by means of judicial activism. This is seen as the inevitable result of blurring the boundaries of competence at the expense of legal certainty.[113] On the other hand, ambiguity could be used as an instrument that the CJEU uses to improve the EU legal system and create opportunities for negotiating the division of competences through exercising judicial restraint. The detrimental effect of ambiguity on legal certainty could be mitigated through the CJEU's teleological and meta-teleological reasoning[114] and the end goal would be to promote greater acceptability and coherence.[115]

Both positions share a starting point: ambiguity has an adverse effect on legal certainty. However, there is clear disagreement on their proposed solutions to this problem. While the former stance is uncompromising and insists on the expulsion of ambiguity from the legal text, the latter allows for the possibility to limit the damage caused by ambiguity. Consequently, each of these theories envisions the relationship between the CJEU and the national courts differently. If the first logic is to be followed, ambiguity seems to be a mere means for the CJEU to fulfil its activist agenda and to prevail in the inevitable conflict of norms,[116] which will ultimately transform its dynamic of interaction with the national courts "from a *horizontal* and *bilateral* to a *vertical* and *multilateral* relationship".[117] In effect, this theory presupposes that the CJEU will inevitably engage in judicial activism when dealing with ambiguity. The second theoretical contribution seems to imply that ambiguity could be used to achieve greater acceptability and coherence on a systemic scale through judicial co-operation. This goal is achieved by means of effective conflict management aimed at conflict

111 Friedbach, 1996: 236; De Sousa, 2012b: 87.
112 Smith 2010: 365.
113 Conway 2010: 337–339.
114 Paunio & Lindroos-Hovinheimo 2010: 396–397; Maduro 2007: 142–143.
115 Leczykiewicz 2008: 781–785; Paunio 2013: 192, 157, 175–176, 191.
116 Martinico 2015: 1344.
117 Craig & De Burca 2011: 482.

avoidance.[118] The dialogue between the CJEU and the national courts aims to mould "a shared legal paradigm through judicial reasoning"[119] through fortifying and enhancing the "systemic compatibility"[120] between the legal systems of the EU and of the Member States.

Ultimately, neither of these two strands of theory supports their claims with concrete examples of the CJEU's treatment of ambiguity, which limits the discussion to a general, abstract level. This book will fill in this gap by challenging these theories by providing evidence in the form of concrete examples of ambiguity from the CJEU's jurisprudence. On the basis of this evidence, a third theory emerges on the last pages of this book that presents a more accurate and complete account of the strategic value of ambiguity for the authority of EU law.

The Relevance of EU Multilingualism for the CJEU's Jurisprudence

In a multilingual system of law, there exist at least two versions of a single law, each drafted in one of its official languages. In general, an official language of a legal system is "a language recognised for use by official bodies and organs in their documents and communications, whether written or oral".[121] For a language to be deemed 'official' in a particular country, it simply must be declared so in a legislative and judicial act, ideally accompanied by clarifications as to the scope of its use and application.[122] The citizens are at liberty to decide which language version to use.[123] Both versions are presumed equal in that they convey the same message and bring about the same consequences.[124] This is done to ensure that citizens that have selected one language version are not placed in a more advantageous position in comparison to those that have opted for the other.[125] As a result, all language communities within a multilingual system of law are informed of their rights and responsibilities and have equal access to law in their preferred language.[126]

However, multilingualism proves to be a challenge to legal interpretation. In a multilingual system of law, the adjudicator typically would consider the different language versions and issue a ruling that is legally binding in relation to all of them.[127] The problem arises where there are small divergences in literal meaning to be found between the language versions.[128] Although some such linguistic

118 Voßkuhle 2010: 183–184; Kuo 2013: 739–740; Tridimas 2015: 409, 427.
119 Paunio 2013: 192, 157, 175–176, 191.
120 Maduro 2007: 149.
121 Robertson 2016: 116.
122 Robertson 2016: 118.
123 Robertson 2016: 12.
124 Robertson 2016: 12.
125 Robertson 2016: 12.
126 Robertson 2016: 13–14.
127 Robertson 2016: 117.
128 Robertson 2016: 117. Here Robertson also refers to one of his earlier works and Case C-265/03 *Simutenkov*.

divergences might be interpreted as a mere error in translation,[129] others may be indicative of a more substantial difference between the meanings of a term or an utterance, as it appears in each language version. The latter scenario may give rise to ambiguity ("inter-lingual ambiguity") in certain circumstances, as it will be shown below.

The existence of different language versions of equal standing and the possibility of linguistic divergences pose a particular challenge to the principles of legal certainty and legitimate expectations.[130] To understand the law in its entirety, both the adjudicator and the average citizen will have to be able to compare and contrast all the linguistic versions, which is a laborious exercise in interpretation that usually also requires expertise in linguistics.[131] The following section will show how the tension between legal certainty and legal interpretation in a multilingual system of law are managed by the CJEU in practice.

Multilingual Analysis in the CJEU's Jurisprudence

Multilingual analysis relies on the comparison between a range of language versions of the Treaty text (EU primary law). This has long been adopted as a valid interpretative approach by the CJEU since *Stauder* (1969, Case 29/69) and operates under the presumption that statutory language that finds expression in a multilingual environment "provides a somewhat unique kind of evidence of purpose".[132] Thanks to the equal authenticity rule (Article 55 TEU), the examination of the Treaty text in one of the official EU languages is in theory considered to be as good as any of the other 23 language versions, and thus sufficiently authoritative. The equal authenticity rule holds special value, since it ensures that an equal measure of respect is given to each of the official languages of the Member States.[133] It could also be seen as a means of protecting the legitimate expectations of EU citizens that seek to rely on EU legislation to launch an action before the CJEU.[134]

Lawrence Solan[135] stressed the importance of determining the legislator's intent through the CJEU's multilingual approach to statutory interpretation and dubbed this adjudicative practice "the Augustinian approach".[136] This method requires the interpreter to compare and contrast a range of language versions of the legislative text, in order to delineate the scope of the statutory provision and eliminate the linguistic interpretations that represent the legislative will

129 Robertson 2016: 117.
130 Derlén 2009: 51.
131 Robertson 2016: 117.
132 Solan 2009: 283, 287.
133 Solan 2009: 280.
134 Mańko 2016: 144, 156–157.
135 Solan 2009: 290.
136 Here Solan (2009: 290) references St. Augustine, the author of *On Christian Doctrine* (396 AD).

inaccurately.[137] The comparison of language versions yields an "important clue" or "privileged evidence" about the intent of the legislator.[138] In this manner, EU translation has established itself as a decisive factor in the shaping of EU law, since it allows the CJEU to ensure the uniformity of the EU legal order and the *effet utile* of EU law through the comparison of language versions for the purposes of statutory interpretation.[139]

When multilingual analysis is applied in the context of statutory interpretation, linguistic divergences aid the interpreter in identifying the areas of linguistic conflict in need of resolution. The linguistic divergences discussed in the Case Studies at hand could be categorised as lexical conceptual linguistic divergences[140] or could be attributed to a lack of consistency.[141] The extent of linguistic divergence is fundamental to the multilingual analysis presented in this book, since it proves that the meaning of terms Y and Z is sufficiently dissimilar for a finding of "inter-lingual ambiguity" to be justified.

The empirical evidence provided by Coernelis J. W. Baaij[142] indicates that the CJEU has consistently relied on the practice of finding linguistic divergences between the different language versions of the EU legislative acts to provide justification or foundation for its decisions. Having analysed the CJEU's practice on diverging language versions, Mattias Derlén distinguished three main approaches.[143] Firstly, 'classical reconciliation' entails "a genuine comparison of the language versions, after which they will be reconciled based on some principle, for example preference for the clear meaning".[144] Secondly, the technique of "reconciliation and examination of the purpose" begins with reconciliation and then proceeds with an examination of the outcome with respect to "the purpose and/or context" of the legal rule.[145] Thirdly, the "radical teleological method" focuses on "the purpose and/or context" of the legal rule and, as soon as the divergence between the language versions is established, abandons the linguistic analysis.[146] In the end, Derlén concludes that "no single method" dominates the CJEU's jurisprudence: "The court employs several different techniques, and it is not possible to create a watertight theory of when it will use each method".[147]

137 Solan, 2009: 290. Here Solan (2009:290) makes a reference to the Opinion of Advocate General Stix-Hackl on *Igor Simutenkov v Ministerio de Educación y Cultura and Real Federación Española de Fútbol*, Case C-265/03, delivered on 11 January 2005, ECLI:EU:C:2005:6.
138 Solan 2009: 283, 285.
139 Burr 2013: 1497, paragraph 65.
140 Aljanati 2015: 291–309.
141 Aljanati 2015: 309–314.
142 Baaij 2012: 219.
143 Derlén 2009: 43– 50. Derlén (2009: 49) admits that there exist other approaches by the CJEU to the same problem.
144 Derlén 2009: 43. See Derlén (2009: 44–45) for examples from the CJEU case-law.
145 Derlén 2009: 45. See Derlén (2009: 46) for examples from the CJEU case-law.
146 Derlén 2009: 47. See Derlén (2009: 47–48) for examples from the CJEU case-law.
147 Derlén 2009: 49.

That being said, it seems as though the Augustinian approach could only be applied to the Treaty text, since it is covered by the equal authenticity rule. In contrast, a multilingual interpretation of the language used in the Court of Justice's preliminary rulings would be inappropriate, since they are in principle excluded from the remit of the equal authenticity rule. There is only one authentic version of a preliminary ruling of the Court of Justice – the one presented in the language of the case. In a nutshell, a distinction is to be made between "a single meaning" (where all the language versions together comprise the meaning of the legislative text) and "a single text" (the only decisive interpretation of the text is the *de jure* original).[148]

There are good reasons for the strict application of this rule. Arguably, all the language versions taken together produce the same meaning, which binds them in "a relationship of dependency".[149] It is therefore fair to say that a "level of parity" is established between them.[150] The explanation behind this bond could be that a process of "dynamic correspondence" unfolds, in which an EU legal concept emerges from the comparison between the different language versions of EU legislation.[151] In the context of EU law, this means that, under the influence of the equal authenticity rule, all the language versions of a Treaty provision merge into the same uniform text.[152] Legal translation theory also echoes this idea by establishing a rebuttable presumption of equal meaning between the various authentic versions of the same legal instrument, as Susan Šarčević explains.[153]

Nevertheless, it would be imprudent to underestimate the importance of the CJEU's jurisprudence as an absolutely essential source of EU law.[154] Further, McAuliffe's study demonstrated that the CJEU's rulings are often drafted by the exact copying of excerpts from EU legislation and by continually using the same terminology.[155] In the light of this intense exchange of replicated information, it would be unwise to automatically render a crucial piece of judge-made terminology ineligible to be subjected to multilingual analysis, without taking into consideration its background and specific circumstances.

Multilingualism and the Meaning of Autonomous Concepts of EU Law

Let us now concentrate on the issue of how the autonomous concepts of EU law behind the terminology in the CJEU's vocabulary are infused with meaning in a

148 Derlén 2016: 54.
149 Burr 2013: 1477, paragraph 65.
150 Burr 2013: 1506, paragraph 82.
151 Burr 2013: 1506, 1512–1513, paragraphs 83, 93–95.
152 Burr 2013: 1513, paragraph 94.
153 Šarčević 1997: 67.
154 Derlén 2016: 68.
155 McAuliffe 2011: 108.

multilingual environment. For this purpose, it might be useful to first consider the notion of "meaning", especially linguistic and legal meaning, in the context of multilingualism.

Linguistic meaning is associated with semantics, which examines how a text is created through the use of language as well as how a text interacts with other texts.[156] Linguistic meaning is concerned with the literal meaning of words or sentences, as found in dictionaries.[157] Semantic ideas in a multilingual legal system could be examined both 'internally'(within the text in one language version) and 'externally'(across different language versions of the same text).[158] This proves to be true in the EU, where there must be coherence and consistency in respect of terminology used in texts from the past and present, in a variety of different legal and language domains.[159]

Legal meaning is created through drafting and then read and constructed by means of interpretation.[160] Further, legal meaning is constructed by means of drawing inferences from factual circumstances and legal sources to formulate legal concepts or arguments.[161] It would be inaccurate to say that inferring legal meaning from the physical aspects of reality is an inherently linguistic activity.[162] Rather, it acquires a linguistic dimension when "we communicate what we learn and our utterance becomes a site of engagement".[163] This is precisely why one needs to acknowledge the communicative aspects and translation issues associated with drafting in a multilingual system of law, such as the EU.[164]

Having affirmed the autonomy and independence of EU law in the landmark judgments of *Costa v ENEL* and *CILFIT*, the CJEU made sure to secure the privilege of defining the substance and meaning of autonomous concepts of EU and keep it outside the reach of the national courts.[165] However, the Court of Justice was then faced with the problem of "multiple references of legal concepts": adjudication on behalf of a legal system that insists on claiming an independent status, though it has no independent legal language of its own making.[166] Even though the Court has made an effort to achieve a certain standardisation of terminology by elaborating on the definition and legal interpretation of terms, this problem

156 Robertson 2016: 144. Robertson (2016: 143–144) also discusses semiotic meaning in the context of multilingualism. However, since the analysis presented in this book focuses on the linguistic and legal aspects of a sample of ambiguity, a more detailed examination of 'linguistic meaning' and 'legal meaning' would be more helpful.
157 Robertson 2016: 145.
158 Robertson 2016: 145.
159 Robertson 2016: 145.
160 Robertson 2016: 146.
161 Robertson 2016: 145.
162 Robertson 2016: 145.
163 Robertson 2016: 145.
164 Robertson 2016: 146.
165 Engberg 2016: 170–171.
166 Kjær 2007: 80.

continues to persist.[167] It appears that autonomous concepts of EU law are still a work in progress.[168]

In this context, Anne Lise Kjær argues autonomous concepts of EU law could be instilled with meaning by means of translation, in a continual "transfer of … knowledge".[169] This notion refers to the continuous process of interaction between legal practitioners within the structures of the EU, which gives every member of the discourse community the opportunity to contribute with legal knowledge from their respective Member State.[170] Jan Engberg's idea to examine autonomous concepts of EU law with the help of Knowledge Communication has yielded similar results, albeit from the perspective of cognitive science.[171] Both authors appear to support the idea that the autonomous concepts of EU law are infused with meaning primarily through official translations by lawyer-linguists. Thus, lawyer-linguists are responsible not only for ***documenting*** meaning, but also for *creating* meaning through their work. The autonomous concepts of EU law are enriched with greater depth and nuance thanks to the diverse range of national perspectives reflected in these official translations. That is precisely why multilingual analysis would be a suitable methodological approach for exploring the full semantic meaning behind a term of EU law.

167 Kjær 2007:81–82.
168 Kjær citing Sandrini 2007: 81.
169 Kjær 2016: 105.
170 Kjær 2016: 105.
171 Engberg 2016: 175–180.

4 A Framework for Analysis

This book was written in response to the undeniable need for concrete examples, in pursuit of greater clarity as to the CJEU's strategic treatment of ambiguity as a means for ensuring the implementation of the authority of EU law. Such an ambitious endeavour, however, is bound to run into a number of serious methodological challenges. Some of the major hurdles included adapting a workable model of ambiguity; factoring in the constitutional peculiarities of the EU legal order, especially in regard to the CJEU's singular adjudicative style and multilingualism; and working out a coherent and systematic classification of the examples found.

The Selection of Case Studies

It is fair to say that spotting the multitude of ambiguities scattered across the EU legislative text or the CJEU's preliminary rulings is not a particularly taxing task for the trained eye of a linguist. The potential of ambiguity to acquire relevance in the future extends beyond the immediately obvious, if one further considers the possibility of latent ambiguity becoming patent, should the appropriate set of material facts be brought before the CJEU.[1] The search for relevant samples of ambiguity therefore appears to be at serious risk of devolving into a needle-in-a-haystack scenario.

Most of these ambiguities, however, merely hold the *promise* of relevance. Their meaning may or may not become subject to legal dispute, the resolution of which will test the interpretative prowess of the CJEU and will directly impact the lives of millions of EU citizens. This is why this book is strictly interested in samples of ambiguity that are central, and not peripheral, to the ultimate resolution of the legal case. They must also have actual, and not hypothetical or future, ramifications for the CJEU's decision-making. Although there is no need for an

1 Anthony Ossa-Richardson explains, citing Sir Francis Bacon, that "[p]atent ambiguity 'is that which appears to be ambiguous upon the deed'", while "[l]atent ambiguity is 'that which seemeth certain and without ambiguity, for anything that appeareth upon the deed, but there is some collateral matter out of the deed, that breedeth the ambiguity'" (Ossa-Richardson citing Bacon 2019: 86).

DOI: 10.4324/9781003294870-5

express acknowledgement of the presence of ambiguity by the CJEU as explained earlier, it is vital that the relevant example of ambiguity is both linguistically and legally plausible. A complete correspondence between the legal and linguistic aspects of a sample of ambiguity, in the spirit of Maduro's maxim cited earlier, guarantees that the linguistic readings of ambiguity (i.e. Paraphrase 1 and Paraphrase 2) actually match workable legal rules whose effects make sense in the pragmatic context of the EU legal order.

Even with all of these limitations in place, it is only a select few of these ambiguities that have changed the trajectory of the evolution of the EU legal order by substantially facilitating the implementation of the authority of EU law. This is why the search for examples concentrated on case-law from the preliminary rulings procedure under Article 267 TFEU. This singular mechanism for the interpretation of EU law not only constitutes a key form of judicial dialogue between the Court of Justice and the national courts,[2] but also is "arguably the most important measure for enforcing EU law against Member States".[3] On a systemic scale, the preliminary ruling procedure is of "pivotal" significance, since it has kept a faithful record of the "evolution and stasis" of the legal integration process in the EU throughout the years.[4] It is no wonder then that Derlén and Lindholm's empirical study on the characteristics of precedent confirmed that the highest number of CJEU's most important judgments originate from the preliminary ruling procedure.[5] This finding reinforces the impression that the preliminary ruling procedure, and not infringement proceedings and/or direct actions, has the greatest contribution towards establishing CJEU's case-law as a particularly impactful source of law in the EU.[6]

Furthermore, Derlén and Lindholm's study[7] uses network analysis to identify the areas of case law within the preliminary ruling procedure that hold the greatest value for the implementation of the authority of EU law. It was established that cases concerning the internal market and competition law have high precedential and persuasive value, with the latter outscoring the former.[8] Within the area of fundamental freedoms, cases concerning the free movement of capital take the lead, contrary to the established view within the academic community that this position belongs to cases about the free movement of goods.[9] Further, with the exception of jurisprudence regarding the internal market and competition law, it is preliminary rulings dedicated to "principles, objectives and tasks of the Treaties" that have the greatest precedential and persuasive value.[10] Lastly, there

2 Rosas 2008: 125–126.
3 Broberg 2017: 111.
4 De la Mare & Donnelly 2011: 365.
5 Derlén & Lindholm 2015: 1082–1083.
6 Derlén & Lindholm 2015: 1083, 1087–1088.
7 Derlén & Lindholm 2015.
8 Derlén & Lindholm 2015: 1088.
9 Derlén & Lindholm 2015: 1088–1089.
10 Derlén & Lindholm 2015: 1089.

were a number of formal requirements that would make a CJEU preliminary reference more embedded in the network of case-law and/or enhance its persuasive and precedential power: a higher number of observations, a case being decided by a Full Court or the Grand Chamber or the Court dealing with a legal problem that is "particularly complicated or concerns a large portion of society – without necessarily being politically controversial".[11]

The aforementioned empirical study certainly provides a helpful set of guidelines, since it adds a much-needed degree of specificity and systematisation to the process of selection of examples. Indeed, the selection of Case Studies broadly conforms to these instructions. However, the final choice of Case Studies departs from Derlén and Lindholm's guidelines (2015) in a number of significant ways.

To begin with, despite its clear superiority in terms of persuasive and precedential power in Derlén and Lindholm's empirical study (2015), EU competition law was completely excluded from the scope of this book. According to Article 3 TFEU, competition law is an area in which the EU has exclusive competence. The authority of EU law meets its greatest challenge when conflict arises between the CJEU and the national courts regarding the distribution of competences. Therefore, areas of exclusive competence are unlikely to provide appropriate examples for understanding how ambiguity could be used by the Court strategically to tackle this challenge.

Furthermore, it would be more prudent to concentrate on areas of law where the EU enjoys shared competence with the Member States (Article 4 TFEU), namely the internal market and the area of freedom, security, and justice. Moreover, the area of fundamental rights was originally left out from the distribution of competences in the EU Treaties. The Charter of Fundamental Rights of the EU codified the CJEU's continuous struggle to assert its jurisdiction in the area of fundamental rights protection through case law. The same is true for the entrenchment of the provisions on EU citizenship in the TFEU. Therefore, the selected Case Studies are representative of the most contentious and challenging areas of law for the implementation of the authority of EU law from the perspective of acceptability. As such, they provide an appropriate environment in which the strategic value of ambiguity could be explored in a fruitful and constructive manner.

Finally, Derlén and Lindholm's study (2015) provides only the initial point of departure for a general overview of the preliminary references by the CJEU. In the interest of greater accuracy, the definition of a leading case should be made conditional on the specific circumstances of each case and its reception by the legal community. This is where Urška Šadl's (2015) suggested criteria for identifying a leading case in EU law could prove to be helpful.

In order to provide a satisfactory answer to the central questions raised in this book, one must necessarily have a systematic approach to examining the different

11 Derlén & Lindholm 2015: 1092, 1096–1097.

manifestations of ambiguity in the EU legal order. The Case Studies presented in this work are certainly intended to lay the foundation in this respect, but cannot be said to constitute a complete and exhaustive account.

Constructing a Typology of Examples

For the purposes of this book, the three-dimensional model of ambiguity forms the base for the typology of ambiguity in the EU legal system.[12] Since the main aim of this book is to investigate the strategic value of ambiguity, the search for examples aimed to provide samples of ambiguity that fall into one of two categories: '*strategic production of ambiguity*' or '*strategic perception of ambiguity*'.[13] The former category describes circumstances where the CJEU strategically produces ambiguous language in its preliminary ruling. The latter category refers to a scenario where the CJEU strategically perceives ambiguity produced by the legislator in the legislative text, which means the Court resolves the ambiguity by means of judicial interpretation (referred to in this study as '*strategic resolution of ambiguity*').[14] It is important to stress that the classification is adapted to suit the perspective of the Court of Justice. Thus, where the strategic perception of ambiguity (i.e. the strategic resolution of ambiguity by the Court) is concerned, it would be irrelevant whether the legislator has produced the ambiguity in the Treaty provision strategically or not. The same goes for the national courts perceiving ambiguity in the legislative provision or in the rulings of the Court of Justice. The point of view of the national courts here matters only insofar as, in cases of strategic perception of ambiguity, the referring court also perceives the ambiguity in the same EU legislative provision as the Court of Justice but could interpret it in a dramatically different manner. The misalignment in perception of the legislative text, which manifests itself in their two contrasting interpretations, could constitute further evidence for the existence of ambiguity. Although the perspectives of the EU legislature and the national courts might be intriguing enough to merit further investigation, they fall outside of the remit of this book.

Furthermore, it was paramount that the typology design addressed the role of ambiguity in the CJEU's efforts to ensure the implementation of the authority of EU law. Therefore, the traditional divide between judicial activism and judicial

12 A graphical representation of the three-dimensional model of ambiguity can be seen in Winkler 2015: 6. Winkler (2015: 6, footnote [4]) clarifies that the three-dimensional model of ambiguity was the product of collaboration between M. Bauer, J. Knape, P. Koch, C. Landmesser, J. Leonhardt, T. Susanka, S. Winkler, E. Winter-Froemel, R. Zigler, & A. Zirker, with the graphical representation being provided by T. Susanka.

13 In the three-dimensional model of ambiguity, the *strategic production of ambiguity* is indicated by "PS^+" and the *strategic perception of ambiguity* is marked with "RS^+" (Winkler 2015: 5–6).

14 Here the term "strategic resolution of ambiguity" is used in a manner similar to "ambiguity resolution" (Winter-Froemel & Zirker 2015: 315, 317, 321, 332) and "strategic ambiguity" (Winter-Froemel & Zirker 2015: 313).

restraint was integrated in the typology design. This distinction is helpful in terms of marking the fluctuations in the expansion or in the limitation of EU competences because of the Court of Justice's treatment of ambiguity.

Consequently, the following classification of examples emerged:

Type 1: Strategic resolution of ambiguity and judicial activism
Type 2: Strategic resolution of ambiguity and judicial restraint
Type 3: Strategic production of ambiguity and judicial activism
Type 4: Strategic production of ambiguity and judicial restraint

This typology reflects all the possible combinations between two pairs of features: *ambiguity resolution v. ambiguity production* and *judicial activism v. judicial restraint*. By the end of this study, each of these types will have been illustrated by at least one example, with the exception of Type 4. During the search for examples, a range of CJEU preliminary rulings were considered to fulfil that vacant spot, but none of them made a strong enough case to merit inclusion on the list. The reasons for this unsatisfactory outcome will be explored in the Conclusion.

Finally, the third element that had to be reflected in the typology design was a means of characterising the mechanics of the Court's strategic behaviour. Shai Dothan's tactics for increasing the reputation of international courts describe the Court's exercise of discretionary reasoning and the one-off issuance of demanding or less demanding judgments as part of the "*walking on the brink of non-compliance*" tactic[15] as well as the Court's gradual advancement of its judicial agenda by means of "*incrementalism*".[16] Type 1 includes the Case Studies of *Melloni* (a demanding judgment in the spirit of "walking on the brink of non-compliance") and *Ruiz Zambrano/Dereci* (an example of "incrementalism" at first, later followed by a demanding judgment as part of "walking on the brink of non-compliance"). In Type 2 (*Keck*), the CJEU exhibits judicial restraint by issuing a less demanding judgment in the style of "walking on the brink of non-compliance". Finally, Type 3 (*Åkerberg Fransson*) is also a demanding judgment in the spirit of "walking on the brink of non-compliance". Since this book offers no example of Type 4, the question of which of Dothan's judicial tactics is applicable here remains open.

Methods of Analysis

Semantic Analysis of Treaty Provisions in English

Each Case Study in this book benefits from a method of analysis tailored to their type and individual characteristics – a semantic analysis of Treaty provisions or multilingual analysis. Both of these investigative approaches are conducted in English. While the former scrutinises the English language version of the relevant

15 Dothan 2014: 117–122.
16 Dothan 2014: 131–136.

Treaty provision, the latter relies on English as the point of reference for the comparison between the language versions or official translations of the CJEU's rulings.

The Case Studies of *Melloni* and *Ruiz Zambrano/Dereci*[17] underwent semantic analysis of Treaty provisions in English. Both examples belong to Type 1 and illustrate syntactic ambiguity[18] found in Treaty provisions in the Charter of Fundamental Rights of the European Union (CFREU) and in the Treaty on the Functioning of the European Union (TFEU), respectively. As a primary source of EU law, the Treaty text is the most authoritative legal text in the hierarchy of sources of EU law. Therefore, the strategic resolution of ambiguity integrated in a Treaty provision would have the greatest potential to impact the implementation of the authority of EU law on a systemic level, especially where the CJEU is invited to interpret Treaty provisions of vital constitutional importance.

At this stage, an argument could be made that a semantic analysis in French would be a more appropriate choice than English, given the customary reliance on French as the working language in the drafting and deliberation processes at the CJEU.[19] Such a choice would not necessarily be unproblematic. The French adopted by the Court of Justice is dissimilar from the French of everyday communication.[20] Further, it may well be that the drafting process is conducted in French, but the "thinking process" that precedes it is often conducted in the mother tongue of the judge's *référendaires*,[21] which explains why the final product amounts to "a stilted and awkward text".[22] This is also the reason why the judge's *référendaires* typically engage in the repetition of expressions or in copying straight from the Court's preceding case-law or the EU legislative text.[23]

Moreover, there are concrete reasons why English is a perfectly legitimate choice for the purposes of the semantic analyses in *Melloni* and *Ruiz Zambrano/Dereci*. Thanks to the equal authenticity rule, the French language loses the

17 The preliminary rulings of *Ruiz Zambrano* and *Dereci* are combined in the same Case Study, since they share a close conceptual link – together they comprise an example of the Court's strategic resolution of ambiguity which unfolds in two stages.

18 The linguistic rule applicable in these Case Studies concerned collectivity-distributivity parallels giving rise to ambiguity. Whether this is a case of phrasal (syntactic) or lexical ambiguity is, however, debatable (see Champollion 2017: 161; MacDonald, Pearlmutter, & Seidenberg 1994: 682). Nevertheless, a more convincing case could potentially be made for syntactic ambiguity in *Melloni* and *Ruiz Zambrano/Dereci*. It is questionable exactly which part of the grammatical construction gives rise to ambiguity. Further, in both Case Studies, a compelling argument could be made in favour of ambiguity arising as a result of the entire grammatical construction, and not a single element thereof. This is why to break the entire construction down to its components (individual parts of speech), in order to subject them to multilingual analysis, would have not only been superfluous, but would have also contradicted the logic of the analysis in these two Case Studies.

19 McAuliffe 2011: 98, 104.

20 McAuliffe 2011: 98–99.

21 McAuliffe 2011: 104.

22 McAuliffe 2011: 98.

23 McAuliffe 2011: 98–99, 107–109.

aforementioned advantage over English when it comes to analysing the EU Treaty text. More importantly, in both cases, it was established that ambiguity in at least one language version of the EU Treaty text (i.e. the English one) was a close match for the CJEU's reasoning in that preliminary ruling. There is a full correspondence between the linguistic and legal (normative) interpretations of ambiguity in these instances. The mirroring between the two is so exact that it is highly unlikely that this is mere coincidence. The Court has clearly perceived the provision as ambiguous. The ambiguity in the English version has probably served as a template for the CJEU's argumentation, but it is also possible that the CJEU might have been looking at other language version(s) that contain(s) the same ambiguity. Even if no other language version contains the same ambiguity, this does not detract from the strength of the argument: one language version suffices to prove that the Court perceived the text of that EU Treaty provision as ambiguous and strategically resolved the ambiguity found there. The fact that the Court's reasoning follows closely the contours of ambiguity in that particular language version speaks for itself.

Multilingual Analysis

The other method of investigation, applicable to the Case Studies of *Åkerberg Fransson* (Type 3) and *Keck* (Type 2), is multilingual analysis based on the peculiar terminology used by the EU legislature and the CJEU. In *Åkerberg Fransson*, the CJEU strategically produced ambiguity by pragmatically enforcing the interchangeable use of terms, thus disregarding the legislative intent behind Article 51(1) CFREU. In *Keck*, the terminological distinction that the CJEU drew might seem puzzling and therefore objectionable, until one discovers that the Court was likely strategically resolving an ambiguous term in Article 34 TFEU.

Multilingual analysis is used to (a) establish the *individual* semantic meaning of the each of the terms X, Y, and Z, and (b) to prove that that the *relationships* between the terms amount to a specific variety of ambiguity – 'inter-lingual ambiguity'.[24] Although ambiguity is customarily discussed within the context of lexical units belonging to a single language ("intra-lingual ambiguity"),[25] the Case Studies at hand contain ambiguity arising between the functional equivalents of lexical units in an array of languages concurrently ("inter-lingual ambiguity").[26] In this sense, one speaks of "inter-lingual uncertainty" in scenarios when:

> two languages are considered or when one language is translated into another language. In such cases, a word, phrase or sentence in one language may not

24 Cao 2007: 71, 75, 78

25 Here the term "intra-lingual ambiguity" originates from the term "intra-lingual uncertainty" (Cao, 2007: 71, 74).

26 Cao 2007: 71, 75, 78.

> be uncertain, but additional uncertainty may become present when they are considered across two or more languages.[27]

Inter-lingual uncertainty arises when lexical, syntactical or grammatical ambiguity is at play, which gives the Court a chance for disambiguation (Cao, 2007: 70, 73, 78). It is important to note that 'intra-lingual ambiguity' and 'inter-lingual ambiguity' ultimately share the same model of ambiguity. There is one ambiguous term (X) which could be associated with two mutually exclusive interpretations (Y, Z) at the same time. The difference lies in the source of the evidence for the semantic meaning of the terms – the former category relies on a single-language text, whereas the latter category derives that information from the comparison of a selection of language versions or official translations.

At this stage, one cannot help but wonder: if 'intra-lingual ambiguity' manifests itself within the boundaries of a single language, on which linguistic plain is 'inter-lingual ambiguity' actually realised? In the EU legal order, the concept of 'meta-text' provides one plausible answer to this question:

> in the context of European multilingualism, the text disappears and is replaced by meta-text synthesizing twenty-three different texts … Thus, the norm is the result of a meta-text deriving from a set of legal texts in order to ensure the existence of a common norm.[28]

The idea of the totality of meaning being derived from all the language versions at once is similar to the notion of a 'hybrid text', which "[consists] of a blend of cultural and linguistic patterns, constrained by a rigid formulistic drafting style and put through many different permutations of translation".[29] In addition, it could also be the case that the legal concepts endemic to a certain legal system are resultant from the "stratification of different meanings" across legal traditions with the passage of time.[30] Each of these theories seems to convey the idea that 'inter-lingual ambiguity' is realised when all of the selected language versions (and arguably official translations) are taken together at once.

Having determined that a finding of ambiguity is the end goal of the multilingual analysis in this book, let us concentrate on describing the mechanism of the multilingual analysis in practical terms. The semantic meaning of a term, taken from the EU Treaty text or the CJEU's preliminary rulings, is revealed by means of a comparison between the iterations of the term in a selection of different language versions or official translations, respectively (see Appendix A for *Åkerberg Fransson* and Appendix B for *Keck*). In an ambiguous term (X), the multilingual analysis will show that the language versions (or official translations) could

27 Cao 2007: 71.
28 Gambaro 2012: 410.
29 McAuliffe 2011: 99.
30 Pozzo 2016: 74.

roughly be divided into two groups,[31] indicating the existence of two semantically meaningful interpretations. The question then becomes whether the semantic meaning of the other two terms (Y, Z) in the model of ambiguity, established through multilingual analysis, will necessarily (a) match the interpretations of X, and (b) show that Y and Z are also mutually exclusive. For the latter requirement, the presence of non-negligible linguistic divergences must be established between the semantic meaning of Y and Z, again ascertained through comparison between the language versions/official translations corresponding to both terms.

The selection of languages was universal for each stage of the multilingual analysis and was intended to include representatives from the main language families in the EU, namely Germanic, Romance, Slavic/Slanovic, Uralic and Hellenic. It was paramount that two languages be selected to represent each category: French and Spanish for Romance[32], Bulgarian and Polish for Slavic/Slavonic,[33] German and English for West Germanic[34] and Danish and Swedish as North Germanic[35] languages. This was done in the hope of ensuring greater accuracy of the outcome of the analysis. The only exceptions to that rule were the latter two language versions, since each category contains a single language – Finnish and Greek, respectively.

In *Åkerberg Fransson*, the ambiguous term invented by the Court seems to share a close association with the terms chosen by the legislator and appears to stem from long-standing terminology in the CJEU case-law that is deeply entrenched in the practice of EU law. In *Keck*, multilingual analysis is applied to the relevant term in the Treaty text, to prove its ambiguous nature. Nevertheless, the official translations of the terms invented by the Court of Justice that correspond to its readings constitute a veritable treasure trove of information about the way these terms are perceived by lawyer linguists of each legal tradition represented in the mix of translations. Even though these official translations are not as authoritative as the language of the case, they are still carriers of valuable data that must not be dismissed lightly. This is why the multilingual analysis in this book is practically applied both to terms invented by the CJEU and to terms from the EU Treaty text.

31 In the Case Studies displayed in this book, there are two interpretations of the ambiguous term, which is the minimum requirement for a finding of ambiguity. Theoretically speaking, however, there could be more than two interpretations of an ambiguous term, which is also valid in cases of inter-lingual ambiguity (established through multilingual analysis.

32 Encyclopaedia Britannica: www.britannica.com/topic/Romance-languages. Last accessed on 28 July 2019.

33 Encyclopaedia Britannica: www.britannica.com/topic/Slavic-languages. Last accessed on 28 July 2019.

34 Encyclopaedia Britannica: www.britannica.com/topic/Germanic-languages. Last accessed on 28 July 2019.

35 Encyclopaedia Britannica: www.britannica.com/topic/Germanic-languages. Last accessed on 28 July 2019.

Part 1 presented a brief overview of the suggested solutions to the theoretical and methodological challenges that accompanied the search for the strategic value of ambiguity for the authority of EU law. What follows is four chapters dedicated to each of the Case Studies mentioned above. In Part 2, Chapter 1 on the Case Study of *Melloni* will show how the CJEU's strategic resolution of ambiguity found in the EU Treaty text will provide evidence to question the traditional grounds for accusations in judicial activism. Chapter 2 of Part 2 presents the Case Study of *Åkerberg Fransson* which demonstrates how the CJEU strategically produces ambiguity on the pages of its preliminary ruling in an ingenuous attempt to fulfil its activist agenda by circumventing the demands of the legislative intent behind an EU Treaty provision. Chapter 3 of Part 2 focuses on the Case Study of *Keck* which will provide evidence for the CJEU's ability to exercise judicial restraint when engaging in the strategic resolution of ambiguity in the EU Treaty text. In Chapter 4 of Part 2, the Case Study of *Ruiz Zambrano/Dereci* will reveal how the CJEU uses the strategic resolution of ambiguity in an EU Treaty provision to execute a long-term agenda of judicial activism. The final instalment, Part 3, is dedicated to a critical assessment of these findings with respect to the two clashing strands of existing theories on the CJEU's relationship with ambiguity. More importantly, a third theory on the strategic value of the authority of EU law, one that reflects more accurately and completely the conclusions drawn from the evidence presented in this book, will emerge. The concluding chapter will also offer a brief summary of the advantages and disadvantages associated with the CJEU's use of ambiguity-based reasoning, in comparison to other alternatives.

Part 2

The Case Studies

1 Judicial Activism Reconsidered? The CJEU's Strategic Resolution of Ambiguity in *Melloni* (Case C-399/11)[1]

Introduction

On 26 February 2013, the Grand Chamber of the CJEU issued two preliminary rulings – *Melloni* and *Åkerberg Fransson* – that have altered "the blueprint for the fundamental rights architecture in the European Union ('EU') for years to come".[2] This significant advancement of EU law, however, came at a steep price. The Court's interpretations of key provisions of the Charter of Fundamental Rights in the EU (CFREU) – Articles 53 and 51 CFREU, respectively – gave rise to severe accusations in judicial activism from the national constitutional courts and the EU legal community alike.

Although *Melloni* has been generally overshadowed by its more interventionist counterpart, the case certainly stands as a paragon example of judicial activism in its own right.[3] The outcome of *Melloni* had a profound adverse impact on the relationship between the Spanish Constitutional Court (*Tribunal Constitucional*) and the CJEU: "as the story unfolded, the actors grew more entrenched and quite one-sided".[4] This is why the CJEU's treatment of the principle of primacy of EU law in *Melloni* is said to have marked the rekindling of constitutional conflict in the EU, which had been dormant since the Treaty of Lisbon.[5]

The following chapter will reveal that the CJEU strategically resolved ambiguity found in Article 53 CFREU, the full text of which goes as follows:

> Nothing in this Charter shall be interpreted as restricting or adversely affecting human rights and fundamental freedoms *as recognised*, in their respective fields of application, *by Union law* and international law and by international

1 This case study presents a revised version of my earlier publication: Kartalova, Sofiya (2018). The Scales of Justice in Equilibrium: The ECJ's Strategic Resolution of Ambiguity in *Stefano Melloni v Ministerio Fiscal* 2013 (Case C-399/11). *International Journal of Language and Law*, 7, 25–46. DOI: 10.14762/jll.2018.025.
2 Schima 2015: 1098.
3 Schima 2015: 1105–1106.
4 Torres Perez 2014: 309.
5 Besselink 2014: 1169–1170.

DOI: 10.4324/9781003294870-7

> agreements to which the Union, the Community or all the Member States are party, including the European Convention for the Protection of Human Rights and Fundamental Freedoms, *and by the Member States' constitutions.*
>
> (Article 53 CFREU, emphasis added.)

It is argued that the construction "as recognised ... by Union law ... and by the Member States' constitutions" is ambiguous. The Court of Justice was presented with two equally plausible interpretations of the legislative text, in both linguistic and legal terms. The provision could be interpreted to mean that Union law and the Member States' constitutions are to be considered "together and jointly" or "together and separately".

The linguistic and legal analysis of this sample of ambiguity will provide a more profound understanding of the circumstances in which the CJEU had to make its choice of interpretation as well as its priorities in adjudication. As a result, the grounds for making these accusations in judicial activism will have to be reconsidered. The presence of ambiguity left the CJEU with little to no guidance as to the EU legislator's intent on a crucial point of law. The wording of the provision was ambiguous as to whether the applicable standard of fundamental rights protection under the Charter was that of the Union ("together and jointly") or that of the Member State in question ("together and separately"). The presence of this ambiguity in Article 53 CFREU compelled the Court to engage in an extreme level of meta-teleological interpretation. Will this finding suffice to completely absolve the CJEU of its blame for having committed judicial activism? The following pages will show.

Let us begin with a brief summary of the preliminary ruling of *Melloni*. Mr Melloni was convicted of bankruptcy fraud *in absentia* by an Italian national court, which led to the activation of the European Arrest Warrant (EAW) procedure and the subsequent apprehension of the offender by the Spanish authorities.[6] As a means of resisting the execution of the EAW, Mr Melloni filed a petition for constitutional protection with the Spanish Constitutional Court.[7] Since there is no right to appeal against convictions *in absentia* under Italian procedural law,[8] Mr Melloni contended that his right to fair trial under the Spanish Constitution would be violated and his human dignity would be undermined, should his surrender to the Italian authorities take effect.[9]

The main problem was that the issuing Member State, Italy, offered a lower standard of protection of fundamental rights (with respect to the right to appeal against convictions *in absentia*) than the executing Member State, Spain. The disparity between these two standards of fundamental rights protection posed a threat to the principle of mutual trust, which is at the heart of the effectiveness of

6 *Melloni*, Case C-399/11: paragraphs 14 and 15
7 *Melloni*, Case C-399/11: paragraph 16 and 17.
8 *Melloni*, Case C-399/11: paragraphs 16 and 18.
9 *Melloni*, Case C-399/11: paragraph 18.

the EAW system. At the same time, the Spanish constitution provided a superior degree of protection of fundamental rights in comparison to the EU, which brought into question the principle of primacy of EU law.

Recognising the overall complexity and constitutional sensitivity of these issues, the Spanish Constitutional Court sought guidance on the interpretation of Article 53 CFREU in the third question of its first preliminary reference to the CJEU. The Spanish Constitutional Court requested a clarification as to a possible interpretation of the provision that would allow the Member State to review the compulsory execution of the EAW, to avoid restricting or affecting the fundamental rights recognised in its constitution.[10]

In response, the CJEU confirmed that the obligation to execute the EAW applies without exception, thus dismissing any possibility for review thereof.[11] The Court of Justice was particularly alarmed by the prospect that a Member State could be left to disapply legal provisions of EU law that come into conflict with its constitution, but are otherwise completely in line with the CFREU, as this would have a detrimental effect on the principle of the primacy of EU law and the effectiveness of EU law.[12] The CJEU also sought to prevent any interference with the uniformity of the standard of fundamental rights protection with respect to promoting mutual confidence on the basis of judicial co-operation and harmonisation in the Area of Freedom, Security, and Justice.[13] As a result, the Court of Justice held that the national courts can continue to apply their national standard of protection of fundamental rights, under the condition that "the level of protection provided for by the Charter, as interpreted by the Court, and the primacy, unity and effectiveness of EU law are not thereby compromised".[14]

The accusations in judicial activism rest on the CJEU's perceived disregard for the wording of Article 53 CFREU and its reliance on an extreme mode of meta-teleological interpretation, which stresses the importance of the principles of EU law in the context of the EU legal system.[15] To begin with, a more extensive introduction to the application and purpose behind Article 53 CFREU would have been appropriate, since the case of *Melloni* constituted the debut of this tremendously significant provision in the Court's jurisprudence.[16] The CJEU made no effort to employ techniques of syllogistic, historical, comparative or linguistic analysis that could help alleviate the Court's perceived abrasiveness in judicial dialogue that comes with an extreme display of meta-teleological interpretation.[17] The Court has instead fuelled

10 *Melloni*, Case C-399/11: paragraph 26.
11 *Melloni*, Case C-399/11: paragraph 56, 57.
12 *Melloni*, Case C-399/11: paragraphs 58 and 59.
13 *Melloni*, Case C399/11: paragraphs 62–63, 37.
14 *Melloni*, Case C399/11: paragraph 60.
15 Maduro 2007:140.
16 Torres Perez 2014: 318.
17 Maduro 2007: 145.

criticism by delivering argumentation that is "short and cursory and extremely self-referential".[18]

This was certainly a missed opportunity for the Court to enhance the acceptability of the outcome in *Melloni* by directly engaging with the Spanish Constitutional Court's suggested solution and by offering a comprehensible explanation for its choice to favour the EU standard of fundamental rights protection above all else.[19] Instead, the Court confidently referred to its previous case-law without properly justifying the connections.[20]An argument could be made to the effect that these references were all aimed at reinforcing the link between the principle of primacy and the effectiveness of EU law.[21] The Court of Justice seemed preoccupied with using the principle of primacy of EU law to re-conceptualise fundamental rights protection in the EU.[22] This could be seen as a fitting solution to the conflict between the Spanish right to fair trial and the effectiveness of the EAW, since systemic problems of supranational nature tend to be best resolved by means of the same origins, if the autonomy of the legal order and the legality of its rules are to be preserved.[23]

However, the Court of Justice revealed very little of its thought process, leaving EU legal community to read between the lines. In essence, the Court's unclear and insufficient justificatory reasoning and excessive reliance on meta-teleological interpretation led to accusations of judicial activism. Without any further insight into the Court's possible decision-making process in the preliminary ruling of *Melloni*, the "black box of European law" remains as impenetrable as ever. The discovery of ambiguity at the heart of Article 53 CFREU is the first step towards obtaining this much-needed insight.

The Legislative Intent Behind Article 53 CFREU

More so than any other legal text mentioned in *Melloni*, Article 53 CFREU holds the key to unlocking the mystery behind CJEU's reasoning there. Both the Spanish Constitutional Court and the CJEU consistently and exclusively refer to this provision as the legal basis of their reasoning. This is evident from the explicit reference made to Article 53 CFREU and the snippets of language borrowed from the provision itself and integrated in the formulation of the third question of the preliminary reference.[24] The preliminary ruling also evoked Article 53 CFREU to hold that the proposed interpretation is rejected and a new interpretation was issued in its place.[25]

18 Rauchegger 2015: 114.
19 Rauchegger 2015: 114.
20 For this purpose, the Court refers to *Internationale Handelsgesellschaft* (Case 11–70) and *Winner Wetten* (Case C-409/06) as well as to Opinion 1/91 (ECR I-6079: paragraph 21) and Opinion 1/09(ECR I-1137: paragraph 65).
21 *Melloni*, Case C-399/11: paragraph 59.
22 Rauchegger 2015: 113.
23 Rauchegger 2015: 113; Itzcovich 2012: 365.
24 *Melloni*, Case C-399/11: paragraph 26.
25 *Melloni*, Case C-399/11: paragraphs 57 and 64.

However, a certain peculiarity in the judicial dialogue becomes apparent at this stage. Although both actors were looking at the same legal text, their interpretations of its contents differed. This is hardly unusual in and of itself in the practice of adjudication, but the difference in opinion in this case was stark and beyond reconciliation. Essentially, the actors put forward interpretations of the same legal text that are ***diametrically opposed*** to each other. It is also noteworthy that neither the preliminary reference, nor the preliminary ruling, contained textual evidence from the wording of the relevant provision in support of either court's reading. Even at this initial stage, a suspicion takes root in one's mind: could it be that ambiguity at the heart of Article 53 CFREU is to blame for this extreme divergence between the available interpretations of the provision?

Before examining the ambiguity at the centre of *Melloni*, let us first discuss the possibilities regarding the purpose and function of Article 53 CFREU. Seeing as the *Melloni* preliminary ruling was historically the first time Article 53 CFREU was applied by the CJEU[26], there had been little information in the way of preceding case-law to aid any interpretive efforts at the time. In circumstances such as these, the chief, if not only, guiding principle becomes legislative intent. This is a particularly aggravating factor in a situation where the presence of ambiguity at the heart of Article 53 CFREU would further deprive the Court of Justice of the means for inferring legislative intent.

To gain basic understanding of the possible legislative intent behind Article 53 CFREU, let us compare it with Article 53 ECHR. What these two provisions have in common is that they are both seen as "safeguard rules".[27] The Charter provision could also be called a "savings clause", which is ordinarily designed to confer protection on the individual by virtue of the international law instrument it belongs to, without impinging on the protection available by preceding legislative texts.[28] Although Article 53 CFREU was originally intended to echo Article 53 ECHR and regulate the levels of protection provided by the Charter and ECHR, it was soon repurposed.[29] This change, as well as the reasons for it, were made evident in the choice of wording, which brought about two substantial corrections. Both of these amendments to the original formulation will prove to be of vital importance for the linguistic analysis of ambiguity.

Firstly, the addition of a special subordinate clause ("in their respective fields of application") was necessitated by the successful application of Article 53 CFREU on a supranational level.[30] Presumably, the inclusion of the subordinate clause was aimed at addressing the problem of the overlap between the national and supranational layer of fundamental rights protection[31] and to prevent

26 Alkema et al. 2015: 8, 20.
27 Alkema et al. 2015: 8.
28 Widmann 2002: 349.
29 Liisberg 2001: 1172, 1174–1181.
30 Widmann 2002: 349.
31 Widmann 2002: 349.

any interference with the principle of the primacy of EU law.[32] Despite the lack of conclusive evidence to this effect, it might very well be a matter of safeguarding the principle of primacy by ensuring that "the revised wording would make it clear that national constitutions could prevail only in the sphere of exclusive national competence".[33] In this sense, its function is most likely to serve as a tangible guarantee that the delineation of powers and competences between the Union and the Member States as well as the scope of EU law would remain unaffected by the Charter.[34] The first part of the linguistic analysis presented below will show that, even if this were indeed the intention behind this drafting choice, the EU legislator's attempt at introducing greater clarity was unsuccessful. The addition of the subordinate clause had no effect on the ambiguity found in Article 53 CFREU.

Secondly, the expression "the Member States' constitutions" was included in Article 53 CFREU as a substitute to "under the laws of any High Contracting Party" in Article 53 ECHR.[35] The former alternative is much more specific than the latter, since the latter seems to extend to statutory instruments and delegated legislative acts.[36] It would appear that the drafters of Article 53 CFREU anticipated that the provision is likely to be relied on in circumstances of constitutional conflict, where the preservation of national constitutional rights is on the line. This lends credence to the assumption that from the very beginning the drafters were largely aware of the high constitutional value of the provision, the possible practical circumstances of its application and the strategic importance of its wording. In the end, this expression contributed to the ambiguity found in Article 53 CFREU.

Despite these amendments in the wording of the clause, it seems that its contents are no clearer than before. The clash of interpretations occurring between the Spanish Constitutional Court and the CJEU was not an isolated instance of confusion with respect to guidance as to the hierarchical order established between the national and supranational standard of fundamental rights protection. For instance, Anne-Marieke Widmann put forward three options to describe the interaction between these two tiers of protection – "the local standard" (EU law as a minimum level of protection, while recognising the superiority of a higher national standard in cases of conflict), "uniform fixed standard" (EU law being representative of both the minimum and maximum level of protection) and "uniform moveable standard" (national constitutional courts are entrusted with setting a maximum level of protection).[37] Similarly, Advocate General Bot concurred and supplemented this division of possible interpretations with the notion of the Charter claiming supremacy only within the scope of EU law and

32 Opinion of Advocate General Bot 2012: paragraph 100.
33 Liisberg 2001: 1175–1176.
34 Alkema et al. 2015: 10.
35 Alkema et al. 2015: 10.
36 Alkema et al. 2015: 10.
37 Widmann 2002: 346–348.

leaving the rest to national constitutional courts to handle.[38] Thus, it seems to be the case that Article 53 CFREU has had a similarly perplexing effect both on those who concentrate solely on the legislative text, like Widmann, and those who let the circumstances of *Melloni* guide their reasoning, such as Advocate General Bot. This implies that the lack of clarity is inherent in the drafting of this provision. The specifics of the case at hand merely serve to further highlight its deficiencies.

At this stage, one begins to wonder why, if the EU legislator was aware of the provision's vulnerabilities, the ambiguity at the heart of Article 53 CFREU was not properly removed? After the wording of the provision was redacted as detailed above, no further steps were taken to shed light on these issues during later discussions at the Convention.[39] Given the extraordinarily high stakes, it is certainly puzzling that the issue of primacy integrated in Article 53 CFREU, which clearly posed problems of interpretation on a textual level at the very first attempt of application, was not fully resolved by the EU legislator.

It could be that the EU legislator was simply confident that the amendments made reliably ensured that the wording of the provision contained no ambiguity. However, there is another plausible explanation. It might be the case that the discussions got terminated, once it was established that the draft provision balanced the interests of all parties concerned in a sufficiently satisfactory manner. Leonard Besselink argues that it is certainly plausible that ambiguity might have contributed to reaching this mutually favourable outcome:

> The state of affairs as to the intention of [Article 53 CFREU] was entirely open and left ambiguous, perhaps consciously. From the EU perspective, one was perhaps able to say primacy was not given up, from the national constitutional perspective, the prevailing national standard of protection was not given up either.[40]

Besselink's proposition was disputed by Bruno de Witte on grounds that there is no evidence in the preparatory work prior to the Charter that the legislator had any intention to deal with the issue of primacy and that, even if that were the case, the provision would have been drafted "in less ambiguous terms".[41] Besselink[42] responded by highlighting the fact that the Charter was at the time envisioned to be an instrument with no binding effect, which left the drafters with substantial liberty as to its contents. Further, it would be highly improbable for the drafters to incorporate the doctrine of absolute primacy into a legislative act with binding power.[43]

38 Opinion of Advocate General Bot 2012: paragraphs 91–95.
39 Liisberg 2001: 1190.
40 Besselink 2014: 1181.
41 De Witte 2013: 213.
42 Besselink 2014: 1181.
43 Besselink 2014: 1181.

While Besselink seems to perceive the presence of ambiguity in Article 53 CFREU as beneficial for reaching agreement between the parties, De Witte favours the setting of clear-cut boundaries in communication. Regardless of the difference in opinion regarding the utility of ambiguity, however, both commentators seem to agree that the wording of Article 53 CFREU is indeed ambiguous.

Linguistic Analysis

Article 53 CFREU as the Source of Ambiguity

Let us now direct our attention to the wording of Article 53 CFREU, to discuss precisely how ambiguity emerged here:

> Nothing in this Charter shall be interpreted as restricting or adversely affecting human rights and fundamental freedoms as recognised, in their respective fields of application, by Union law and international law … and by the Member States' constitutions.

It is argued that the relevant sample of ambiguity is most likely to be found in the entire construction "*as recognised by … and by …*" (i.e. "as recognised … by Union law … and by the Member States' constitutions"). On this basis, the construction could be given two mutually exclusive interpretations: "as considered together and jointly" (Paraphrase 1) or "as considered together and separately" (Paraphrase 2).

The guiding linguistic principle seems to rely on the differentiation between collectivity and distributivity as the underlying rationale of ambiguity. In this context, let us examine Brendan S. Gillon's idea that:

> [I]n English, plural noun phrases in subject position give rise to so-called collective and distributive construals. An example of this is found in the sentence given below which is, in fact, true on both a distributive and a collective construal: (1.0) Whitehead and Russell wrote a book. (1.1) Whitehead and Russell wrote a book together. (1.2) Whitehead and Russell wrote a book each.[44]

This parallel[45] between the collective and distributive construals of plural noun phrases leads to ambiguity in Gillon's estimation.[46] To refer back to Article 53 CFREU, Paraphrase 1 could be seen as a collective construal, while Paraphrase 2 could be said to correspond to a distributive construal.

44 Gillon 1996: 443–444.
45 The shift from active to passive voice, as expressed by the *by*-phrase, of the agentive verb is of no consequence for establishing this parallel (Gillon 1996: 450).
46 Gillon 1987: 199, 215–216.

The existence of the phenomenon of "collective-distributive ambiguity", as predicated on Gillon's definition of ambiguity,[47] was also later recognised by Chinatsu Aone.[48] Furthermore, Roger Schwarzschild[49] discusses a similar idea, based on the "sets theory" and "union theory" of plural noun phrases linked by term conjunction. Although the distinction is only conditionally applicable,[50] this condition is satisfied by the inclusion of the plural form of "the Member States' constitutions" contained in Article 53 CFREU, so the example at hand could still be framed in those terms.

There is some disagreement among scholars on whether ambiguity originates from the plural noun phrase or the verb phrase. Gillon is clearly a proponent of ambiguity found in the plural noun phrase.[51] However, Peter Lasersohn argues exclusively for verb phrase ambiguity.[52] If Lasersohn is indeed correct, the verb "to recognise" from Article 53 CFREU must be scrutinised more closely. The verb "to recognise" is not considered capable of intensifying the contrast between collective and distributive readings,[53] so this means that it allows for their simultaneous existence. Further, it is likely to be viewed as an ambiguous verb that gives rise to collectivity-distributivity parallel interpretations, according to Dowty's classification.[54]

Lastly, ambiguity may arise by virtue of the use of the conjunction "and", to unite "Union law" and "the Member States' constitutions". In this case, ambiguity emerges on account of the relationship established between nouns or adjectives linked with "and", since this conjunction "can convey that the members of a group are to be considered together, but it can also convey that they are to be considered together and separately".[55] The same idea has been expressed in the context of legal drafting as follows: the phrase "A and B" could be interpreted to mean "A and B, jointly or severally" or "A and B, jointly but not severally".[56]

It seems that the construction "as recognised ... by Union law ... and by the Member States' constitutions" contains ambiguity leading to collectivity-distributivity parallels, regardless of the true source of ambiguity – the plural

47 Gillon adopts the following definition of ambiguity for this purpose: "A sentence is ambiguous if, with respect to a given state of affairs, the sentence can be both truly affirmed and truly denied" (Gillon 1987: 202).

48 Aone 1991 32–33.

49 Schwarzschild 1996: 6.

50 The condition is that the sentences "contain a conjoined noun phrase one of whose conjuncts is itself a plural (formed by conjunction or common noun pluralization)" (Schwarzschild 1996: 8).

51 Gillon 1996; Gillon 1990b. Note that Gillon recognises the significance of the relationship between the noun phrase and the verb phrase for the collectivity-distributivity parallels (Gillon 1996: 449–450).

52 Lasersohn 1995: 83, 124.

53 Gillon 1996: 449–450.

54 Dowty 1987: 98.

55 Adams & Kaye 2006: 1172.

56 Dunahoo 1970: 146.

noun phrase, the verb phrase or the conjunction "and". In other words, all paths lead to the same conclusion.[57] Could it be that these interdependent elements contribute to the emergence of ambiguity *simultaneously*? That may very well be the case, if ambiguity flows from the noun phrase united by the conjunction "and", but is only made legally meaningful through the verb "to recognise". Thus, ambiguity is produced and resolved exclusively in a single legal and linguistic plain, namely identifying *by whom* the act of recognition is performed.

Finally, the construction of this theory hinges on the inclusion of plural noun phrase "the Member States' constitutions" in the sample of ambiguity. This result conforms to the expectations formed by the drafting amendments to Article 53 CFREU made by the EU legislature, the circumstances of which were detailed earlier. It may be safe to conclude then that there is a great likelihood that the sample of ambiguity thus framed has a strategic purpose with respect to the problem of the primacy of EU law.

The Subordinate Clause "in Their Respective Fields of Application"

As previously discussed, the inclusion of the subordinate clause "in their respective fields of application" by the EU legislator in Article 53 CFREU most probably has direct relevance to the issue of the primacy of EU law. Its function seems to be clarify the legislator's position on this matter beyond any doubt. The following section questions to what extent the EU legislator was successful at this supposed attempt at removing some perceived indeterminacy in the legislative text.

At first glance, it would seem that the EU legislator placed great reliance in the disambiguating properties of the adjective "respective". To this effect, let us consider the following example: "Jill and Ben visited their uncles".[58] This sentence gives rise to two alternative interpretations: "Jill visited her uncles and Ben's uncles, and Ben visited his uncles and Jill's uncles" and "Jill visited her uncles, and Ben visited his uncles".[59] The insertion of the adjective respective in the example sentence ("Jill and Ben visited their respective uncles") has the power to force the latter interpretation.[60] This example demonstrates that, where collectivity-distributivity parallels are concerned, the addition of the adjective "respective" is capable of resolving its ambiguity in favour of a distributive construal of the adjacent plural noun phrase. At this point, it must be noted that the well-established view that the adjective "respective" could successfully work as

57 It must be noted, however, that Lasersohn dismisses the claim that ambiguity might originate from the plural noun phrase (1995: 104, 97–98, 93) or even from interaction between the two (1995: 115–116). Although Lasersohn puts forward the same argument in his earlier work (1989: 133), his contention is later effectively challenged by Gillon (1990: 482). Therefore, this idea still remains contentious.

58 Gillon 1996: 452–453.

59 Gillon 1996: 452–453.

60 Gillon 1996: 452.

a distributive operator with respect to predicates[61] has now been refuted, which suggests its function could only be described as a nominal distributive operator.[62]

The use of the adverb "respectively" is considered to present a reading that is antithetic to a collective reading.[63] Thus, one might attempt to argue that the adjective "respective" automatically acquires the same disambiguating effect by association with the adverb "respectively". However, this claim would be inaccurate, since they fulfil different semantic functions: "*Respective* is an attributive adjective whose scope of modification is restricted to the noun phrase in which it is embedded, and *respectively* is an adverb that directly affects the semantics of the predicate of a sentence".[64] While the use of "respectively" guarantees the desired clause-level respective reading as a rule, the same is only sometimes true for the use of "respective".[65] On this basis, it is fair to say that the disambiguating effect of the adverb "respectively" cannot be automatically transposed onto the adjective "respective", since the "respective" modifier is much narrower in scope than the "respectively" modifier. This means that the adjective "respective" has to be targeted with great precision at a particular part of the sentence, in order to achieve the desired disambiguating effect.

Let us now return to the wording of Article 53 CFREU: "human rights and fundamental freedoms ... as recognised, in their respective fields of application, by Union law and international law ... and by the Member States' constitutions". It is evident that the subordinate clause "in their respective fields of application" that contains the adjective "respective" is intended as a response to the question: "Where do the Member States' constitutions and Union law recognise human rights and fundamental freedoms?". The role of the adjective "respective" is then relegated to a mere forcing of the distributive construal of the relationship between the fields of application of Union law and the Member States' constitutions (i.e. Member States' constitutions and their own field(s) of application; Union law and its own field of application). In other words, the use of the adjective "respective" guarantees an unambiguous reading of the subordinate clause, but does nothing to remove the ambiguity in the main sentence.

Now let us consider if the ambiguity in the main sentence survives. It is argued that the ambiguity in the construction "to be recognised ... by Union law ... and by the Member States' constitutions" remains unresolved by the use of the adjective "respective". To this effect, one need simply ask: "By whom are human rights

61 In grammatical terms, a predicate is "the part of a sentence that contains the verb and gives information about the subject: In the sentence, "*We went to the airport*", "*went to the airport*" is the predicate". Cambridge Dictionary, https://dictionary.cambridge.org/dictionary/english/predicate last accessed on 18 January 2022.

62 Okada 1999: 877–879.

63 Gawron & Kehler 2002: 87. Predication based on the adverb "respectively" is considered to be another form of plural predication (Gawron & Kehler 2002: 87), which, in this respect, is similar to distributivity (Fast 2005: 17–18).

64 Okada 1999: 872, emphasis added.

65 Gawron & Kehler 2002: 88.

and fundamental freedoms recognised?" The appropriate answer then would be: "by Union law ... and by the Member States' constitutions". It remains unclear whether the act of recognition is performed together and jointly (collective construal) or together and separately (distributive construal). The use of "respective" makes no difference here. In the light of these findings, it seems safe to conclude that the subordinate clause "in their respective fields of application" was unsuccessful at resolving the ambiguity inherent in Article 53 CFREU.

To summarise, the linguistic analysis has proven that ambiguity in Article 53 CFREU survived, despite the use of the adjective "respective" in the subordinate clause. If that were not so and ambiguity in Article 53 CFREU were in fact fully removed, then the issue of primacy would be resolved outright and even the theoretical possibility of an overlap between the two regimes of fundamental rights protection would be dismissed. Further, such a straightforward interpretation would rob Article 53 CFREU of its *effet utile*[66] and render the preliminary reference of *Melloni* pointless. This line of thought logically suggests that the ambiguity, which gave rise to the contrasting interpretations issued by the CJEU and the Spanish Constitutional Court of Article 53 CFREU, must lie elsewhere in the text of the legal provision. It was further established that the unresolved ambiguity in the main sentence of Article 53 CFREU (i.e. in the construction "as recognised ... by Union law ... and by the Member States' constitutions") opens up two feasible possibilities in linguistic terms: "as recognised together and separately" or "as recognised together and jointly". Let us now explore if the ambiguity in Article 53 CFREU, thus formulated, makes sense in legal terms.

Legal Analysis

The *Melloni* case turns on defining the terms of the interaction between the national and the supranational layers of fundamental rights protection in the EU. The constitutional dilemma in the *Melloni* preliminary ruling is illustrative of a trend where treaties often fail to regulate the overlap between different regimes, which results in the absence of a clear hierarchical order between parallel sources of authority.[67] In the absence of clear guidance, two possibilities emerge. As a result, a peculiar form of pluralism manifests itself according to the legal text,[68] which suggests that the same "human rights and fundamental freedoms" gain recognition by two sources at the same time, with each of these sources claiming ultimate supremacy in its own domain. This model of pluralism is reminiscent of Neil MacCormick's non-hierarchical notion of "radical pluralism" which outgrows the framing in terms of primacy and emphasises the lack of communication between the national and the EU legal systems.[69] It is unnecessary for these

66 Lenaerts 2012: 398; De Boer 2013: 1092–1093.
67 Alter, Helfer, & Madsen 2016: 4–5.
68 Walker, Maduro, Kumm, & Komarek cited in Lenaerts, 2012: 398.
69 Eleftheriadis citing MacCormick 2010: 371–372; Eleftheriadis 2010: 371–374.

sources to overstep the limits of their respective fields of application to engage in a confrontation. It is their mere existence as competing alternatives to each other that inevitably leads to their conflict. This leaves ambiguous the issue of which of these competing sources of authority would prevail in cases of overlap.

Thus, the full correspondence between the linguistic and normative dimensions of the sample of ambiguity has been clearly demonstrated. In other words, there is a meaningful legal interpretation that matches the linguistic paraphrase of the ambiguous language in Article 53 CFREU. The centrality of the act of ambiguity resolution to the CJEU's decision-making in *Melloni* is also guaranteed, which means the ambiguity found in Article 53 CFREU is highly likely to have been essential to the ultimate outcome of said preliminary ruling.

Based on the two readings of ambiguity in Article 53 CFREU presented earlier, the Charter of Fundamental Rights could be interpreted by the CJEU as affording a homogenous level of protection of fundamental rights ("together and jointly") or a heterogeneous level of protection ("together and separately"). In the former case, there could only be one uniform standard of protection of fundamental rights at EU level, under which any national standard of protection would necessarily be subsumed. The latter scenario allows for the parallel coexistence of a Union standard alongside the national standards of protection of fundamental rights.

The case of *Melloni* demonstrates how this ambiguity created an opportunity to gain insight into the Court of Justice's decision-making as it makes the strategic choice between imposing a conditional or an absolute model of primacy of EU law in the execution of the European Arrest Warrant with respect to trials *in absentia*. The CJEU's ambiguity resolution also reveals its strategic priorities when it comes to the implementation of the authority of EU law, since the Court was faced with the dilemma of upholding mutual trust or protecting fundamental rights. Admittedly, the Court of Justice was familiar with this scenario, as it had previously encountered a similar dilemma in the cases of *Jeremy F* and *Radu*, where priority was given to mutual trust, i.e. the effectiveness of the European Arrest Warrant.[70] However, *Melloni* illustrates a rare situation where the clash between fundamental rights and mutual trust had never before been directly and explicitly linked to the principle of the primacy of EU law. This makes *Melloni* a particularly high-profile case, the outcome of which has tremendous impact on the authority of EU law.

On a more global and theoretical scale, the CJEU's interpretation of ambiguity is indicative of its preferred strategy for the implementation of the authority of EU law on a systemic scale – "*system-building*" *through concepts*[71] or *system-maintenance through acceptability*.[72] The former approach concentrates on upholding the rule of law and the coherence within the EU legal system through the

70 Montaldo 2016: 966–967, 976, 984.
71 Leczykiewicz 2008: 782–785.
72 Paunio 2013: 157, 191, 176.

development of legal concepts in the CJEU's jurisprudence.[73] The latter method relies on a discursive model of legal certainty, in which "a shared legal paradigm through judicial reasoning" gradually emerges, to enhance the acceptability in the dialogue between the CJEU and the national courts.[74] Although ideally these two strategies would complement each other, the *Melloni* scenario exemplified one of their rare, but calamitous, clashes.

A choice of interpretation of Article 53 CFREU in favour of *system-building through concepts* would mean the Court is interested in prioritising mutual trust and the absolute model of primacy. Conversely, a choice of interpretation of this Treaty provision for *system-maintenance through acceptability* would indicate the Court's preference for fundamental rights protection and the conditional model of primacy. Judging from the reaction of the national constitutional courts to the outcome in *Melloni*, it is clear that the CJEU opted for the former at the expense of the latter. The Court appeared to deem this an acceptable constitutional cost for its ultimate decision and seemed to prefer it to other solutions.

The Constitutional Cost of the CJEU's Strategic Resolution of Ambiguity

Ultimately, the Court of Justice implicitly established the absolute primacy of EU law with respect to the European Arrest Warrant in *Melloni*.[75] Since its preferred interpretation of ambiguity in Article 53 CFREU was tantamount to a dismissal of both a lower and a higher national standard, the Court of Justice effectively asserted that the EU standard remains the only valid option for protection of national rights in the EU. *Melloni* demonstrates that the Charter "is not just a floor, but it might also become in practice a ceiling".[76]

The CJEU was evidently intent on achieving this strategic end at all costs. The list of sacrifices is impressive: dismissal of the best interests of the individual, disturbances in the CJEU's dialogue with the Spanish Constitutional Court and other national constitutional courts to the detriment of acceptability, and damage to the CJEU's relationship with the ECtHR. At this stage, one begins to wonder whether establishing absolute primacy with respect to the EAW was a worthwhile strategic end in itself or if there was some grander purpose behind it that would justify the tremendous constitutional price the Court was willing to pay.

To begin with, in so resolving ambiguity in Article 53 CFREU in *Melloni*, the CJEU showed total disregard for the interests of the individual. The Court of Justice's relentless pursuit of absolute primacy in relation to EAW cost Mr Melloni the opportunity to enjoy the higher standard of protection of his fundamental rights provided by the Spanish constitution. This outcome illustrates the

73 Leczykiewicz 2008: 782–785.
74 Paunio 2013: 157, 175–176, 191.
75 Besselink 2014: 1180–1183; Torres Perez 2014: 317.
76 Torres Perez 2014: 317.

great lengths to which the CJEU is prepared to go to protect its core systemic values – "the primacy, unity and effectiveness of EU law".[77] It seems to be the case that "the court settles for absolute primacy as a greater concern than substantive rights".[78]

Furthermore, the CJEU's choice of interpretation of ambiguity at the heart of Article 53 CFREU was done at the expense of acceptability, as it inflicted incalculable damage on its relationships with the Spanish Constitutional Court and the national constitutional courts of some of the other EU Member States. With respect to the latter, it was evident that the *Melloni*, especially when combined with *Åkerberg Fransson*, was met with disapproval in one form or another by other constitutional courts – the UK Supreme Court, the Austrian Constitutional Court and the German Constitutional Court, to name but a few.[79] Most notably, the *Antiterrordatei* judgment[80] by the *Bundesverfassungsgericht* could be seen as "a clear warning signal towards the [CJEU]", while its *Identitätskontrolle* judgment[81] showed its unwillingness to accept the Court of Justice's forceful imposition of a uniform standard of protection of EU fundamental rights.[82]

At the same time, the relationship between the CJEU and the Spanish Constitutional Court also suffered. Previously to *Melloni*, the Spanish Constitutional Court had generally demonstrated a willingness to avoid direct contact, probably in the hope of minimising the possibility of confrontation, with the CJEU. Between 1991 and 2011 the guiding principle consistently employed and "rigidly applied" by the Spanish Constitutional Court in its relationship with the European Court of Justice was that matters of EU law did not constitute constitutional issues.[83] This meant that the Spanish Constitutional Court left it solely to the ordinary courts to apply EU law and engage in the preliminary ruling procedure.[84] This approach had a dual effect, namely a combination of conflict avoidance and an implicit claim as the ultimate authority on fundamental rights protection in the Spanish constitutional system.[85] It is this policy of disassociation from EU law matters that explains the Spanish Constitutional Court's refusal to avail itself of the preliminary ruling procedure until *Melloni*. Finally, in Declaration 1/2004, the Spanish Constitutional Court found an ingenious way to avoid constitutional conflict in the form of a potential clash between the Spanish Constitution and the Constitutional Treaty by drawing a distinction between "supremacy" and "primacy".[86] This means that,

77 *Melloni*, Case C-399/11: paragraph 60.
78 Besselink 2014: 1189.
79 Edenharter 2018: 397–398.
80 BVerfGE 133, 277–377.
81 BVerfGE 140, 317–376.
82 Edenharter 2018: 395–397.
83 Rodriguez-Izquierdo Serrano 2015: 1515.
84 Rodriguez-Izquierdo Serrano 2015: 1513–1514.
85 Rodriguez-Izquierdo Serrano 2015: 1514.
86 The author of this book has previously argued that the distinction drawn between "supremacy" and "primacy" in Declaration 1/2004 was a strategic act of ambiguity resolution by the Spanish Constitutional Court as means of constitutional conflict avoidance (Lunch seminar

from the perspective of the Spanish Constitutional Court, there was a significant amount of good will and willingness to co-operate accumulated over the years. This explains why the Spanish Constitutional Court was particularly sensitive to the sudden change of tone, from co-operation to confrontation, exhibited by the Court of Justice in *Melloni*.

It took more than a year for the national constitutional court to confirm the outcome of *Melloni*, which hinted at the growing tension between the participants in the judicial dialogue.[87] When the Spanish Constitutional Court eventually issued its judgment, it implicitly, but firmly, affirmed its authority as the final arbiter in instances of constitutional conflict on grounds of fundamental rights protection by treating the CJEU's reasoning in *Melloni* as "a mere hermeneutic tool".[88] Then, it proceeded to revise the right to fair trial on the basis of national constitutional argumentation, which was not without serious deficiencies.[89] Perhaps it is worth noting that the Spanish Constitutional Court remained "strikingly defiant" when it came to elaborating on its interpretation of Article 53 CFREU.[90] This approach was in all likelihood designed to undercut the significance and binding effect of the *Melloni* preliminary ruling as a manifestation of the authority of EU law on the national constitutional stage.[91] Nevertheless, the Spanish Constitutional Court's attempt to conceal the true origins of the impetus for revisiting its position on the right to fair trial was largely unsuccessful.[92] Nevertheless, the damage caused by the CJEU's decision-making in *Melloni* to its relationship with the Spanish Constitutional Court in terms of acceptability is evident.

However, the CJEU's dialogue with the national constitutional courts of the EU Member States is not the only judicial relationship at stake here. The CJEU's preferred interpretation of ambiguity in *Melloni* revealed that, in contrast to its counterpart – Article 53 ECHR, Article 53 CFREU has become a means not of negotiating agreement, but of asserting dominance. The jurisprudence of the European Court of Human Rights (ECtHR) suggests that the Court only very rarely relies on Article 53 ECHR expressly or out of its own initiative.[93] When the safeguard clause is nevertheless invoked with respect to a conflict of norms,

at iCourts, University of Copenhagen, on the topic of "Strategic Ambiguity Resolution as an Opportunity to Explore the Dynamics of Trust in the Dialogue between the European Court of Justice and the Spanish Constitutional Court" (28 February 2018); Presentation at International Society of Public Law (ICON-S), "Courts, Power, Public Law" Conference (ICON-S Annual Meeting), Copenhagen, on the topic of "The Strategic Value of Ambiguity for the Authority of EU Law in the Dialogue between the European Court of Justice and the National Courts", as part of Panel 123: "The Limits of Judging" [5–7 July 2017]).

87 Torres Perez 2014: 319; Pliakos & Anagnostaras 2015: 119.

88 Torres Perez 2014: 320, 323.

89 Torres Perez 2014: 322–323.

90 Torres Perez 2014: 320.

91 Pliakos & Anagnostaras 2015: 119–120.

92 Pliakos & Anagnostaras 2015: 120; Perez 2014: 322–323.

93 Alkema et al. 2015: 12.

the ECtHR usually seeks a compromise or, alternatively, evades the problem by outright ignoring any reference to the rule or by distinguishing the case where it appeared.[94] In general, the ECtHR treats Article 53 ECHR not as a binding legal principle, but as a helpful rule of interpretation that promotes greater flexibility and harmonisation and helps with striking a balance between conflicting interests.[95]

The CJEU's approach to implementing Article 53 CFREU in *Melloni* exposed its intent of 'weaponising' Article 53 CFREU for the purposes of enforcing the primacy of EU law against any competitive provider of fundamental rights protection in Europe. This became apparent as the CJEU issued Opinion 2/13 of 2014 which postulated that Article 53 CFREU and Article 53 ECHR should be reconciled in such a way that

> the power granted to Member States by [Article 53 ECHR] is limited ... to that which is necessary to ensure that the level of protection provided for by the Charter and the primacy, unity and effectiveness of EU law are not compromised.[96]

By so doing, the CJEU seems to have acted pre-emptively in terms applying its reasoning in *Melloni* to draw firm lines in the potential conflict with the ECtHR. This assertive move was in all likelihood designed to undercut the permissive treatment Article 53 ECHR affords higher standards of fundamental rights protection under the national laws of the High Contracting Parties.[97] However, such a "wide notion of conflict" is unsustainable in the practice of international law-making[98] and lacks appreciation for some fundamental tenets of fundamental rights protection on the international scene.[99] As a result of the CJEU's actions, the relationship between the two courts has arguably suffered a serious blow.[100]

Last but not least, there are important systemic implications for the EU legal order that flow from the CJEU's preferred choice of interpretation of ambiguity in Article 53 CFREU. Advocate General Bot clearly stressed the necessity to ensure the effectiveness of the European Arrest Warrant in his opinion on *Melloni*.[101] A necessary precondition for the successful implementation of the European Arrest Warrant is a significant enhancement of mutual confidence, achieved by promoting and speeding up judicial co-operation.[102] The Court of Justice is to help "the European Union to become an area of freedom, security

94 Alkema et al. 2015: 12.
95 Alkema et al. 2015: 12.
96 Opinion 2/13 2014: paragraph 189.
97 Eeckhout 2015: 967.
98 Eeckhout 2015: 967–958.
99 Alkema et al. 2015: 17–18.
100 Eeckhout, 2015: 990.
101 Opinion of Advocate General Bot 2012: paragraph 114.
102 Opinion of Advocate General Bot 2012: paragraph 115.

and justice by basing itself on the high degree of confidence which should exist between the Member States".[103] Advocate General Bot recognised the difficulties the EU legal system might encounter in this context:

> In the absence of harmonisation of procedural guarantees, it would be difficult for the European Union to progress in the application of the principle of mutual recognition and in the construction of a real area of freedom, security and justice.[104]

In this sense, the European Arrest Warrant is simply the procedural expression of the struggle to achieve a much greater systemic goal. It could very well be the case that the Court of Justice intentionally adopted the well-established language and rhetoric of primacy to carve out a place for the comparatively young and vulnerable concept of mutual trust in the EU legal order.

Ultimately, the CJEU also prioritised its preferred outcome over the individual's best interests in this instance, condemning them to a lower level of fundamental rights protection. Further, the CJEU's assertive approach to implementing Article 53 CFREU also soured its relationship with the ECtHR. Finally, the CJEU's strategic decision-making in *Melloni* was arguably aimed at reinforcing the position of the doctrine of mutual trust within the Area of Freedom, Security, and Justice by enforcing an uncompromising vision of the principle of the primacy of EU law, while showing disregard for the national constitutional courts' response in the process.[105] This was the constitutional cost the CJEU was willing to pay for its preferred interpretation of ambiguity in Article 53 CFREU.

The Long-term Ramifications of the CJEU's Strategic Resolution of Ambiguity

Now let us see how the CJEU's ultimate strategic goal in its ambiguity resolution in *Melloni* – upholding the EAW by all means – stood the test of time. The CJEU's ambiguity-based solution showed tremendous resilience in the face of the challenges posed by subsequent case-law, namely in *Aranyosi and Căldăraru* (Joined Cases C-404/15 & C-659/15 PPU) and in *M.A.S.* (Case C-105/14).

The challenge posed by Aranyosi and Căldăraru

Following their arrest,[106] Mr Aranyosi and Mr Căldăraru, resisted the activation of the simplified surrender procedure under EAW.[107] Since it was questionable whether the conditions of imprisonment in their respective Member States met

103 Opinion of Advocate General Bot 2012: paragraph 115.
104 Opinion of Advocate General Bot 2012: paragraph 117.
105 Ostropolski 2015: 175–176.
106 Joined Cases C-404/15 & C-659/15 PPU, 2016: paragraphs 28, 30, 32, 47–48, 52.
107 Joined Cases C-404/15 & C-659/15 PPU, 2016: paragraphs 33, 53.

the European standards, a violation of Article 3 ECHR (which corresponds to Article 4 CFREU)[108] and Article 6 TEU might occur, should the applicants be extradited under EAW to their home countries.[109] Focusing on the first question of the preliminary reference, the national court sought clarification from the CJEU on Article 1(3) of the Framework Decision on the matter of whether the surrender procedure is rendered impermissible in such circumstances.[110] The referring court also requested guidance on the duty of the executing Member State to ascertain the extent of compliance with the minimum EU standards of detention conditions.[111]

The Grand Chamber of the CJEU recognised, citing Opinion 2/13, that

> the principle of mutual trust requires, particularly with regard to the area of freedom, security and justice, each of those States, save in exceptional circumstances, to consider all the other Member States to be complying with EU law and particularly with the fundamental rights recognised by EU law.[112]

At the same time, the Court also affirmed that the prohibition of inhumane and degrading treatment enshrined in Article 4 CFREU (Article 3 ECHR) was absolute and binding on the Member States when implementing EU law, which is the case with the transposition of the Framework Decision into national law.[113] On this basis, the Court of Justice held that, where there is evidence of "a real risk of inhuman or degrading treatment of individuals detained in the issuing Member State", the EU standard of fundamental rights protection, set by Article 4 CFREU, *Melloni*, and Opinion 2/13, calls for an assessment of that risk before surrender of the individual sought by the EAW takes effect.[114] The Court also issued detailed guidance to help the executing judicial authority ascertain whether there is a risk of inhuman or degrading treatment.[115]

Now let us explore how *Aranyosi and Căldăraru* fit in the CJEU's EAW jurisprudence, the development of which could be said to be comprised of a total of three evolution phases.[116] At the first stage, to which *Melloni* belongs, mutual

108 Article 3 ECHR shares the same wording, meaning and scope with Article 4 CFREU, as per [p. 17] of the Explanations to the Charter (Joined Cases C-404/15 & C-659/15 PPU, 2016: paragraph 8, 86).
109 Joined Cases C-404/15 & C-659/15 PPU, 2016: paragraphs 34, 42, 59.
110 Joined Cases C-404/15 & C-659/15 PPU, 2016: paragraph 63.
111 *Aranyosi and Căldăraru*, Joined Cases C-404/15 & C-659/15 PPU, 2016: paragraphs 63.
112 *Aranyosi and Căldăraru*, Joined Cases C-404/15 & C-659/15 PPU, 2016: paragraphs 78, 82.
113 *Aranyosi and Căldăraru*, Joined Cases C-404/15 & C-659/15 PPU, 2016: paragraphs 83–87.
114 *Aranyosi and Căldăraru*, Joined Cases C-404/15 & C-659/15 PPU, 2016: paragraphs 88.
115 *Aranyosi and Căldăraru*, Joined Cases C-404/15 & C-659/15 PPU, 2016: paragraphs 89–90, 91–94.
116 Xanthopoulou 2018: 492–493.

trust was treated with such utmost reverence by the CJEU that it appeared as though the executing national courts were invited to exercise "blind trust" towards their counterparts when activating the EAW procedure.[117] In the following phase, marked by *Aranyosi and Căldăraru*, the CJEU continues to prioritise mutual trust above all (including fundamental rights protection), but maintains control by allowing for narrowly defined exceptions that ultimately seem to serve as a confirmation to the rule, rather than its alternative.[118] The third stage of adjudication based on the individual circumstances of each EAW case is yet to come.[119]

The aforementioned breakdown of the development of the CJEU's EAW jurisprudence highlights the role of *Aranyosi and Căldăraru* as its natural and inevitable consequence of *Melloni*. According to this account, one might conclude that the CJEU committed to a top-down approach in moulding the EAW jurisprudence that entails issues of fundamental rights protection. In other words, the Court of Justice laid down the overarching principle from the outset – the absolute primacy of EU law as a guarantee for the effectiveness of the EAW – and then proceeded to very carefully and selectively adjudicate on an *ad hoc* basis on possible derogations thereof. This means *Melloni* marked the highest point of the evolution of the EAW leading to that moment and serves as the benchmark for the implementation of mutual trust. The succeeding cases like *Aranyosi and Căldăraru*, although themselves Grand Chamber preliminary rulings, continue referring back to *Melloni* as a starting point and a source of guidance, cementing its status as a landmark ruling.

Nevertheless, it could be argued that *Aranyosi and Căldăraru*'s influence is not to be underestimated. The decision could be viewed a sign of change in the CJEU's attitude in the wake of the *Identity Review Order*[120] by the *Bundesverfassungsgericht* – where the Court was once resolute in applying the *Melloni* rationale, it now appeared "shaken" and "fragile".[121] The outcome in *Aranyosi and Căldăraru* could also serve as an indication of the growing autonomy of national courts when it comes to putting the fundamental rights protection standards in other Member States into question, which would perhaps lead to a broader practical application of Article 53 CFREU and a decline in the CJEU's influence with respect to national courts.[122]

However, this is unlikely to be the case. It is seems more feasible to conclude that the main contribution of *Aranyosi and Căldăraru* was an affirmation to the effect that "mutual confidence is not to be interpreted as blind trust, and that the presumption that Member States observe the fundamental rights

117 Xanthopoulou 2018: 493–494.
118 Xanthopoulou 2018: 494–495.
119 Xanthopoulou 2018: 496–498.
120 BvR 2735/14.
121 Korenica & Doli 2016: 553.
122 Korenica & Doli 2016: 554.

requirements is not actually irrefutable".[123] This achievement was secured on exceedingly strict terms – under "rigorous requirements ... that may practically prove very challenging to meet outside the particular factual scenario of *Aranyosi and Căldăraru*".[124]

There are two main arguments that support this conclusion. Firstly, *Aranyosi and Căldăraru* is a preliminary ruling of comparably limited influence, due to one key difference that sets it apart from *Melloni*. While *Melloni* dealt with the conflict between the principle of primacy of EU law and the standard of fundamental rights protection at national level, *Aranyosi and Căldăraru* addressed the extent of obligation of the issuing Member State to comply with the standard of fundamental rights protection set by the Charter and its ramifications for the EAW procedure.[125] In other words, the outcome in *Melloni* was central to the resolution of the former problem of tremendous constitutional value, whereas the implications of the situation in *Aranyosi and Căldăraru* were of only secondary importance. Secondly, the CJEU demonstrated its commitment to *Melloni* in another highly authoritative Grand Chamber ruling in 2017 – *M.A.S.* Even though the factual and legal situation in *M.A.S.* differed from *Aranyosi and Căldăraru*, the principles laid out in *Melloni* concerning the primacy of EU law were deemed relevant and applicable all the same. Given the CJEU's preoccupation with ensuring coherence at a systemic level, this is unlikely to be a coincidence. For these reasons, despite the controversy surrounding *Melloni*, *Aranyosi and Căldăraru* essentially failed at overthrowing its authority.[126]

The challenge posed by M.A.S.

Let us now discuss how the ambiguity-based outcome in *Melloni* was treated in *Taricco* in 2015 and *M.A.S.* (also known as *Taricco II*) in 2017. The case of *Taricco* concerned the limitation periods on VAT fraud as means of tax evasion in the champagne industry.[127] The impetus behind the preliminary reference was that the limitation periods prescribed by the Italian Penal Code may indirectly lead to unfair competition, in violation of Article 101 TFEU, and thus interfere with the effectiveness of EU law.[128]

Although the national court sought clarification in its third question on another provision of EU law, the CJEU redirected the discussion to Article 325 TFEU.[129] In response, the Court of Justice held that, provided the fundamental rights of the individual were respected, it was for the national authority to establish a potential violation of Article 325 TFEU by deciding whether the national measures qualify as "effective and dissuasive penalties in a significant

123 Anagnostaras 2016: 1684.
124 Anagnostaras 2016: 1684.
125 Anagnostaras 2016: 1687.
126 Anagnostaras 2016: 1687.
127 *M.A.S.*, Case C105/14, 2015: paragraphs 18–25.
128 *M.A.S.*, Case C105/14, 2015: paragraphs 25–26.
129 *M.A.S.*, Case C105/14, 2015: paragraphs 34–39.

number of cases of serious fraud affecting the financial interests of the European Union".[130]

However, the Italian legal system dictates that rules pertaining to limitation periods belong to substantive criminal law and the Italian constitution prohibits the retroactive effect of such provisions on account of the principle of legality.[131] The outcome in *Taricco* demanded that the option of retroactivity was available in a situation where the national authority deemed the penalties not sufficiently "effective and dissuasive".[132] Further, in paragraph 46 of *Taricco*, the Court gave "clear indications" that the Italian limitation period measures would be so regarded.[133]

Consequently, the Court of Cassation and the Court of Appeal, Milan, made a reference[134] to the Italian Constitutional Court, voicing doubts as to whether the Italian constitution is compatible with *Taricco*.[135] The Italian Constitutional Court then triggered the preliminary ruling procedure, in order to find out whether Article 325(1) and (2) TFEU necessitated the disapplication of national provisions on limitation periods, even in the absence of a "sufficiently precise legal basis" and in contravention of the principle of legality of criminal proceedings in the Member State constitution.[136]

Without making explicit mention of *Melloni*, the Court of Justice affirmed on the basis of *Åkerberg Fransson* that the national courts and authorities have the liberty to apply the national standard of protection of fundamental rights, as long as the "the primacy, unity and effectiveness of EU law" are preserved.[137] However, the CJEU acknowledged the central role of "the principle that offences and penalties must be defined by law, as to its requirements concerning the foreseeability, precision and non-retroactivity of the criminal law applicable", which in the Court's estimation seems to be rooted not only in the "constitutional traditions common to the Member States", but also in the EU legal order (as per Article 49 CFREU).[138] As such, this principle must be given priority over the "obligation to ensure the effective collection of the Union's resources".[139] Therefore, the CJEU allowed for lack of precision and retroactivity to become grounds for the national authority's taking exception to the obligation of disapplication.[140]

130 *M.A.S.*, Case C105/14, 2015: paragraphs 47–48, 53, 58.
131 *M.A.S.*, Case C-42/17, 2017: paragraphs 13–16.
132 Bonelli 2018: 361.
133 Bonelli 2018: 360.
134 The reference by the Italian Court of Cassation and the Court of Appeal in Milan was made on the basis of two cases that entailed potentially serious infringements of Decree No 74/2000 (Case C-42/17, 2017: paragraph 10–11).
135 *M.A.S.*, Case C-42/17, 2017: paragraphs 10–12.
136 Here description is given of questions (1) and (2) out of three questions in the *M.A.S.* preliminary reference. Case C-42/17, 2017: paragraph 20.
137 *M.A.S.*, Case C-42/17, 2017: paragraph 47.
138 *M.A.S.*, Case C-42/17, 2017: paragraph 51–53.
139 *M.A.S.*, Case C-42/17, 2017: paragraph 52.
140 *M.A.S.*, Case C-42/17, 2017: paragraph 58–62.

In *M.A.S.*, the Italian Constitutional Court gave the CJEU a "second chance" to avoid constitutional conflict and the potential triggering of the *controlimiti* doctrine in the wake of *Taricco I.*[141] A change of tone – from the allegedly confrontational pronouncement in *Melloni* to a more co-operative attitude shown in *M.A.S.* – was needed, if the CJEU was to encourage the national constitutional courts to continue approaching it with preliminary references in the future.[142] *M.A.S.* is a testament to the Court's willingness to explore national constitutional issues, including the national standard of fundamental rights protection, fully and with the requisite degree of respect.[143]

In this sense, the CJEU made good use of this opportunity for reconciliation with the Italian Constitutional Court. The CJEU achieved this goal by shifting the emphasis of the debate from national identity to the 'constitutional traditions common to the Member States', leading to a "consolidation of judicial dialogue" in the EU.[144] The Italian Constitutional Court took great care to reframe the *controlimiti* doctrine on the basis Article 4(2) TEU, so as to secure its recognition in EU law.[145] Here the Italian Constitutional Court conjures a potent strategic combination between the 'constitutional identity' and *controlimiti* doctrines in a bid to renegotiate the boundaries of the principle of primacy of EU law by placing restrictions on the transfer of powers to the EU by safeguarding the "hard core" of its domestic constitution.[146] This "hard core" is vaguely defined, with a wide array of formulations in the national constitutions, so as to afford a Member State maximum discretion in drawing those lines.[147]

Nevertheless, the CJEU ignored the carefully laid setup of national identity and proceeded to carve its own path along the lines of the principle of legality as the common denominator between the constitutions of the Member States.[148] The principle of legality enjoys universal recognition across the Member States constitutions.[149] As such, it was probably perceived by the Court of Justice as a far more solid, reliable, and coherent legal foundation than the vague and diverse descriptions of 'national identity' inhabiting the national legal orders. Even though the Court of Justice took a leaf from the Italian Constitutional Court's book and favoured co-operation over confrontation, its choice of legality as the legal basis indicates its determination to do so *on its own terms.* The choice made by the CJEU shows where its strategic priorities lie – in selecting the solution with the greatest potential for endurance in the long run.

141 Bonelli 2018: 361, 365.
142 Bonelli 2018: 365–366.
143 Bonelli 2018: 366.
144 Bonelli 2018: 358–359, 364–366, 370–371.
145 Bonelli 2018: 370.
146 Paris 2018: 210–213.
147 Paris 2018: 212–213.
148 Bonelli 2018: 371–365.
149 Bonelli 2018: 365.

At first glance, it would appear that *M.A.S.* marked a regression with respect to the CJEU's advance in *Melloni*, based on its willingness to allow for an exception to the principle of primacy of EU law. The outcome of *Melloni*, with its uncompromising treatment of primacy, was a hard-earned victory for the CJEU, since the ruling provoked the discontent of not only the Spanish Constitutional Court, but also of the *Bundesverfassungsgericht* and the UK Supreme Court.[150] *Åkerberg Fransson* was also met with a similar unfavourable response.[151] Consequently, it could be presumed that with its next step, the Court would be keen to deflate the tensions, so as not to risk causing long-term damage to its relationship with the national constitutional courts. Indeed, the Court of Justice relied on the combined effect of Article 49 CFREU and the Italian iteration of the principle of legality (while leaving the nature of the relationship between the two unspecified) to allow the national court to use the Charter as the "minimum standard" of protection of fundamental rights on this occasion.[152] However, this move is not to be mistaken for a sign of remorse for the Court of Justice's previous activism.

It must be borne in mind that the CJEU was likely willing to afford the concession in *M.A.S.* because the relative constitutional impact of *Melloni* appears to be far greater than that of *M.A.S.*. Firstly, the absence of harmonisation through EU secondary legislation of limitation rules on criminal proceedings with respect to VAT fraud in *M.A.S.* is to be contrasted against the presence of such with respect to the application of EAW to trials *in absentia* in *Melloni*.[153] Secondly, criminal law in *M.A.S.* is intended to serve as a means towards promoting the financial and economic interests of the Union, while in *Melloni* the EAW is meant to foster judicial co-operation on a constitutional scale.[154] Finally, the set of circumstances in *M.A.S.* is confined within the Italian legal order, whereas the EAW in *Melloni* ensures its relevance for mutual recognition in the interstate relations in the EU.[155] These points of differentiation suggest that *Melloni* has an additional, systemic dimension that *M.A.S.* lacks. Thus, in *M.A.S.*, the CJEU crafted a rule applicable "only exceptionally, in a specific and narrowly confined situation", which means this result "does not pose a substantial threat to the effective implementation of EU law".[156]

Moreover, it might be that the Italian Constitutional Court's behaviour was intended not to challenge, but to *uphold*, the authority of EU law by enhancing the pluralistic nature of the EU legal order and the search for a common ground in judicial dialogue based on shared values.[157] Davide Paris[158] maintains that the

150 Edenharter 2018: 396–398.
151 Edenharter 2018: 396–398.
152 Rauchegger 2018: 1537–1539.
153 Rauchegger 2018: 1533–1534.
154 Rauchegger 2018: 1534.
155 Rauchegger 2018: 1534.
156 Rauchegger 2018: 1545.
157 Paris 2018: 224.
158 Paris 2018: 223.

doctrines of 'constitutional identity', *controlimiti* and *ultra vires* were adopted by the national constitutional courts "not as a rebellion but as an act of true fidelity to EU law". According to this reading, *M.A.S.* stands as evidence of the Italian Constitutional Court's desire "to convince the Court of Justice that its understanding of EU law is more faithful to EU law than the Court of Justice's own perception".[159] In support of this theory, one need only remember that the Italian Constitutional Court made sure that its proposal was fully compliant with the uniform application of EU law and the superior standard of fundamental rights protection offered by the EU, per Article 53 CFREU.[160] Essentially, the "challenge" posed by the *Taricco I* and *M.A.S.* was not defending the authority of EU law *in general*, but ensuring that the *Melloni* reasoning *in particular* has the staying power to become firmly entrenched in the EU legal order.

For all of these reasons, although some maintain that *M.A.S.* has "watered down" the joint effect of *Melloni* and *Åkerberg Fransson*,[161] others are still left unconvinced. The core of the Court's reasoning in *Melloni* – "the primacy, unity and effectiveness of EU law" – remained unaffected.[162] *M.A.S.* seemed to function not as a modification, but as a "specific application", of the rules of constitutional conflict laid down in *Melloni* and *Åkerberg Fransson*.[163] In this sense, the CJEU managed to transform *M.A.S.* from a potential challenge to the rationale of *Melloni* into a mere opportunity for softening its rough edges. Thus, the flexibility (in the sense of adaptability) of *Melloni* proved to be essential to its survival.

To sum up, in *Aranyosi* and *Căldăraru*, the Court was invited to reconsider its prioritisation of the EAW over fundamental rights or at least recognise an exception thereof. In *M.A.S.*, the Court of Justice was presented with an opportunity to ameliorate the effects of the unconditional assertion of primacy in *Melloni* in the dialogue with the national constitutional courts. The ultimate decision taken by the Court of Justice in *M.A.S.* suggested that, despite some minor refinements, *Melloni* had tremendous staying power as the reigning principle of CJEU adjudication in this area. Moreover, the high strategic value of ambiguity resolution in *Melloni* was showcased in practice, as the formula proved to be sufficiently flexible to allow for further adjustments and thus, avoid being abandoned at the first signs of trouble.

Conclusion

Ultimately, the example of *Melloni* illustrates a situation where the CJEU is faced with a choice of interpretation of a Treaty provision with grave systemic implications for the implementation of the authority of EU law. In the presence of a

159 Paris 2018: 223.
160 Bonelli 2018: 370.
161 Edenharter 2018: 394.
162 Rauchegger 2018: 1531–1532.
163 Rauchegger 2018: 1532.

sample of ambiguity in Article 53 CFREU, the Court of Justice is faced with two readings that are equally plausible in linguistic and legal sense, which left little to no traces of the legislator's intent. The EU legislator was either unable or unwilling to remove the ambiguity at the heart of Article 53 CFREU, which left a key constitutional issue unresolved on the face of the legislative text. This omission led to a situation where the CJEU was simply responding to the "non-sense", defined in linguistic terms, that was produced by the EU legislator in the multilingual environment of the EU legal order.[164] Therefore, it could be argued that the CJEU "is not to blame for disrespecting the literal meaning of the texts, because there is no such meaning".[165] This new finding suggests that the Court of Justice engaged in meta-teleological interpretation out of necessity for effective adjudication, and not out of sheer wilfulness or desire for power. If that be the case, the traditional understanding of the Court's judicial activism should be revised, so as to more accurately reflect the challenges of adjudication in the EU legal order.

Nevertheless, the CJEU cannot be fully absolved of blame for its decision-making in *Melloni*. Although an equally plausible alternative was available, the CJEU still opted for the interpretation the ambiguity in Article 53 CFREU that would expand the remit of EU competence. Taking into consideration the specific context and circumstances of the CJEU's decision-making, accusations of judicial activism could be mounted on grounds that the CJEU's choice would be injurious to 'system-maintenance through acceptability' on a systemic scale, in the presence of an equally worthy alternative – 'system-building through concepts'. In the end, the prioritisation of an absolute model of primacy was a necessary prerequisite for ensuring the effectiveness of the European Arrest Warrant. In the end, the strategic act of ambiguity resolution in the *Melloni* example contributed towards the implementation of the authority of EU law by making use of the judicial tactic of "walking on the brink of non-compliance".[166] Thus, the discovery of ambiguity in the legislative text forces us to re-examine *the grounds* for the accusations in judicial activism, not the fact of the accusations themselves.

The CJEU was willing to pay the constitutional cost of this choice – the aggravation of the relationship with the Spanish Constitutional Court and the discontent of other constitutional courts in the EU. Despite the initial backlash, the CJEU was adamant in upholding the *Melloni* formula, even in the face of the challenges posed by the subsequent preliminary rulings of *Aranyosi and Căldăraru* and *M.A.S.* This gives us strong indication that a strategic act of ambiguity resolution has extraordinary staying power and longevity.

164 Kjær 2010: 298–300, 315.
165 Kjær 2010: 298.
166 Dothan 2014: 117–122.

2 Judicial Activism Reinvented?

The CJEU's Strategic Production of Ambiguity in *Åkerberg Fransson* (Case C-617/10)[1]

Introduction

26 February 2013 marked a momentous turning point in the CJEU's jurisprudence on fundamental rights protection in the EU legal order. The CJEU's strategic act of ambiguity resolution in the preliminary ruling of *Melloni* was by no means the sole reason why this was the case. By strategically producing ambiguity in the Grand Chamber preliminary ruling of *Åkerberg Fransson* on the same date, the Court of Justice certainly succeeded in dispelling the myth that 'lightning never strikes the same place twice'.

An identical birth date and a singular connection with ambiguity, however, are not the only common characteristics these two rulings share. Both *Melloni* and *Åkerberg Fransson* dealt with fundamental questions of federal nature.[2] *Melloni* dealt with the problem of whether to protect the EU interest by means of precluding the introduction of a higher standard of protection of fundamental rights in national law under Article 53 CFREU. *Åkerberg Fransson* explored the possibility of safeguarding the EU interest by activating the CJEU's jurisdiction under Article 51 CFREU.[3] The provision, titled 'Field of application', reads as follows:

> 1. The provisions of this Charter are addressed to the institutions, bodies, offices and agencies of the Union with due regard for the principle of subsidiarity and to the Member States *only when they are implementing Union law*. They shall therefore respect the rights, observe the principles and promote the application thereof in accordance with their respective powers and respecting the limits of the powers of the Union as conferred on it in the Treaties.
>
> 2. The Charter does not extend *the field of application of Union law* beyond the powers of the Union or establish any new power or task for the Union, or modify powers and tasks as defined in the Treaties.
>
> (Article 51 CFREU, emphasis added)

1 This case study presents a revised version of my earlier publication: Kartalova (2018).
2 Von Papp 2018: 523.
3 Von Papp 2018: 523.

DOI: 10.4324/9781003294870-8

There was nothing to suggest on the face of the facts in *Åkerberg Fransson* that the outcome of this case would eventually have a tremendous impact on the constitutional evolution of the EU. After a fisherman from Sweden by the name of Åkerberg Fransson was sentenced on grounds of grave tax offences, he was compelled to pay a VAT tax surcharge on the basis of the same criminal act, i.e. providing false information.[4] This problem prompted a preliminary reference by a Swedish national court which sought clarification regarding the lawfulness of imposing VAT penalties on an individual twice, in breach of the *ne bis in idem* principle in Article 50 CFREU.[5] In response, the CJEU discussed the matter of jurisdiction on the basis of Article 51 CFREU in greater depth.[6]

It should come as no surprise that the interventionist approach taken by the Court of Justice in the interpretation of Article 51 CFREU provoked the discontent of the national constitutional courts of the EU Member States and academics alike.[7] The seemingly innocuous setup for *Åkerberg Fransson* turned out to constitute 'the perfect storm' of circumstances that might enable judicial activism. The case entailed a high-stakes preliminary reference that addressed an issue with grave financial implications for tax collection in the EU[8] and direct impact on the CJEU's jurisdiction in fundamental rights protection, which is ultimately decided on the basis of a key Charter provision of dubious terminological clarity.

The main interpretative issue with regards to Article 51(1) CFREU was that, depending on the meaning attributed to the expression "implementing EU law", a narrow and a broad interpretation of the provision could be discerned.[9] The former reading would enable the Member States to act *solely* as agents of EU law with respect to the application of EU law, whereas the latter reading would encompass within the remit of the provision situations of derogations of EU law.[10] Faced with a choice between the two, the CJEU opted for the broad interpretation.[11]

The main reason *Åkerberg Fransson* was met with criticism was the relationship established between "implementing EU law" and acting/falling "within the scope of EU law". Prior to *Åkerberg Fransson*, these terms used to be treated as

4 Case C-617/10: paragraphs 12–13.
5 Case C-617/10: paragraphs 14–15.
6 Case C-617/10: paragraphs 17–18, 23.
7 Schima 2015: 1105–1107.
8 It might be that the Court was exceptionally emboldened to put forward an "expansive interpretation" in *Åkerberg Fransson*, since (a) VAT regulation has been harmonised at EU level, and (b) the sanctions for VAT infringement are directly connected to the matter of VAT collection that is of great significance for the EU budget (Spaventa 2016: 17). The latter circumstance is greatly reminiscent of the situation in *Taricco*, discussed in Chapter 2, where the Court exhibited a similar uncompromising stance when the effectiveness of VAT fraud actions was jeopardised (Spaventa 2016: 17). For more information on the relevant tax issues, see: Bernitz 2015: 205–208.
9 Brittain 2013: 277–278.
10 Brittain 2013: 277–278.
11 Case C-617/10: paragraphs 17–21.

distinctly separate in the CJEU's jurisprudence. The differentiation between the two used to be the norm in the case-law before the Charter on account of the *Wachauf* and *ERT* jurisprudence.[12] Given the interchangeability of these terms demonstrated by the Court in *Åkerberg Fransson*,[13] one could now reasonably conclude that the distinction should be viewed as immaterial in practical terms.[14] This is precisely why *Åkerberg Fransson* is credited with being a turning point in the CJEU's jurisprudence.

The general absence of precise and correct use of the terminology of Article 51 CFREU and "the lack of depth" of the Court's analysis in *Åkerberg Fransson*[15] could have serious constitutional repercussions in the light of this judicial choice. If the expression "implementing EU law" in Article 51(1) CFREU is interpreted broadly, its synonymy with the phrase "within the scope of Union law" would be established, which would grant the Charter of Fundamental Rights a virtually all-encompassing scope.[16] The terminological issues associated with interchangeability inherent in Article 51 CFREU have a tremendous impact on the contentious interaction between the Charter and the general principles of EU law[17] and the delimitation of CJEU's competences.[18]

These are the parameters of the main problem of EU constitutional law presented in *Åkerberg Fransson*. What was most notably absent from the set of available solutions was an in-depth analysis that explains precisely *how* the relevant terms from the legislative text of Article 51 CFREU and the Court's own jurisprudence interact. The linguistic and legal analysis of ambiguity detailed below will fill this gap in the knowledge.

Firstly, the analysis will contain a concrete and exhaustive description of the patterns of interchangeable use of these terms traced in the text of the preliminary ruling of *Åkerberg Fransson*, which would help advance the notion of interchangeability beyond an obscure intuition and a passing remark.[19] Secondly, the analysis will elaborate on the Court of Justice's strategic insight in adding the term "applicability" into the mix of relevant terms, which is a heretofore overlooked aspect of the Court's decision-making. For instance, Emily Hancox[20] only briefly commented on the term, without attempting a multilingual analysis, while concentrating mainly on the term "the implementation of EU law". In addition, both the ideas of interchangeability of terms and "applicability" were noticeably missing from Stephen Brittain's multilingual investigation of the terms "implementing EU law" and "within the scope of Union law", which concluded

12 Hancox 2013: 1418–1421.
13 Dougan 2015: 1204–1206.
14 AG Opinion on *Åkerberg Fransson*, 2012: paragraph 34; Sarmiento 2013: 1277–1278.
15 Schima 2015: 1111.
16 Brittain 2013: 277–278.
17 Hancox 2013: 1411–1412, 1418; Dougan 2015: 1205–1206.
18 Hancox 2013: 1425–1426; Dougan 2015: 1209.
19 E.g. Dougan 2015: 1204, 1206.
20 Hancox 2013: 1425.

with disproving their synonymy, but offered no alternative explanation as to their interaction.[21]

Most importantly, the analysis will focus on investigating in greater detail the role of ambiguity. The potential ambiguity arising between the terms used in Article 51(1) CFREU and the Explanations to the Charter of Fundamental Rights[22] was only briefly acknowledged without substantial elaboration by Daniel Sarmiento.[23] Sarmiento also makes a very short reference to the difference in the language versions of these terms.[24] Johannes Masing[25] also recognises the ambiguity created with the juxtaposition between Article 51(1) and the corresponding information provided by the Explanations to the Charter of Fundamental Rights. Further, Damian Chalmers[26] notes that there is ambiguity arising between the implementation of EU law and "acting within the field of Union law", which amounts to an "ambiguous test" of EU jurisdiction. Despite being very informative and thought-provoking, none of these studies was successful at piecing together the entire picture. In other words, none of them put forward a concrete, exhaustive, and evidentially substantiated theory as to the exact nature of the *relationship* between all of the relevant terms.

This chapter proposes the analytical framework of a strategic act of ambiguity production as one viable explanation to the CJEU's decision-making in *Åkerberg Fransson*. This ambiguity production made it possible for the Court to resolve the ambiguity it single-handedly created in the very same preliminary ruling, in favour of a more strategically advantageous outcome, one that would support the unwarranted expansion of EU competences.

As previously discussed, the interchangeable use of a given pair of predicates does not necessarily entail synonymy.[27] This is why it would be premature to assume that simply because the CJEU enforces the interchangeable use of a set of terms on a pragmatic level, they are actually synonymous on a semantic level. In fact, the results of a multilingual analysis (Annex A), which were conducted on the basis of the relevant terms used in Article 51 CFREU and the preliminary ruling of *Åkerberg Fransson*, will disprove this notion with respect to the terms "applicability", "(scope/field of) application", and "implementation". In other words, their semantic meaning suggests the relationships between them fit the model of polysemy (as a form of ambiguity), and not of synonymy. More specifically, it will be shown that the ambiguous term "applicability" could be semantically understood as "implementation" (Paraphrase 1) or "(scope/field of) application" (Paraphrase 2), with the latter two terms being mutually exclusive.

21 Brittain 2013: 305.
22 Explanations to the Charter, 2007.
23 Sarmiento 2013: 1277.
24 Sarmiento 2013: 1277, 1275–1276, footnote [31].
25 Masing 2016: 501.
26 Chalmers 2010: 143.
27 Gardner 2009: 97.

The outcome of the multilingual analysis will discover non-negligible linguistic divergences between terms previously regarded as interchangeable by the Court, which will suffice to establish "inter-lingual ambiguity".[28] As previously explained, this phenomenon could be said to arise on a multilingual plain, from a "meta-text"[29] or a "hybrid text"[30] of the language versions of Article 51 CFREU or the official translations of the preliminary ruling of *Åkerberg Fransson*.

How does the strategic treatment of ambiguity serve the Court's activist agenda? The CJEU was interested in validating the strategically advantageous term "the scope of Union law" ("[scope/field of] application") as a legitimate alternative to "implementing Union law" ("implementation") – the term chosen originally by the EU legislator. The Court of Justice achieved this goal by coming up with an ambiguous term of its own ("applicability"), the semantic meaning of which allowed for the two aforementioned terms to function as its paraphrases. Through the interchangeable use of divergent terms, the Court of Justice essentially supplanted the semantic (and pragmatic) meaning the EU legislator infused in the provision with pragmatic meaning of its own.

Ultimately, the linguistic and legal analysis of ambiguity in this chapter will add more specificity and depth to the accusations of judicial activism mounted against the CJEU's decision-making in *Åkerberg Fransson* by demonstrating precisely how the Court has executed the unsanctioned expansion of competence. *Åkerberg Fransson* is a particularly suitable example of the Court's capacity to achieve this end by strategically exploiting and aggravating (to the point of ambiguity production) the indeterminacy initially produced by the EU legislator in the context of the interaction between the legislative text and the Explanations to the Charter of Fundamental Rights.

Finally, the ambiguity production in *Åkerberg Fransson* serves as evidence of strategic behaviour exhibited by the Court of Justice, which reached its culmination in the very same preliminary ruling, when the Court's strategically resolved the ambiguity it had just produced. Such conduct appears to match Dothan's description of the judicial tactic for increasing the reputation of international courts by the name of "walking on the brink of non-compliance", which was implemented through the Court's discretionary reasoning.[31]

Legal Analysis

Before commencing with the linguistic analysis of the ambiguity found in Article 51(1) CFREU, it is important to consider the legislative intent and pragmatic context of Article 51(1) CFREU. For this purpose, one must first take account of the terminological challenges associated with the interpretation of the provision

28 Cao 2007: 78.
29 Gambaro 2012: 410.
30 McAuliffe 2011: 99.
31 Dothan 2014: 8, 117–122.

in the CJEU's jurisprudence preceding *Åkerberg Fransson*. Then, the drafting history of the provision must be investigated. Finally, it would be helpful to closely examine the purpose and function of the Explanations to the Charter as well as the British and Polish Protocol No. 30.

The Terminological Challenges in the CJEU's Jurisprudence Preceding Åkerberg Fransson

The CJEU's jurisdiction in the area of fundamental rights protection has been a material item on the Court's agenda even prior to the drafting of the Charter of Fundamental Rights. That is why the discussions surrounding the multiple revisions of the draft Article 51 CFREU, detailed later in this chapter, were interlaced with references to the CJEU's jurisprudence.

In particular, the drafters of Article 51 CFREU seem to rely mainly on the CJEU's language in *Wachauf* regarding situations where the Member States "implement Community rules".[32] Mr Wachauf was a tenant farmer who sought compensation for discontinuance of milk production upon the expiration of his tenancy on the basis of the German Law of 17 July 1984 implementing Regulation No 857/84.[33] The referring court, the *Verwaltungsgericht* (Administrative Court) Frankfurt am Main, sought clarification on narrow points of terminology and applicability.[34] Although the referring court doubtlessly initiated the preliminary ruling procedure in the hope of receiving guidance on the underlying issue of fundamental rights in this case, there was no apparent indication of that in the way the reference was worded.[35]

Nevertheless, the Court of Justice responded by imposing an obligation to comply with the EU standard of fundamental rights protection not only where the EU institutions are concerned, but also in situations where the Member States "implement Community rules".[36] The outcome of *Wachauf* constitutes a significant extension of the scope of EU law in practice, since in the majority of cases it is the Member States that are tasked with implementing EU law.[37] The *Wachauf* decision was also indicative of the Court's growing willingness to expand its influence by engaging in a direct and meaningful manner with issues of fundamental rights, rather than seeking to reject such preliminary references or avoid such issues contained therein.[38]

32 *Wachauf*, Case 5/88: paragraph 19.
33 *Wachauf*, Case 5/88: paragraph 2.
34 *Wachauf*, Case 5/88: paragraphs 1–7, 12. In particular, the referring court sought clarification on the terminology used in Article 12(d) of Regulation No 857/84 and the factual circumstances in which Article 5(3) of Regulation No 857/84 applies.
35 Jacobs 2010: 136.
36 *Wachauf*, Case 5/88, paragraph 19.
37 Jacobs 2010: 137.
38 Jacobs 2010: 137–138.

In other words, the CJEU made it clear in *Wachauf* that the yardstick for national legislation implementing EU law would be an EU standard of fundamental rights protection, rather than a national constitutional one.[39] Thus, the CJEU's reasoning in *Wachauf* was intended to safeguard the principle of "the uniform application of EU law" by obviating the need to nullify or set aside EU legal rules on a domestic level.[40] In so doing, the CJEU enhanced the impact of its fundamental rights protection jurisprudence on the basis of a "decentralised system [of fundamental rights review]", which is characterised by a close co-operation with the ordinary national courts.[41] This means that the CJEU was more interested in fostering a more intensive relationship of collaboration with the national courts and setting an example, rather than usurping their functions of review or establishing a form of control over them.[42]

In the case of *ERT*, the CJEU introduced a second type of situation to contrast with *Wachauf*, namely scenarios where a legal rule "[falls] within the scope of Community law".[43] The case of *ERT* dealt with a legal dispute between 'ERT', a Greek radio and television enterprise with exclusive rights for broadcasting on the territory of the Greek state, and 'DEP', a competitor company operating at municipal level in Thessaloniki that was allegedly in breach of these rights.[44] After ERT sought to obtain an injunction and an order for seizure and sequestration from the Thessaloniki Regional Court, the proceedings were stayed and a preliminary reference was made to the CJEU.[45] For the present purposes, the response given by the Court of Justice to the ninth and the tenth question of the preliminary reference would be considered the most pertinent.[46]

In the *ERT* preliminary ruling, the CJEU described the circumstances in which it would have to make a pronouncement that is *indirectly* related to the relationship between national rules on fundamental rights protection and the ECHR. The Court conceded it was unable to review the compatibility between the ECHR and "national rules which do not fall within the scope of Community law".[47] However, if such rules "fall within the scope of Community law" and a preliminary reference is made on that basis, the CJEU would be compelled to supply the national court with "all the criteria of interpretation" necessary

39 Kühn 2010: 153.
40 Kühn 2010: 153.
41 Kühn 2010: 151, 153–154.
42 Cruz Villalón 2010: 164–165.
43 *ERT*, Case C-260/89: paragraph 42. No reason was discovered to make a normative or linguistic distinction between "[falling] within the scope of [EU law]" and "[acting] within the scope of [EU law]", such that would contribute to this analysis in any meaningful way.
44 *ERT*, Case C-260/89, paragraphs 2–3.
45 *ERT*, Case C-260/89, paragraph 4.
46 *ERT*, Case C-260/89, paragraphs 5, 41. These questions concern the compatibility of this broadcasting monopoly with the social objective laid out in Article 2 and the Preamble of the EEC Treaty as well as Article 10 of the European Convention of Human Rights (ECHR).
47 *ERT*, Case C-280/89, paragraph 42.

to ascertain the compatibility with fundamental rights.[48] Earlier the Court had explained that EU fundamental rights and the ECHR share common ground in the form of general principles of law derived from "the constitutional traditions common to the Member States" and the regulation of human rights by guidelines provided in international treaties in which the Member States partake.[49] For this reason, the CJEU's obligation to guarantee the observance for fundamental rights necessarily entailed a consideration of these national rules in the light of the ECHR.[50] The Court held that the Member State's attempt to justify the obstruction to the freedom to provide services must be conditioned on compliance with the general principle of freedom of expression.[51] The assessment on this point with respect to EU law will be done by the national court, "and if necessary" by the CJEU.[52]

The case of *ERT* has earned a reputation for being an important milestone in the CJEU's jurisprudence, since this is where the expression "to fall within the scope of Community law" appears for the first time. The CJEU then proceeds to assign it an excessively broad interpretation by making it clear that derogations made by Member State must be interpreted with reference to the general principles of law and must be compatible with the EU standard of fundamental rights protection.[53]

In the period preceding *ERT*, the CJEU was interested in pursuing a policy based on "the principle of non-violation", meaning that it would demonstrate respect for human rights as regulated by other bodies and institutions, such as the Member States.[54] The *ERT* preliminary ruling contributed towards a change of direction by supplying "a legal basis and a justification for EU institutions to develop internal human rights policies" as well as a fragmented system of fundamental rights on a global scale within the EU legal order.[55] Furthermore, *ERT* played a key role in making fundamental rights "more salient and more present" in the activities conducted on the legal and political stage in the EU.[56] In this sense, the importance of fundamental rights for legitimising the EU beyond the limits prescribed by the institutions of the nation state must not be underestimated, on account of their immediate relationship with the individual autonomy ascribed to the EU citizen.[57] However advantageous the *ERT* principle might appear for the CJEU on a systemic level, its actual application in practice seems to be problematic:

48 *ERT*, Case C-280/89, paragraph 42.
49 *ERT*, Case C-280/89, paragraph 41.
50 *ERT*, Case C-280/89, paragraph 42.
51 *ERT*, Case C-280/89, paragraphs 43–45.
52 *ERT*, Case C-280/89, paragraphs 44.
53 *ERT*, Case C-280/89, paragraph 43.
54 Chalmers 2010: 145.
55 Chalmers 2010: 145.
56 Chalmers 2010: 149.
57 Chalmers 2010: 148.

> as a practical matter, but also due to subsidiarity and legitimacy requirements, the *ERT* type of cases would require a wide margin of national discretion, the burden of responsibility to balance conflicting rights, values, policies and principles is effectively placed on *all* national courts which would challenge some deeply embedded conceptions of the judiciary and the separation of powers in many Member States.[58]

The excessive amount of pressure on the national courts was bound to wreak havoc in the judicial systems both at a domestic and at a supranational level. In addition, the obvious jeopardy associated with an expansion of competences must be considered. Thus, it comes as no surprise that the EU legislator would ultimately show a clear preference for the terminology adopted in *Wachauf*, as opposed to the one in *ERT*, in the drafting of Article 51 CFREU.

The Drafting History of Article 51(1) CFREU

The Charter of Fundamental Rights is now a legal instrument with "the same legal value as the Treaties" (Article 6(1) TEU). However, that was not initially the case since the matter of its legally binding nature and justiciability was uncertain in the early days of the Charter initiative.[59] The Charter was originally drafted "as if" it were ultimately to become an integral part of the Treaties, even though the properties in question could only be ascribed to it subject to the approval of the European Council, which at the time appeared to be a "highly unlikely" prospect.[60] The Charter was seen by the European Council as a means of consolidation of pre-existing sources of fundamental rights protection in the EU, and not as a means of innovation or constitutional reform.[61] It would seem that it was not any real necessity for superior fundamental rights protection that provided the political impetus for drafting the Charter.[62] In this sense, the Charter was a mere "performative [statement] claiming legitimacy" in an attempt to bolster the Union's legitimacy.[63] Thus, the Charter was simply an opportunity for the European Union to reconnect with the EU citizen by displaying its accomplishments and reaffirming its commitments.[64]

Nevertheless, the main purpose and function of the Charter are arguably more substantial than that, namely:

58 Kühn 2010: 160–161.
59 De Burca 2015: 801.
60 De Burca 2015: 801.
61 De Burca 2015: 803. Here De Burca refers to the ECHR, the "common constitutional traditions" of the EU Member States and some legal instruments of more limited influence (e.g. the European Social Charter and the Community Charter of Fundamental Social Rights of Workers).
62 De Burca 2015: 803.
63 Baquero Cruz 2008: 66, 72.
64 De Burca 2015: 802.

> to include within a single, easily understandable document a catalogue of fundamental rights that limits the authority of the European Union, its bodies and institutions, and the exercise of their authority in the same way in which, at the national level, the authority of Member States is bound by the fundamental rights included in their respective constitutions.[65]

The introduction of the Charter was supposed to remedy the lack of clarity and legal certainty resultant from the disorderly and fragmented fashion in which rights were heretofore dispersed across the jurisprudence of the CJEU and other legal documents.[66] In other words, the creation of the Charter was motivated by "a genuine demand for uniform application of EU law", which entails avoiding "the risk of having twenty-seven different standards of protection of fundamental rights within the European Union, and therefore a heterogenous application of the EU law".[67] However, it is dubious to what extent the Charter was successful in this endeavour, especially seeing as using a "network of normative cross-references" to the ECHR, other sources of international law and the national constitutions of the Member States as the basis for its construction has led to a multitude of contradictions and clashes.[68]

The excerpt cited above also highlights the use of fundamental rights as a means for restricting power.[69] A distinction between *rights* and *powers* could be made: while *rights* are normally "contrasted with obligations", *powers* are occasionally viewed as "norms regulating competences".[70] Thus, on a national level, individual rights could be used to render unconstitutional legal measures inapplicable.[71] Further, in federal systems like the US or, to a certain extent, the EU, such practice awakens fears of a potential illegitimate appropriation of the functions of the legislature as well as of the possibility that the federal constitutional court may unduly interfere with state powers.[72] It is precisely this rationale that links the discussion on fundamental rights protection and the problem of delimitation of competences between the EU and the Member States.[73] In this context, the "federal question" emerges: the problematic justification of the necessity to add an extra layer of EU fundamental rights protection on top of the one provided by the Member States, especially since judicial review is already conducted by the national courts, national constitutional courts and the European Court of

65 Von Danwitz & Paraschas 2012: 1400.
66 Baquero Cruz 2008: 66.
67 Von Danwitz & Paraschas 2012: 1401. It is worth noting that this idea aligns well with the CJEU's strategic act of resolving the ambiguity in Article 53 CFREU in favour of a homogenous (and not heterogenous) standard of fundamental rights protection afforded by the Charter in *Melloni*, as argued previously in the *Melloni* Case Study.
68 Baquero Cruz 2008: 66–67.
69 Von Danwitz & Paraschas 2012: 1400.
70 Von Papp 2018: 512–513.
71 Von Papp 2018: 513.
72 Von Papp 2018: 513.
73 Von Papp 2018: 513.

Human Rights.[74] Now let us see how Article 51 CFREU addresses the federal question, thus defined.

The idea behind Article 51(1) appears to be an attempt to justify the CJEU's highly contentious power of judicial review over Member State acts.[75] At the same time, Article 51(2) CFREU amounts to a solemn resolution to the effect that harmonisation on the basis of fundamental rights protection must not be conducted without the inclusion of the political actors.[76] Seeing as the very subject matter of Article 51 CFREU demands a pronouncement with grave ramifications for the highly controversial issue of delimitation of competence, the stakes with the drafting of Article 51 CFREU were extraordinarily high.

That is why a lenient approach to the drafting of the provision would probably incite doubts of the seemingly benign, non-activist intention behind the Charter initiative. Conversely, the unequivocal and exact formulation of Article 51 CFREU was likely to alleviate those fears and increase the chances that the Charter would be met with acceptance in the EU community. The uncompromising insistence on clarity that is inherent in the use of the adverb *only* in the expression "only when [the Member States] are implementing Union law" in Article 51(1) CFREU[77] certainly supports this conclusion. The use of such a "categorical term" is rather unconventional in EU law,[78] especially given its notoriously abstract, convoluted and sometimes obscure means of expression. The peculiarly agitated verbosity[79] characterising the manner in which Article 51(2) CFREU was drafted reveals a strong desire to ensure that the wording is precise and exhaustive. Only then could the drafters rest assured that the provision is capable of effectively restricting the scope of the Charter. On the whole, it would appear that "[t]he entire statutory environment ... reads like a valiant, almost imploring, effort to base the protection of fundamental rights on existing powers instead of on new ones".[80]

Having understood the constitutional challenges inherent in the drafting of Article 51 CFREU, let us now examine its drafting process in greater detail. The drafting process of said provision was a prolonged and complicated affair, which is helpfully outlined by Grainne de Burca.[81]

To begin with, De Burca invites us to first consider a rough draft of "the Preamble or Article 1" to the Charter of February 2000 that reads: "[The following provisions] are binding on the Member States only where the latter transpose or apply the law of the Union".[82] Then, she draws our attention to a revision

74 Von Papp 2018: 513.
75 Von Papp 2018: 514.
76 Masing 2016: 500.
77 Von Danwitz & Paraschas 2012: 1401.
78 Von Danwitz & Paraschas 2012: 1401.
79 Baquero Cruz 2008: 70.
80 Masing 2016: 499.
81 De Burca 2015: 808–809.
82 De Burca 2015: 808. CHARTE 4123 /1/00, 15 February 2000: 9.

of this wording from April 2000: “The provisions of this Charter are addressed … to the Member States exclusively within the framework of implementing Community law”.[83] These formulations seem to be “reasonably restrictive” in nature, to be then supplanted by a version that is broader in character and much closer to the stance taken in the CJEU’s jurisprudence, especially in *Wachauf*.[84] In particular, this version[85] reads as follows: “The provisions of this Charter are addressed to … the Member States exclusively within the scope of Union law”.[86] This leads us to the final version[87] of Article 51 CFREU: “The provisions of this Charter are addressed to … the Member States only when they are implementing Union law”.[88] De Burca[89] argues that the final formulation is much stricter than even the CJEU’s own case-law and notes the use of a “looser and broader term” in the explanations to the same version in the draft from October 2000: “the requirement to respect fundamental rights defined in a Union context is only binding on the Member States when they act in the *context* of Community law” (emphasis added), accompanied by a reference to *Wachauf* and *ERT*.[90] Finally, De Burca summarises her findings as follows:

> This somewhat tedious tracing of the convoluted path taken by what might seem like a fairly innocuous “horizontal” clause, from its earliest and reasonably strict interpretation by the secretariat’s guideline, through several broader intermediate formulations, and reverting ultimately to an even stricter version, illustrates an emergent reluctance to commit the Member States to observing the norms of the Charter other than in the cases which are most closely linked to the European Union where the Member States have little or no autonomy, i.e. in the actual implementation of European Union legislation.[91]

The sheer number of versions under discussion and the attention to detail shown in the drafting of this excerpt of the provision certainly stand as testament to the

83 De Burca 2015: 808. CHARTE 4235/00, 18 April 2000: 2.
84 De Burca 2015: 808.
85 De Burca (2015: 809) cites the text of the amended text as presented here, but the reference she gives for it reads “CHARTRE 4360/00 of June 14, 2000” (De Burca, 2015: footnote 41). No document corresponding to such a reference in the list of meetings was found here: www.europarl.europa.eu/charter/activities/calend1_en.htm. Last accessed on 13 May 2019.
86 CHARTE 4316/00, 16 May 2000.
87 De Burca (2015: 809) cites the text of the amended text as presented here, but the reference she gives for it reads “CHARTRE 4470/00, September 14, 2000” (De Burca, 2015: footnote 47). No document corresponding to such a reference was found in the list of meetings here: www.europarl.europa.eu/charter/activities/calend1_en.htm. Last accessed on 13 May 2019.
88 CHARTE 4422/00, 28 July 2000: 15; CHARTE 4487/00, 28 September 2000: 22.
89 De Burca 2015: 809.
90 CHARTE 4473/00, 11.10.2000: 46.
91 De Burca 2015: 809.

drafters' growing awareness of the importance of the choice of terminology to describe the extent of obligation imposed on the Member States. The fluctuations in the level of strictness, with which the obligation of the Member States is delineated, are also interesting to observe. The original intention was to describe the desired effect by means of the acts of "transposition" or "application" of EU law, united by the conjunction "or". As a next step, the descriptive approach is abandoned in favour of using a concrete term of EU law – "implementation". This creates the impression that most probably, in the minds of the drafters, the verb "to implement" is not some generic placeholder, but a technical legal term with a very specific function and usage in EU law. This commitment to specificity is mirrored in the final version of Article 51 CFREU in the Charter ("only when [the Member States] are implementing Union law").

The drafters only show any interest in imprecision or leniency in their drafting choices twice – in the "exclusively within the scope of Union law" version and in the draft Explanations to the final version. Both times occur when the drafters attempt to bridge the gap and establish a certain level of correspondence between the legislative text and the CJEU's case-law. Nevertheless, as is evident from their final choice of formulation, the drafters' temporary preoccupation with ensuring the consistency between the legislative text and the Court's jurisprudence eventually gave way to the more important constitutional objective of drawing firm lines of delineation of competencies. In other words, the drafting process of Article 51 CFREU shows that the drafters' commitment to a restrictive drafting approach wavers when an attempt to reconnect with the CJEU's jurisprudence is made. This evidence suggests that the agendas of these two actors are at odds with each other, which in turn increases the chances that, on a pragmatic level, the Court's expansive interpretation of Article 51 CFREU contradicts the legislator's intent.

A similar undercurrent of discord in the otherwise normal drafting process has been detected by Piet Eeckhout: "one can see the strong tension between keeping the brakes on, as regards scope, and the accelerator effect of drafting a general, up-to-date charter of fundamental rights".[92] In other words, the Charter is "paradoxical" in that "it contains indivisible fundamental rights, but of strictly limited scope".[93] This internal friction seems to be caused by the clash between the drafters' commitment to restricting the effect of the Charter and the insistence of fundamental rights groups and non-governmental organisations[94] on pushing their vision for the Charter as the latest human rights legal instrument with a broad scope and binding nature in Europe.[95] This commentary provides affirmation of the drafter's commitment to precision and clarity of drafting even in the face of external pressures.

92 Eeckhout 2002: 956.
93 Eeckhout 2002: 957–958.
94 Eeckhout (2002: 956–957) names in particular a wide Platform of European Social NGOs, the ETUC, Amnesty International.
95 Eeckhout 2002: 956–957.

The Explanations to the Final Version of Article 51 CFREU

The main source of guidance as to the legislative intent behind the final version of Article 51 CFREU are the Explanations to the Charter,[96] which were meant to introduce greater clarity and facilitate the interpretation of the Charter text. Unfortunately, in the case of this provision the Explanations achieved the exact opposite effect. The Explanations to Article 51 CFREU contain an explicit assurance, followed by references to *Wachauf*, *ERT*, and *Annibaldi*, to the effect that:

> it follows unambiguously from the case-law of the Court of Justice that the requirement to respect fundamental rights defined in the context of the Union is only binding on the Member States when they *act in the scope of Union law*.[97]
>
> (emphasis added)

Confusingly, this pronouncement suggested the equivalence between "implementing Union law" (Article 51(1) CFREU) and "[acting] in the scope of Union law" – two fixed terminological constructions that were heretofore treated as distinctly separate by the exact same string of case-law cited in support of their conflation. The EU legislator offered no further clarification or reasonable justification for this sudden deviation from the CJEU's well-established jurisprudence in the Explanations.

Is the CJEU bound to comply with this bewildering declaration of equivalence made by the Explanations then? Formally speaking, the Explanations "do not as such have the status of law, they are a valuable tool of interpretation intended to clarify the provisions of the Charter".[98] Although no further guidance on this matter is available, Koen Lenaerts makes a persuasive case for an affirmative response to this question.[99] Lenaerts asserts that the Explanations "have a higher interpretative value that that of travaux préparatoires", despite not being legally binding.[100] This idea follows from the fact that the authors of the Treaty of Lisbon and the Charter of Fundamental Rights were firmly convinced of the importance of the Explanations.[101] Lenaerts also contends that the CJEU would be engaging in judicial activism, if the Court were to interpret the provisions of the Charter of Fundamental Rights in a manner that contravenes the Explanations.[102] Therefore, the CJEU may resort to alternative methods of interpretation only if the Explanations "provide no (complete) answer" to the question of interpretation at hand.[103]

96 Explanations to the Charter, 2007.
97 Explanations to the Charter, 2007: C 303/32.
98 Explanations to the Charter, 2007: C 303/17.
99 Lenaerts 2012: 402.
100 Lenaerts 2012: 402.
101 Lenaerts 2012: 402.
102 Lenaerts 2012: 402.
103 Lenaerts 2012: 402.

If the unhelpful contribution of the Explanations indeed carries such a substantial weight, the Court seems to have found itself in a singular predicament in *Åkerberg Fransson*. Due to the blatant lack of understanding shown by the EU legislator in the Explanations for the established use of the said terms in the Court's preceding jurisprudence, the Court was essentially 'caught between a rock and a hard place'. The CJEU could not retrospectively erase the distinction made in *Wachauf* and *ERT*, as this would undermine its own authority. At the same time, the Court of Justice was equally unable to challenge the authority of the legislator as expressed in the Explanations, as this would constitute judicial activism. Thus, it is fair to say that one of the main aims of the CJEU's decision-making process in *Åkerberg Fransson* was to ensure the reconciliation between its preceding jurisprudence and the Charter.[104]

By engaging in ambiguity production in *Åkerberg Fransson*, the Court was able to ensure the precariously balanced co-existence between these terms, without outright resolving this problem. In this sense, the CJEU's strategic act of ambiguity production in *Åkerberg Fransson* could be said to fall in line with the following behavioural pattern: "The Court's constant manipulation of law as language and language as law simultaneously produces nonsense and combats nonsense".[105] In other words, the Court generates nonsense in the form of ambiguity in *Åkerberg Fransson*, in the hope of "making sense of [the] nonsense"[106] produced in the Explanations and superimposed over the original wording of Article 51 CFREU by the EU legislator by the EU legislator itself.

The British and Polish Protocol No. 30

It seems to be precisely this unpredictability in the Court's behaviour with respect to the interpretation of Article 51 CFREU that left some of the Member States uneasy, despite the precautions taken by the EU legislator in the form of an overtly strict drafting approach and providing the Explanations to the Charter. To alleviate their rising anxieties over this uncertainty, the United Kingdom and Poland[107] subscribed to Protocol No. 30 to the Charter.[108]

It is worth noting that Poland and the UK had different motivations to adopt Protocol No. 30. The UK seemed to have harboured hopes that Protocol No. 30 would discourage the EU from legislating in new areas of law – more

104 Sarmiento 2013: 1277.
105 Kjær 2010: 311.
106 Kjær 2010: 315.
107 The Czech Republic also expressed a wish to follow the British and Polish example with Protocol No. 30 in 2009 but withdrew its request in 2014 because of changes in its national political scene (Borowski 2018: 395–396).
108 Nevertheless, following the ratification of the Treaty of Lisbon, the Polish judiciary appeared to ignore the existence of the Protocol (Duff 2013: 9). In response, constitutional arrangements were set in place for a possible amendment or withdrawal of Poland from the Protocol (Duff 2013: 9).

specifically, on labour law – on the basis of the Charter, so that the need to compromise on its stance on key matters.[109] The UK was particularly disconcerted about the right to strike as well as other economic and social rights enshrined in Title IV of the Charter.[110]

In contrast to the UK, Poland took no issue with social and labour rights as presented in the Charter but supported them "fully" (Declaration 62 of 2016), due to its long-standing historical commitment in that regard, especially with respect to trade unions in modern times.[111] At the same time, Poland was mainly interested in protecting from the influence of the Charter its right to legislate[112] in "the sphere of public morality, family law, as well as the protection of human dignity and respect for human physical and moral integrity".[113] The concerns that motivated the creation of Protocol No. 30, detailed above, help us gain an appreciation of the concrete practical implications of a broad interpretation of Article 51 CFREU, according to the specific circumstances of each Member State.

Arguably the most important contribution of Protocol No. 30 on an EU constitutional plain was the explicit guarantee it provided, to the effect that:

> [t]he Charter does not extend the ability of the Court of Justice of the European Union, or any court or tribunal of Poland or of the United Kingdom, to find that the laws, regulations or administrative provisions, practices or action of Poland or of the United Kingdom are inconsistent with the fundamental rights, freedoms and principles that it reaffirms.
>
> (Article 1(1), Protocol No. 30)

By virtue of its Article 1(1), Protocol No. 30 supports a narrow interpretation of the phrase "when [the Member States] are implementing Union law" of Article 51(1) CFREU, in contrast to the broader reading given in the Explanations to the Charter.[114] Its chief value lies in solidifying the status quo when it comes to the delimitation of the jurisdiction of the national and supranational courts to review national laws and in precluding the possibility of an extension of the scope of the Charter.[115]

Here it is important to briefly note that a fundamental misunderstanding about the effect of Protocol No. 30 threatened to take root in the British political discourse in 2007, namely that Protocol No. 30 provided the option of an all-encompassing opt-out from the Charter.[116] The case of *NS* (Joined Cases C-411/10 and C-493/10) corrected this misconception by clarifying that the

109 Duff 2013: 9.
110 Borowski 2018: 397.
111 Borowski 2018: 398, footnote [69].
112 Duff 2013: 9.
113 Declaration 61 of 2016.
114 Belling 2012: 261.
115 Belling 2012: 263–264.
116 Duff 2013: 9.

exemption established by Article 1(1) of Protocol No. 30 was strictly confined to the obligations of Poland and the UK associated with Article 51 CFREU, and not with the entire Charter.[117] This was also the conclusion Steve Peers[118] reached after producing a comprehensive summary of the academic commentary in support of that point.[119] Although at first glance this amendment might appear slight, its actual impact must not be underestimated. To secure the opt-out granted by Protocol No. 30, the UK and Poland were prepared to risk great political backlash within the EU community. Protocol No. 30 appears to have caused a great deal of political turmoil and legal uncertainty as well as to have posed a threat to the uniformity of the protection of fundamental rights provided at EU level.[120]

The mere existence of the necessity to explicitly limit the effects of Article 51 CFREU through a separate protocol shows that a broad interpretation of Article 51 CFREU, as it appears on the page, could grant the Court of Justice such extensive discretion that the Member States felt the need to 'insure' against its potentially devastating ramifications. The fact that the Member States expressly and exclusively referred to limiting the influence of the Court of Justice, as opposed to any other EU governmental institutions, may be viewed as especially significant, as it indicates that Article 1(1) of Protocol No. 30 is "a particular expression of distrust" for the Courts and specifically for the CJEU.[121] In this sense, Protocol No. 30 foreshadows the developments in *Åkerberg Fransson*, where the Court exploited the vulnerabilities in the drafting of Article 51 CFREU.

Indeed, the accusation in judicial activism was hard to avoid in the face of the unwarranted expansive interpretation given to Article 51 CFREU in *Åkerberg Fransson*. As established above, the Court's interpretation contradicts the legislative intent expressed in the final version of Article 51 CFREU and the legislative history of its drafting process. However, the Court of Justice must not be condemned as activist without paying due regard to the mitigating factors detailed above. After all, the fact that Poland and the UK subscribed to Protocol No. 30 hints at a sense of awareness that, despite the drafter's best efforts, the drafting of Article 51 CFREU still leaves a lot to be desired and needs to be further fortified against the Court's activist advances.

Summary of the Findings of the Legal Analysis

Ultimately, it seems that the EU legislator was acutely aware of the high stakes inherent in the drafting of Article 51 CFREU with respect to the 'federal question'. From the outset, the EU legislator was determined to ensure that the

117 Joined Cases C411/10 and C493/10, paragraphs 119–120.
118 Peers 2012, 384–385.
119 Peers citing Craig, Pernice, Bernard, Anderson & Murphy, and Layden & Lock, 2012: 379–380.
120 Duff 2013: 11.
121 Borowski 2018: 414–415.

provision was drafted with extreme accuracy and clarity. However, the necessity to reconcile the language of CJEU's pre-existing case-law with the wording of the Article 51 CFREU caused their resolve to waver. The EU legislator adopted a highly restrictive approach to the terminological choices made in drafting the provision. At the same time, the (legally non-binding, but still highly influential) Explanations to the Charter attached to the final version of Article 51(1) CFREU seemed to have created more problems than they solved. The terminology used in the Explanations introduced a great deal of confusion and uncertainty. These circumstances created an environment of enhanced indeterminacy that prompted the UK and Poland to subscribe to Protocol No. 30, to pre-empt an unwarranted expansion of competences by the CJEU.

Based on this evidence, it is safe to conclude that the EU legislator was preoccupied with ensuring the clear and precise drafting of Article 51 CFREU. The EU legislator seemed to have placed its reliance on the restrictive and specific language used in the drafting of Article 51 CFREU, to exclusively refer to the type of situation envisioned in *Wachauf*. Therefore, there is a very high probability that the legislative intent behind Article 51(1) CFREU was to read the phrase "only when [the Member States] are implementing Union law" according to its plain and ordinary meaning.

To this end, multilingual analysis will be applied to a selection of language versions of Article 51(1) CFREU to demonstrate that the semantic meaning of the provision matches the pragmatic meaning instilled by the legislator. The linguistic analysis will demonstrate that the pragmatic dimension of the Court's interpretation of Article 51(1) CFREU contradicts the overall legislative intent of the EU legislator in drafting the provision, expressed in semantic and pragmatic terms.

Linguistic Analysis

What follows is a detailed description of how the CJEU produced ambiguity on the pages of the preliminary ruling of *Åkerberg Fransson*, to achieve an unwarranted expansion of EU competences.

The Relationships of Interchangeability Established by the CJEU in Åkerberg Fransson

The CJEU treats a set of terms – which were borrowed from the wording of Article 51 CFREU, its own jurisprudence and the Explanations to the Charter – as interchangeable. These relationships of interchangeability are established on a pragmatic level through their use in context.

The terms used to refer to the meaning of Article 51 CFREU were simultaneously validated by a range of sources:

(a) to "implement Community rules" (*Wachauf*, Case 5/88: paragraph 19) / "implementing Union law" (Article 51(1) CFREU);

(b) to "fall within the scope of Community law" (*ERT*, Case C-260/89: paragraph 42) / to "act in the scope of Union law" (Explanations to the Charter, 2007: C 303/32);
(c) "the field of application of Union law" (Article 51(2) CFREU, Explanations to the Charter, 2007: C 303/32).

To begin with, let us concentrate on a range of relevant terms interspersed throughout the text of the preliminary ruling of *Åkerberg Fransson*, namely "the scope of (European) Union law",[122] "the field of application",[123] and "implemen ting"/"implementation".[124] The CJEU made its own contribution to the list by using the term "applicability" with reference both to EU law and to the Charter of fundamental rights.[125]

All of these terms played a decisive role in the CJEU's reasoning in *Åkerberg Fransson*. Advocate General Cruz Villalón pointed to 'scope', 'field of application', and 'implementation' as the terms relevant to resolving the legal dispute at the centre of the case.[126] Furthermore, AG Cruz Villalón maintained that the friction between the terminology employed in the jurisprudence of the Court prior to *Åkerberg Fransson* and the wording of Article 51(1) was mainly due to the terms "field of application" (belonging to the former) and "implementation" (used in the latter).[127] More importantly, AG Cruz Villalón shares the following in respect of the interaction between these two terms:

> At this juncture, I believe that it would be helpful to view the different formulations used as expressions which are not qualitatively different. It is clear that nuances may be identified between them. However, the boundaries are always blurred.[128]

If one reads between the lines, the message comes across that the relationships between the terms should be investigated further, so as to establish precisely how they might be related. One viable explanation of this connection could be interchangeability.

122 *Åkerberg Fransson*, C-617/10: paragraphs 19, 20, 21, 22. There is some significant variation across the board when it comes to the verb with which "the scope of European Union law" collocates, e.g. "to fall" (paragraph 21), to "lie" (paragraph 19), to "come" (paragraph 22), to "act" (paragraph 20, citing the Explanations to the Charter). However, for the purposes of this study, the distinction between them is seen as immaterial.
123 *Åkerberg Fransson*, C-617/10: paragraphs 17, 20, 23. Here the single usage of "application" in paragraphs 28, 33 and 46 is omitted, as it is irrelevant for the purposes of this study.
124 *Åkerberg Fransson*, C-617/10: paragraphs 16 and 17. Here the usage of the terms in paragraph 27, 28, 29 is omitted, as it is irrelevant for the purposes of this study.
125 Case C-617/10: paragraph 21.
126 Opinion of AG Cruz Villalón, 2012: paragraphs 32 and 34.
127 Opinion of AG Cruz Villalón, 2012: paragraph 26.
128 Opinion of AG Cruz Villalón, 2012: paragraph 27.

Interchangeable use is predicated on the equivalence between terms being established in a pragmatic context. Predictably, the Court does not necessarily spell out their equivalence by explicitly labelling it as such. Rather, the relationship of equivalence is mainly discerned by following the Court's line of argument and by scrutinising the legal meaning of its statements. Thus, the discovery of these patterns of interchangeability is primarily a matter of legal judgment, since inference from the legal context is necessary.

Let us now view the relationships of interchangeability from a bird's eye perspective, before commencing with the arduous process of providing evidence for each relationship. *Figure A* presents the pragmatic patterns of interchangeable use of divergent terms established by the CJEU throughout its reasoning in *Åkerberg Fransson*.

Figure A illustrates how the CJEU pragmatically established a network of relationships of interchangeability. **Relationship (A)** was succinctly summarised by the CJEU as follows: "The applicability of European Union law entails applicability of the fundamental rights guaranteed by the Charter".[129] Earlier in the same paragraph, the Court gave a thorough explanation of the content of this formula, to the effect that: "situations cannot exist which are covered in that way by European Union law without those fundamental rights being applicable".[130] Here, "covered in that way by European Union law" actually refers to "national legislation [falling] within the scope of European Union law".[131] The latter is a phrase that the Court plainly admitted to have borrowed from the Explanations to the Charter.[132] This provides evidence in support of **relationship (B)**. Furthermore, with respect to **relationship (C)**, the "applicability of fundamental rights"[133] appears to be equated to "the field of application of fundamental rights".[134] The Court used both of the expressions to denote a situation where "fundamental rights [are] applicable",[135] so there is certainly common ground between the two to justify their relationship. With regards to **relationship (D)**, the CJEU expressly acknowledged that it adopts the terminology of *ERT* and the Explanations to the Charter ("[falling/lying] [outside/within] the scope of European Union law") to define "the field of application of the fundamental rights of the European Union".[136] Finally, in regard to **relationship (E)**, the CJEU made it clear that the wording of Article 51(1) CFREU ("when [the Member States] are implementing Union law") determines "the Charter's field of application".[137]

129 *Åkerberg Fransson*, C-617/10: paragraph 21.
130 *Åkerberg Fransson*, C-617/10: paragraph 21.
131 *Åkerberg Fransson*, C-617/10: paragraph 21.
132 *Åkerberg Fransson*, C-617/10: paragraph 20.
133 *Åkerberg Fransson*, C-617/10, paragraph 20.
134 *Åkerberg Fransson*, C-617/10: paragraph 21.
135 *Åkerberg Fransson*, C-617/10: paragraph 21.
136 *Åkerberg Fransson*, C-617/10: paragraphs 19 and 20.
137 *Åkerberg Fransson*, C-617/10: paragraph 17.

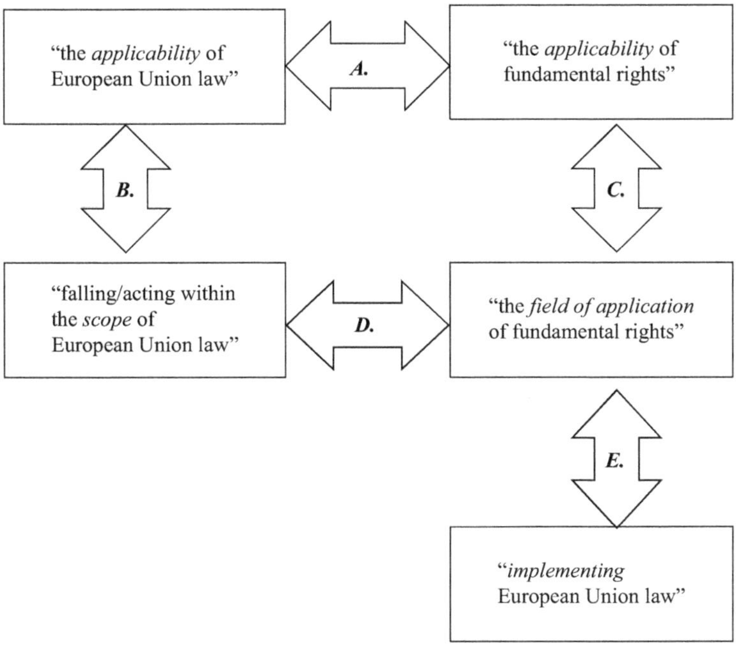

Figure A The relationships of interchangeability established by the CJEU between terms in *Åkerberg Fransson*.

The evidence suggests that the Court established three different classes of relationships of interchangeability, differentiated on the basis of degrees of remoteness. Firstly, a ***direct relationship***, which can be observed between any two terms in *Figure A* above, positioned immediately next to each other (e.g. between "the applicability of European Union law" and "the applicability of fundamental rights"). In contrast, an indirect relationship is more remote (i.e. two terms separated by at least one other term). Secondly, there are ***one-step indirect relationships***, where two terms are separated by one other term (e.g. "the applicability of European Union law" and "the field of application of fundamental rights"). Thirdly, one can also spot ***two-step indirect relationships***, where two terms are separated by two other terms (e.g. "the applicability of European Union law" and "implementing European Union law"). Naturally, the direct relationship is the most immediate connection, while the two-step indirect relationship is the most distant one.[138] It is important to note that, in contrast to the will of the legislator expressed in the Explanations, ***no direct relationship of interchangeability*** was

138 Theoretically, it is also possible to have indirect connections of more steps, but they are typically superseded by a shorter route. For example, there is a three-step indirect relationship between "falling/acting within the scope of European Union law" and "implementing

detected between "falling/acting within the scope of European Union law" and "implementing European Union law" in the Court's reasoning, but rather *a one-step indirect relationship*. Finally, it seems to be the case that all the terms, aside from "implementing European Union law", were bound in what appears to be *a loop of interchangeable terms*.

On this basis, one can draw conclusions about the degree of connectedness of each term, with the greatest weight being attributed to *direct relationships*. In addition, an excessive number of *indirect relationships*, preferably of the *one-step* class, will also be viewed as important. Further, the impact of the relationships will be decided on the basis of their source – the legislative text, the Explanations, the CJEU's case-law (listed from *high* to *low*).

Thus, it has been determined that the terminological construction "the field of application of fundamental rights" has the greatest number of *direct relationships* (3) and the greatest number of *one-step indirect relationships* (3) and a fair number of *two-step relationships* (2). Within *the loop of interchangeable terms*, the term "falling/acting within the scope of European Union law" ranks second in terms of degree of connectedness. This term also has the greatest number of *one-step indirect relationships* (3) and an average number of both *direct* (2) and *two-step indirect* (2) *relationships*. Lastly, the term "implementing European Union law" has the least number of *direct relationships* (1) and has only an average number of relationships in each class (2).

On this basis, the term "field of application of fundamental rights" stands out as the central hub of this array of terms, since it serves as an intersection point between the 'loop' and the expression "implementing European Union law". This is no great revelation, given the fact that Article 51(2) CFREU refers to "the field of application of Union law" and Article 51 CFREU as a whole is titled "Field of application". It is equally unsurprising that "implementing European Union law" is the most isolated term, since it is the clearest and the most legally authoritative representation of the legislator's intent to strictly limit the effect of Article 51 CFREU. Since its direct relationship with "field of application" is entrenched in the legislative text, and therefore is fixed and immutable, it is perhaps the most impactful of them all.

The second *direct relationship* worth discussing in detail is the one between "field of application" and "acting/falling within the scope of European Union law". This is a fairly weak relationship, since it is only rooted in the *ERT* case and the Explanations to the Charter (which are not legally binding). As such, it represents another aspect of the status quo. It is an element of the analysis that the CJEU could not afford to ignore, not least because it represents terminology that made its first appearance in the Court's own case-law.

Finally, the third *direct relationship* of interchangeability of "the field of application" is with "the applicability of fundamental rights". As previously noted, the

---

European Union law"), but it is weaker by comparison with the more immediate one-step indirect connection between the same terms.

term "applicability" was the Court's own contribution to the array of relevant terms associated with Article 51 CFREU. "Applicability" in both of its forms enjoyed only a middling degree of connectedness (2 *direct relationships*, 2 *one-step indirect relationships* and 1 or 2 *two-step indirect relationships*) and a fairly weak impact (as it was only based on the Court's statements in *Åkerberg Fransson*). It is doubtful that there was any real need to introduce this term in the Court's reasoning at all, since it is not a well-established part of the Court's vocabulary in this context and there was no practical necessity to come up with a substitute to "the field of application". The CJEU failed to provide any definition, explanation or justification of its use and left it unsupported by reference to previous case-law. As a purely stylistic solution, it is certainly a bizarre and even reckless choice, given its prominent role in the decisive part of the Court's reasoning in a preliminary ruling of such gave constitutional ramifications like *Åkerberg Fransson*. Therefore, the most feasible explanation is that the use of the term "applicability" is strategic. If that be the case, then there must be a direct causal link between the invention of the Court of this term and the realisation of the Court's ultimate strategic aim.

To sum up, it seems that the careful construction of a confusing tangle of relationships of interchangeability was designed to carve out a space for the meaningful inclusion of the term "applicability". The term was created as a variation of the well-established construction "the field of application", in the hope of drawing normative authority by association. More importantly, this unusual approach of interchangeable use of terms is also likely to have been a clever ploy for side-lining the term "implementing Union law", in favour of attributing greater significance to "the scope of Union law". Given the extremely low level of connectedness of the former term, which stands in stark contrast to its especially high level of impact, this hypothesis is confirmed. The exact opposite is true for "the scope of Union law", which is a term of relatively low impact but of excellent connectedness.

At this stage, it might be useful to consider what problem the CJEU sought to resolve by means of establishing these relationships of interchangeability. Thus far, it has been made clear that the CJEU's previous case-law of *ERT* and *Wachauf* obliges it to distinguish between "falling/acting within the scope of European Union law" and "implementing Union law". At the same time, the Explanations to the Charter conflate the two terms when it comes to determining "the field of application" of the Charter under Article 51 CFREU. This seemingly impossible task is actually a good fit for ambiguity, since this phenomenon allows for (at least) two mutually exclusive alternatives to be equally valid at the same time, without affecting the truth (normative) value of the statement.

Thanks to the 'loop of interchangeability', established by the Court, all of these terms appear to be mutually interchangeable in pragmatic terms. Indeed, this includes even "implementing Union law", as it is mutually interchangeable with one of the elements of the 'loop'. Seeing as the CJEU *explicitly* equates "the applicability of European Union law" and "the applicability of fundamental rights" by stating that the former "entails" the latter in paragraph 21 of *Åkerberg*

Fransson, it is only fair that this instruction is heeded. Therefore, these two versions of applicability will be treated as one – "the applicability of European Union law". Secondly, "the scope of EU law" and "the field of application of fundamental rights" will also collapse into one term – "the (scope/field of) application of European Union law".[139] Lastly, "implementing Union law" will be labelled as "the implementation of European Union law". This is done for practical purposes, to shape the terms into similarly phrased constructions that will facilitate the ensuing multilingual analysis. However, it is also makes normative sense on grounds of this concrete and decisive pronouncement made by the Court.

The main assumption is that interchangeability typically implies synonymy on a semantic level. The evidence provided by the multilingual analysis will show that there is incongruity between the semantic and pragmatic meaning given by the legislator to "implementation" and the relationship of interchangeability established in pragmatic terms between "implementation" and "(scope/field of) application". Further, the addition of the term "applicability" allowed for this array of terms to be rearranged in a model based on ambiguity, rather than synonymy.

Multilingual Analysis

To show that these terms are not bound by synonymy, but by polysemy (as a form of ambiguity), a multilingual analysis was conducted (see Appendix A). It is certainly the case that in the preponderance of the selected translations "implementation" means "putting something into action/effect" and/or "enforcement". Here reference is made to Spanish, Bulgarian and Greek, as well as the entirety of the Germanic languages (English, German, Swedish, and Danish). In this respect, this analysis confirms the outcome of the study conducted by Brittain,[140] namely that the term "to implement" in Article 51(1) CFREU is meant to signify a positive action by a Member State, so that a provision of EU law is put into effect.

However, it is interesting to note that in the Spanish and Swedish (language of the case)[141] translations, the term selected for "implementation" actually overlaps with that for "application" ("field/scope of application"). This is particularly intriguing, since they belong to different language families – Romance and Germanic, respectively. Yet, both of these translations have preferred "implementation" in the sense of "putting into action" or "execution, enforcement", even though the more generic, neutral alternative of "application" was also available.

139 In the preliminary ruling of *Kremzow* of 1997, the Court of Justice uses "the field of application of Community law" and "the scope of Community law" interchangeably (Case C-299/95: paragraph 15).

140 Brittain 2013: 293.

141 The divergence with respect to the Swedish language version was noted by Bernitz (2015: 197).

Further, it was also established that "field/scope of application" appears to mean "coverage", "range", "purview", according to a range of translations – English, German, Danish, and Finnish. The Greek translation refers to "competence", "province".

Now let us consider the newcomer to this array of terms – "applicability". Both the English and Swedish translations suggest that "applicability" is associated with "relevance". Additionally, the German and Bulgarian translations indicate that the applicability of a legal rule is defined by its workability or operation. The Finnish translation reveals that applicability may be characterised by the suitability of fitness for a particular purpose of a legal rule. It is also noteworthy that other translations expose a connection between "applicability" and certain fixed expressions in EU law. More specifically, the Polish translation highlights the link with "uniform application of law", while the Danish translation refers to the expression "to be directly applicable".

At this stage, a quick search in the IATE (InterActive Terminology for Europe), the online terminology database at the EU, sheds light onto the usage of terms in EU law.[142] The results from the IATE database gave a much-needed confirmation that the term "applicability" is included in the following collocations in English:[143] "direct applicability" and "immediate applicability". With respect to these two collocations,[144] the IATE database puts forward the following definition: "a measure created for certain Community acts which are directly applicable and do not have to be transposed beforehand into national law".[145]

The results presented above lead to a reassessment of the semantic relationships between these terms. Firstly, "implementation" cannot be equated to "application". The pragmatic interchangeable use of "implementation" and "application" is not based on synonymy between these terms, as the linguistic divergence between them is too great. "Implementation" carries a very specific, distinct connotation in the sense of enforcement, which is much narrower in scope that "application".[146]

Secondly, "applicability" can be equated to "application". Since "applicability" serves the function of an overarching term denoting practical workability, relevance and fitness for a particular purpose of a legal rule. At the same time, "(field/scope of) application" is associated with the act of delineation of competence. Therefore, it makes sense that "field/scope of application" could be considered to be part and parcel of "applicability", especially if used in the sense of relevance and fitness for purpose.

142 https://iate.europa.eu/home. Last accessed 2 June 2019.

143 Another result also came up ("extraterritorial applicability" in the "Restriction on Competition [Council]" category), but it is considered irrelevant for the present purposes.

144 IATE Database (iate.europa.eu): IATE ID: 1414780. Last accessed on 5 April 2018.

145 IATE Database (iate.europa.eu): EUROVOC, Edition 2, 1987. Last accessed on 5 April 2018.

146 Brittain's analysis (2013) confirms that the verb "to implement" cannot be equated to "the scope of EU law", since it excludes situations of Member State derogations.

Thirdly, "applicability" can also be equated to "implementation". The term "applicability" is connected to the fixed expression "direct applicability" (i.e. the quality of being 'directly applicable'). Logically, this means it is equally associated with "indirect applicability" (i.e. the quality of being 'indirectly applicable'). The latter case refers to the transposition of an EU legal rule into national law (Article 291 TFEU), which confirms that "implementation" is a feature of "applicability".

On this basis, it becomes clear that "the applicability of European Union law" is an overarching concept which is semantically and normatively linked both to "application" and "implementation". At the same time, "application" and "implementation" were determined to be divergent terms, meaning that there is no synonymy between the two on a semantic level. The semantic model of ambiguity production in *Åkerberg Fransson* is as follows: the polysemous (ambiguous) term "applicability" could be interpreted as "(scope/field of) application" (Paraphrase 1) and "implementation" (Paraphrase 2). The two readings are mutually exclusive and equally plausible in both linguistic and legal terms. Thus, in *Åkerberg Fransson* the CJEU produced ambiguity, more specifically "inter-lingual ambiguity".[147]

The Strategic Implications of the CJEU's Ambiguity Production in *Åkerberg Fransson*

Thus, the initial hypothesis of polysemy (as a form of ambiguity), strategically produced by the CJEU on the pages of *Åkerberg Fransson*, has been proven correct. This means the pragmatic model of interchangeability developed by the Court in *Figure A* lacks semantic support. Could it be then that this pragmatic model of interchangeability actually amounts to "*nonsense*"[148] in linguistic terms? More importantly, how does the production of ambiguity on a semantic level contribute towards the fulfilment of the Court's strategic goals?

Throughout this elaborate pragmatic exercise, the Court switches from one term to the other with staggeringly casual ease. As a result, the bewildered reader is left with the lingering suspicion that the terms in question are devoid of actual substance and meaning. Nevertheless, AG Cruz Villalón seems to have identified a 'common thread', based on his observation of the CJEU case-law preceding *Åkerberg Fransson*:

> a common feature of the different formulations used is the requirement that Union law must have a *presence* at the origin of the exercise of public authority; that presence, it should be added, must be as a law, that is with the capacity to determine or influence to some extent the subject-matter of that exercise of public authority in the Member State. However, 'presence' never becomes 'predetermination', in so far as the latter situation scenario should not pose a problem.[149]

147 Cao 2007: 71, 75, 78.
148 Kjær 2010: 315.
149 Opinion of AG Cruz Villalón 2012: paragraph 33.

In other words, even though at face value it might seem that the Court is connecting the dots in a random manner, every move is calculated to gain new ground on the playing field where the Court can assert its "presence". Moreover, the Court is advancing in a cautious manner that would allow it to avoid giving the problematic impression of "predetermination". Further, AG Cruz Villalón comments on the execution of this agenda with respect to the relevant terminology:

> none of the formulations referred to ('scope', 'field of application', and 'implementation') has the capacity, of itself, to restrict the scope of that statement of principle. One way of looking at it is that the formulations have little to do with the idea of *lex stricta*, if that condition is applicable to them. On the contrary, they have all the advantages and difficulties of any essentially open formulation.[150]

It would appear that AG Cruz Villalón intuited the key aspects of the ensuing strategic use of these terms in the Court's preliminary ruling of *Åkerberg Fransson*. Firstly, none of these terms, taken on its own, is capable of producing the desired effect by the Court. Rather, it is the *relationships* between them that make all the difference. Secondly, taken together, they amount to an "essentially open formulation". It is precisely this 'openness' that is conducive to the emergence of ambiguity.

In and of itself, the pragmatic model of interchangeability in *Åkerberg Fransson* is 'nonsensical'. The most likely, albeit obvious, reason for that is simply because the model was not designed to make sense. This model was not intended to clarify meaning, but to draw connections to serve a very specific strategic purpose – an expansion of competences. Its intended effect was to devalue "implementation" and enhance the importance of "scope" and "application", while validating the new term of "applicability".

The conducted multilingual analysis exposed the underlying semantic meaning of these terms, buried beneath their pragmatic functions imposed by the Court. The presence of semantic ambiguity meant that "applicability" could be given two equally plausible interpretations – as "(scope/field of) application" and as "implementation". This discovery explains why the Court was insistent on the otherwise pointless inclusion of the term "applicability" into the mix of terms. The polysemous term "applicability" allows for the validation of "(scope/field of) application" as a semantic alternative to "implementation". This creative bit of judicial law-making allowed the Court to shift the starting point of the legal analysis from the severely restrictive option of "implementation", enshrined in Article 51(1) CFREU by the EU legislator, to the more flexible and thus more advantageous formulation of "the applicability of European Union law/fundamental rights".

Thus constructed, the semantic model of ambiguity with "acceptability" at its apex, meant that the semantic meaning instilled by the legislator was

150 Opinion of AG Cruz Villalón, 2012: paragraph 34.

technically respected: "(scope/field of) application" was *not directly* equated to "implementation". This is where ambiguity is superior to synonymy in strategic terms. A direct assertion of synonymy between these terms would have indisputably constituted grounds for judicial activism, as it clearly contradicts the legislative intent, expressed in pragmatic terms in the drafting history of Article 51 CFREU. At the same time, the Explanations to the Charter suggest *some form* of equivalence between the two that allows for *interchangeability*. The addition of "applicability" into the analysis satisfied both of these contradictory instructions issued by the EU legislator in pragmatic terms, while at the same time fulfilling the Court's ultimate strategic goal of expansion of competence.

That being said, one central question of this Case Study is yet to be answered: precisely on what basis could one mount an accusation of judicial activism against the Court of Justice in the case of *Åkerberg Fransson*? Firstly, the very act of inclusion of the term "applicability" is incriminating in terms of judicial activism, since it appears to be solely intended to fulfil the strategic purpose of expansion of competence. The pragmatic model of interchangeability designed to accommodate for this term generated strategically advantageous 'nonsense' on top of the 'nonsense' created by the EU legislator in the Explanations to Article 51 CFREU. Secondly, the Court could have equally resolved the ambiguity it created in favour of "implementation", and not "(scope/field of) application", had it been inclined to do so. On this latter charge, the *Åkerberg Fransson* follows the logic of examples based on strategic ambiguity resolution, presented elsewhere in this book.

The Aftermath of the CJEU's Strategic Resolution of the Ambiguity Produced in *Åkerberg Fransson*

Thus far, the strategic approach by which the CJEU gradually set the scene for ambiguity resolution in *Åkerberg Fransson* was examined closely. At the beginning, there was only one option available to the Court – using the term "implementing Union law", the legislative intent behind which clearly necessitated a narrow interpretation of Article 51(1) CFREU. At the end of the process, the CJEU had created an opportunity to interpret the polysemous (ambiguous) term "applicability" broadly as "(scope/field of) application". Thus, in *Åkerberg Fransson*, the Court of Justice resolved the ambiguity it single-handedly produced earlier in the same preliminary ruling by strategically affirming its jurisdiction.[151] What did the CJEU manage to achieve through this deft strategic manoeuvring?

The CJEU succeeded in establishing a heretofore unprecedented connection between the scope of application of the Charter of Fundamental Rights and the principle of effectiveness of Union law.[152] It could be argued that the central

151 *Åkerberg Fransson*, Case C-617/10, 2013: paragraphs 21, 22, and 31.
152 Van Bockel & Wattel 2013: 878.

doctrine in *Åkerberg Fransson* was built on the Court's pronouncement[153] that "[t]he applicability of European Union law entails applicability of the fundamental rights guaranteed by the Charter".[154] Consequently, to fall within the scope of EU law and to be subject to regulation under the Charter, a national measure needs to merely pose a risk of undermining the effectiveness of EU law.[155] This new rule seems to apply in any situation where the Member States act under an obligation imposed by EU law, irrespective of how specific or general it might be.[156] In contrast, it would appear that the extent of determination of Member State actions by EU law *does* make a difference in this respect, judging from the Court's direct reference to *Melloni* in paragraph 29 of *Åkerberg Fransson*.[157] If the action of the Member States is "not entirely determined by EU law" in the situation in question, the national authorities and courts are given some leeway in applying national standards of fundamental rights protection, as long as the *Melloni* 'red line' of "the primacy, unity and effectiveness of EU law" is not crossed.[158] This explanation actually confirms the impression that the ultimate strategic aim that informed the CJEU's creative approach to reasoning in *Åkerberg Fransson* is actually the successful implementation of the authority of EU law on a systemic level. In other words, *Åkerberg Fransson* merely adds detail to the picture within the framework set by *Melloni*. The necessity to ensure that both preliminary rulings work in unison to lead to the same overall conclusion certainly seems to have been an operating concern in the Court's decision-making.

Unfortunately, by fixating upon that specific outcome of its analysis, the CJEU seems to have compromised with other aspects of its reasoning in *Åkerberg Fransson*. The new formula offered no greater clarity than the legal rules predating it.[159] This impression was confirmed upon a detailed examination of the treatment of the term "implementation" in the CJEU case-law that followed *Åkerberg Fransson*, conducted by Fontanelli.[160] Having scrutinised five key cases – *Torralbo*, *Turnhout*, *Siragusa*, *Hernandez*, and *Pfleger* – he concludes that:

> the Court seems to be buying time and generally narrowing down Fransson's liberal approach … the Court is acutely aware that a better test for art.51(1) is necessary … the use of formulaic reasoning suggests that the Court is treading lightly, testing the relevance and accuracy of its own case law and playing by ear, rather than experimenting with new tests.[161]

153 Van Bockel & Wattel 2013: 877.
154 *Åkerberg Fransson*, Case C-617/10: paragraph 21.
155 Van Bockel & Wattel 2013: 878.
156 Van Bockel & Wattel 2013: 878.
157 Van Bockel & Wattel 2013: 878–879.
158 *Åkerberg Fransson*, Case C-617/10, 2013: paragraph 29.
159 Van Bockel & Wattel 2013: 877.
160 Fontanelli 2014.
161 Fontanelli 2014: 694.

Fontanelli then highlights the absence of a true will for finding a workable over-arching solution on part of the Court: "the Court's determinations with regard to art.51(1) of the Charter are purpose-driven; they are not concerned with the application or creation of a coherent judicial test".[162]

Finally, Fontanelli delivers a damning assessment of the "applicability" formula from paragraph 21 of *Åkerberg Fransson*, which he dubs "Fransson equivalence":

> In less than 18 months, *Fransson* equivalence has revealed itself for what it is: a tautological red herring. If anything, *Fransson* confirmed that a specific legislative intention is not necessary for a national measure to implement EU law de facto: any contribution to the objectives of EU law can induce the Court to "see" implementation at work.[163]

Thus, it seems that the Court of Justice was never particularly concerned with investigating the true meaning of any of the relevant terms in *Åkerberg Fransson*. Their treatment was simply a means to an end, a retrospective justification of a foregone conclusion. In the wake of the landmark preliminary ruling, the *Åkerberg Fransson* "applicability" formula soon proved to be practically useless in tackling the complexities of the ensuing case-law. Further, the Court failed to initiate a meaningful revision of the formula or to propose a more helpful new interpretation of the wording of Article 51(1) CFREU. This development validates the intuition that the CJEU's invention and subsequent inclusion of the term "applicability" in the reasoning presented in *Åkerberg Fransson* was strategically motivated. Further, this strategic purpose seems to have been contained within the pages of *Åkerberg Fransson*. Therefore, the theory of strategic ambiguity production, immediately followed by strategic ambiguity resolution, in *Åkerberg Fransson* appears to have been substantiated by these findings.

At the same time, the CJEU paid a high constitutional price for its judicial activism in *Åkerberg Fransson*, since this decision was evidently taken at the cost of acceptability. As elaborated in the previous chapter, the Member States' national constitutional courts showed reluctance, to say the least, to accept the combined effect of these two preliminary rulings.[164] Most notably, the German Constitutional Court (*Bundesverfassungsgericht*) expressed its displeasure with the outcome of *Åkerberg Fransson* in its *Antiterrordatei* judgment.[165] The *Bundesverfassungsgericht* fired a "forceful warning shot" by ruling that a federal law that set up a German counter-terrorism database is not determined by EU law and thus not covered by Article 51(1) CFREU in the sense of "implementing Union law".[166]

162 Fontanelli 2014: 697.
163 Fontanelli 2014: 697.
164 Edenharter 2018: 395–399.
165 Edenharter 2018: 395–396.
166 Thym 2013: 396.

The reaction by the German Constitutional Court helps expose the actual root of the accusations of judicial activism in this instance. The crux of the problem is not a matter of negotiating the level of protection of fundamental rights afforded to EU citizens, but whether the CJEU's ruling is to be considered *ultra vires* and undermines *constitutional identity*.[167] To be more specific, an *ultra vires* act would be classified as "[j]udicial interpretation of Treaty articles or EU legislation that is regarded too broad, thereby widening the application of such provisions beyond what is felt to be warranted".[168] Moreover, given the CJEU's insistence on shielding the effectiveness of EU law from unwanted interference reconfirmed in *Åkerberg Fransson*,[169] an accusation in the Court's acting *ultra vires* could also be founded on the following definition:

> [j]udicial decisions that are premised on interpretive principles, such as effectiveness, in order to extend the remit of a Treaty article or provision of EU legislation, where the burden carried by such principles is felt to be overbroad and insufficiently justified.[170]

Daniel Thym argues that the CJEU's decision in *Åkerberg Fransson* is unlikely to have been made *ultra vires*, but was rather "an act of frustration" on part of the German Constitutional Court after the CJEU refused to accept the "olive branch" extended by the former in the *Honeywell* judgment.[171] Thym also maintains that the precautions against such practices taken by the German Constitutional Court in *Honeywell* fail to apply in the case of *Åkerberg Fransson*, since they only pertain to restricting legislative competence.[172] Moreover, Thym stresses that there might be reason to believe that the statutory wording, the drafting history and the Explanations to the Charter present the ultimate decision of the Court as a plausible outcome of the normal course of judicial practice, per the definition of the latter in the *Honeywell* judgment.[173] Furthermore, an argument could be made for a broad interpretation of Article 51(1) CFREU. Paul Craig[174] adduces textual evidence of the equation between "implementing Union law" and "the scope of Union law" in the CJEU's case law (*Caballero*) and the Explanations to the Charter. Additionally, Craig[175] points out that the *ERT* principle is preferable in normative terms, since a narrow interpretation would lead to the need for fine technical distinctions, which would provide a shaky foundation for the development of a coherent doctrine for the application of the Charter. Furthermore, in

167 Thym 2013: 398.
168 Craig 2011: 397.
169 *Åkerberg Fransson*, Case C-617/10, 2013: paragraph 29.
170 Craig 2011: 397.
171 Thym 2013: 399.
172 Thym 2013: 400.
173 Thym citing *Honeywell*, 2013: 399–400.
174 Craig 2011: 430–431.
175 Craig 2011: 431.

case the narrow interpretation had been supported by the Court, the *ERT* case and its related jurisprudence would have still been binding on the Member States, creating a regime that runs parallel to the Charter.[176] For all of these reasons, Thym[177] suggests criticism against *Åkerberg Fransson* be based on the CJEU's failure to respect national constitutional identity or a mixture between national constitutional identity and *ultra vires*.

This brief analysis demonstrates the reigning confusion that the outcome in *Åkerberg Fransson* generated across the board. Identifying the exact grounds for an accusation in judicial activism is important not only from the perspective of accountability, but also as a means of future prevention. Without this essential specificity, any objection has little chance of maturing beyond a mere intuition and any protest inevitably loses its keen sting. This is precisely where the contribution of this example plays a decisive role in the debate. The fact of the matter is that the remit of EU competence was expanded as a result of the Court's decision-making in *Åkerberg Fransson*. The Court's firm determination to achieve this outcome left clear traces in its reasoning as it appears on the pages of the preliminary ruling of *Åkerberg Fransson*. By examining the elaborate model of pragmatic interchangeability and the consequent ambiguity production on a semantic level, this example demonstrated the exact lengths to which the Court was prepared to go to circumvent the instructions of the EU legislator with respect to Article 51 CFREU and realise its activist vision.

The mere fact that the Court chose to take this winding road to its final destination hints at its own awareness that any other more straightforward alternative would not have led to this outcome or would have had a higher constitutional price. As shown above, this strategy has succeeded in shaking the confidence of some of the critics in the Court's activism, despite clear indications that the CJEU has overstepped the EU legislator's intent in drafting Article 51 CFREU, as shown earlier in this Case Study. More importantly, by "walking on the brink of non-compliance", the Court of Justice has enhanced its reputation.[178]

Conclusion

The example of *Åkerberg Fransson* demonstrates that the CJEU is fully capable of creating strategic opportunities for ambiguity resolution for itself, even where there are none to be found on the face of the statutory text. In this instance, Article 51 CFREU was in all likelihood specifically drafted with the legislative intent to preclude the CJEU from abusing the wording of the statute to justify an unwarranted expansion of competences. This was made clear upon a closer inspection of the pragmatic context surrounding the legislative provision. The extreme importance of the 'federal' question, the drafting history and the

176 Craig 2011: 431.
177 Thym 2013: 400–401.
178 Dothan 2014: 8, 117–122.

concerns expressed by the UK and Poland in the form of Protocol No. 30 all suggest that the EU legislator was exclusively interested in a restrictive interpretation of "implementing Union law". The Explanations to the Charter represented a non-binding aberration from this norm, from which the CJEU promptly took advantage in *Åkerberg Fransson*.

The pragmatic model of interchangeable use of relevant terms exposed the CJEU's true intentions behind engaging with this terminology. Far from being interested in providing actual clarification, the Court was more concerned about establishing specific relationships between the terms. The combined effect of these relationships of interchangeability was to cast aside in isolation the term "implementing Union law", which presented an obstacle to the CJEU's activist agenda. At the same time, the CJEU managed to boost the impact of "scope of Union law" and "field of application", while entangling the newly coined term "applicability" into the network of relationships. The combined effect was strategically advantageous in that it was conducive to a broad interpretation of Article 51 CFREU.

This impression was later confirmed by the multilingual analysis conducted on the basis of the relevant terms found in a selection of language versions of Article 51 CFREU and the official translations of *Åkerberg Fransson*. It was established that, on a semantic level, both the terms "(scope/field of) application" and "implementation" are facets of the term "applicability" but cannot be equated to each other. Therefore, this semantic configuration closely resembled the model of ambiguity production, with "applicability" being the ambiguous (polysemous) term. Even though the interchangeability that the CJEU established in pragmatic terms could be easily mistaken for a suggestion of synonymy, the linguistic analysis presented in this chapter demonstrated that the semantic relationships between them match the model of ambiguity production more accurately.

Ambiguity production is strategically advantageous for the Court, since it allows the CJEU to present "(scope/field of) application" as a viable alternative interpretation of "applicability", alongside "implementation". Thus, the Court could sidestep "implementation", without outright rejecting it as a plausible interpretation. Such a rejection would have directly contradicted the legislative intent behind the provision and would have clearly amounted to judicial activism. Establishing synonymy between "(scope/field of) application" and "implementation" would have been both semantically and normatively inaccurate. Therefore, the Court of Justice came up with the ingenious inclusion of the previously inconsequential term "applicability" as a centerpiece of the *Åkerberg Fransson* formula. Thus, the CJEU piled "nonsense" on top of the "nonsense" carelessly generated by the EU legislator in the Explanations to the Charter.

The said formula had little actual utility beyond creating the strategic opportunity for ambiguity resolution within the preliminary ruling of *Åkerberg Fransson*, however. The CJEU failed to put forward a coherent doctrine on its basis in the succeeding case-law. As if conscious of the fragility of its creation, the CJEU avoided revisiting, further clarifying or even substituting it for the purposes of resolving those disputes in a more comprehensive manner. Nevertheless, the CJEU's strategic ambiguity production and subsequent strategic resolution of ambiguity fulfilled its ultimate goal. The Court achieved a tangible and significant expansion of EU competences and an enhancement of the CJEU's reputation, in a manner that made the precise formulation of grounds for criticism for the perpetration of judicial activism a challenging task, until now.

3 Judicial Restraint Reconfirmed?

The CJEU's Strategic Resolution of Ambiguity in *Keck* (Joint cases C-267/91 and C-268/91)

Introduction

The internal market, defined as "an area without internal frontiers in which the free movement of goods, persons, services and capital" is guaranteed (Article 26(2) TFEU), is nowadays considered to be the crowning achievement of the European Union. The construction of the internal market has been primarily, if not exclusively, preoccupied with the advancement of "economic integration" by means of the removal of barriers to free movement that could potentially impede interstate trade.[1] Within this framework, Article 34 TFEU is considered "the clearest embodiment of the principle of freedom of movement of goods within the Treaty".[2] The provision reads as follows: "Quantitative restrictions on imports and all measures having equivalent effect shall be prohibited between Member States" (Article 34 TFEU).[3] Despite its deceptive simplicity, Article 34 TFEU has been recognised as a legal rule with a tremendous constitutional significance:

> [Article 34 TFEU][4] ... is perhaps the chief mechanism employed by the Treaty to advance the economic and social cohesion and solidarity among the Member States. [Article 34 TFEU] is also the structural and doctrinal model for the other "four freedoms" provided for in the Treaty ... This establishes [Article 34 TFEU] as the central jurisprudential impulse for European interdependence. The brevity of [Article 34 TFEU] belies its vigor.[5]

This is why ambiguity found in Article 34 TFEU would be "constitutionally significant" in the context of the distribution of competences between the EU and the Member States in the formation and functioning of the internal market.[6]

1 Lianos 2010: 705–706.
2 Chalmers 1993: 270
3 For the sake of consistency, Article 30 EEC (ex Article 28 TEC) will be referred to with its current designation – Article 34 TFEU – throughout this book.
4 Chriss (1995: 152) originally refers to Article 30 EEC, which is now Article 34 TFEU.
5 Chriss 1995: 152.
6 Horsley 2012: 736.

DOI: 10.4324/9781003294870-9

Indeed, the following chapter will demonstrate that the noun "measure" in the term 'measures having equivalent effect' in Article 34 TFEU is ambiguous (polysemous). The results of the multilingual analysis of a selection of language versions of Article 34 TFEU indicates that the noun "measure" could be interpreted either as "[a] legislative enactment proposed or adopted"[7] (Paraphrase 1) or as "a way of achieving something, or a method for dealing with a situation"[8] (Paraphrase 2).[9] These two readings appear to match the semantic content of the nouns "requirement" (Paraphrase 1) and "arrangement" (Paraphrase 2).

The ambiguity found in Article 34 TFEU became the cornerstone of the CJEU's reasoning in the preliminary ruling of *Keck* (Joined cases C-267/91 and C-268/91). More specifically, by introducing the typological distinction between 'rules that lay down requirements' and 'selling arrangements'[10] the Court committed the strategic act of ambiguity resolution. As a result of its decision-making in *Keck*, the Court of Justice succeeded in limiting the excessively broad scope of 'measures having equivalent effect' to qualitative restrictions (MEQRs) in Article 34 TFEU in an earlier landmark preliminary ruling – *Dassonville* (Case 8–74). Further, the CJEU returned to its customary approach of tackling discrimination in the internal market, which had dominated this area of law before the 'market access' logic was given preference in *Dassonville*.[11]

Despite achieving the status of a leading ruling that successfully remedied the unreasonably wide remit of the *Dassonville* formula, *Keck* has been subjected to severe criticism on account of the Court's chosen means of achieving this end. The distinction between the two categories has been found objectionable for being "artificial and unworkable", infused with "perilous formalism".[12] More specifically, it could be argued that there is an overlap between 'selling arrangements' and 'rules that lay down requirements' in practice, which in effect devalues the distinction and proves these are categories of "indicative value at best, a rough 'rule of thumb'".[13] The category of 'selling arrangements' has been condemned as "merely a convenient label" which lacks legal significance in and of itself.[14]

The air of artificiality that surrounds the distinction drawn in *Keck* inevitably gives rise to suspicions of strategic judicial behaviour. After all, there is nothing to suggest in the wording of Article 34 TFEU that such a distinction already

7 Oxford English Dictionary: www.oed.com/view/Entry/115506?rskey=GdLRPU&result=1&isAdvanced=false#eid last accessed on 15 July 2019.
8 Cambridge Dictionary: https://dictionary.cambridge.org/dictionary/english/measure last accessed on 15 July 2019.
9 The Paraphrases are formulated according to the English language version, since it happened to summarise the findings from the analysis of the other selected language versions well, which are all displayed in Appendix B.
10 *Keck*, Joined cases C-267/91 and C-268/91: paragraphs 15–16.
11 Barnard 2013: 74–75.
12 Weatherill 1996: 894, 896.
13 Enchelmaier 2003: 284–285.
14 Enchelmaier 2003: 283–284, 317.

exists or could reasonably be made. On this basis, the Court of Justice's invention of the category of 'selling arrangements' and its arbitrary differentiation from 'rules that lay down requirements' could be condemned as judicial activism. This impression is further reinforced when one considers the availability of appropriate alternative approaches to the resolution of the legal problem in *Keck*, offered by Advocate General Van Gerven and Advocate General Jacobs in their Opinions on *Keck* and *Leclerc-Siplec*, respectively.

However, one must not assume that any act of judicial law-making is necessarily a matter of judicial activism.[15] Indeed, given how broadly drafted Article 34 TFEU is, a degree of judicial creativity is needed to ensure its practicability. In fact, this chapter will show that the Court of Justice's interpretation of this Treaty provision is actually legitimate. The multilingual analysis[16] of a selection of language versions of this Treaty provisions will provide evidence that the noun "measure" in the term "measures having equivalent effect" is ambiguous (polysemous). Further, a multilingual analysis of an array of official translations of the preliminary ruling of *Keck* will demonstrate that the noun "requirement" in the term "rules that lay down requirements" and the noun "arrangement" in the term "selling arrangements" constitute two distinct readings of the noun "measure", which suggest polysemy as a form of ambiguity. If its semantic interpretations match the interpretation given by the CJEU, there will be a congruity between the semantic meaning instilled by the EU legislator in Article 34 TFEU and the pragmatic use of the terms by the CJEU. Consequently, this evidence will dispel the doubts about the legitimacy of the Court's reasoning in *Keck*.

Moreover, the CJEU's ambiguity-based reasoning in *Keck* is actually an expression of judicial restraint, and not of judicial activism. Todd J. Friedbacher makes a strong case to the effect that the Court of Justice's decision-making in *Keck* was actually strategically aimed at counteracting the "legitimacy crisis" that threatened to undermine the Court's authority in the early stages of the development of the internal market.[17] In this context, *Keck* is viewed as a response to the rising discontent with the Court's performance, experienced by the general public, the Member State governments and national courts in the EU community.[18] By this account, *Keck* is envisioned as "a judgment about precisely where the Community-Member State jurisdictional divide falls, allocating those measures classified as 'selling arrangements' to the Member States, and forcing both

15 Pollicino 2004: 292.

16 "Inter-lingual ambiguity" (Cao, 2007: 78) will be the object of study once again. The research approach applicable here is similar to the one applied in *Åkerberg Fransson*, the difference being that the findings in the present Case Study will be used to provide evidence for ambiguity resolution, and not ambiguity production. Therefore, there will be no reference made to interchangeable use of terms. Additionally, *Åkerberg Fransson* deals with judicial activism, whereas *Keck* is an example of judicial restraint.

17 Friedbacher 1996: 235–236.

18 Friedbacher 1996: 236–238.

the Court and the Community legislature from this particular sphere".[19] Pedro Caro De Sousa also argues that the CJEU's reasoning in *Keck* came about as a result of the Court's commitment to enhancing legal certainty and safeguarding its legitimacy in the wake of its activist decision-making in *Dassonville*.[20] In this context, the CJEU's approach to *Keck* could be characterised as judicial restraint in the manner of a less demanding judgment for the purposes of "walking on the brink of non-compliance"[21].

Legal analysis

The ambiguous drafting of Article 34 TFEU

The legal definition of the internal market is fraught with "a remarkable range of ambiguities", which means that "within those vacant spaces political choices are required to determine its shape and direction".[22] This astute observation could be extended beyond the internal market as an "ambiguous" legal concept in and of itself, to the Treaty provisions regulating free movement, which are ordinarily loosely drafted, in order to leave room for decision-making with respect to the delineation of competences by the Court of Justice.[23] As a result, the CJEU was given significant interpretative leeway in this area of law. In addition, the combination between scarcity of expression and far-reaching constitutional impact in the drafting of Article 34 TFEU could be a prerequisite for the emergence of ambiguity. Indeed, the presence of "a considerable degree of ambiguity" in the definition of MEQRs in Article 34 TFEU has been noted, though not discussed in detail.[24]

A closer inspection of Article 34 TFEU reveals that the provision encapsulates contradictory internal market ideologies. The contrast between these ideas creates a pragmatic context that could easily facilitate the emergence of ambiguity. For instance, the debate on the legislative intent behind Article 34 TFEU has certain systemic implications for the EU legal order, which were articulated by Advocate General Tesauro in the case of *Hünermund*:[25] "Is [Article 34 TFEU][26] a provision intended to liberalize intra-Community trade or is it intended more generally to encourage the unintended pursuit of commerce in individual Member States?".[27]

19 Friedbacher 1996: 240.
20 De Sousa 2012b: 87.
21 Dothan 2014: 124.
22 Weatherill 2017: 125.
23 Weatherill 2017: 125, 127–128.
24 Horsley 2012: 736.
25 Opinion of AG Tesauro, 1993: paragraph 1.
26 At the time of AG Tesauro's Opinion: Article 30 EEC.
27 Catherine Barnard (2013: 120) also reframes this question to assess the potential applicability of Article 34 TFEU to market circumstances rules. The concept of 'market circumstances' was included in the remit of Article 34 TFEU under *Dassonville* (Barnard 2013: 120). Unlike MEQRs, market circumstances rules are non-discriminatory in nature, impose

This formulation echoes the juxtaposition between "economic supranationalism" and "economic constitutionalism".[28] The former interprets Article 34 TFEU as a provision intended to regulate the relationship between the liberalisation of the internal market and national sovereignty.[29] The latter envisions Article 34 TFEU as a guarantee for the right to trade for every trader in the EU in case a conflict with national legislation arises.[30]

Similarly, it could be argued that, when it comes to the internal market, the core conflict in the EU legal order ceases to be that between supranationalism and intergovernmentalism, but that between *centralisation* and *decentralisation*.[31] Article 34 TFEU,[32] along with other key free movement Treaty provisions, could be interpreted as supporting either of these models.[33] On the one hand, they could be read widely, to promote economic freedom and greater centralisation in a unitary system, thus prohibiting almost the entire range of rules that could have adverse effect on the trade of goods and services.[34] On the other hand, they could be given a narrow interpretation, to favour anti-protectionism and greater decentralisation in a federal system, in which Member State legislation is paid due respect, as long as it does not cause disadvantage to imported goods or services.[35] In Snell's estimation, a *narrow* reading of said provision, developed on the basis of "a wide concept of discrimination", is ultimately preferable in terms of the respect afforded to Member State competences and the capacity for overcoming obstacles on the way to the economic prosperity of the Union.[36]

In the light of these findings, it seems that the wording of Article 34 TFEU supports a number of interpretations, which are often contradictory or mutually exclusive. It stands to reason then that it could also give rise to ambiguity that is key to the resolution of the legal problem in *Keck*.

The excessive scope of Article 34 TFEU before *Keck*

The Court of Justice's strategic resolution of ambiguity in *Keck* was intended to be a solution to the plethora of problems created by the preceding case-law, especially by *Dassonville* (Case 8–74). The preliminary ruling of *Dassonville* concerned a situation where a national rule prohibited a trader from importing

no dual regulatory burden and fulfill no protective function, actual or intended, with respect to the market of the home Member State (Barnard 2013: 119–120). The concept will be revisited later in this chapter.

28 Barnard 2013:120.
29 Barnard 2013:120.
30 Barnard 2013:120.
31 Snell 2002: 33.
32 At the time of Snell's writing: Article 28 EC.
33 Snell 2002: 34–35.
34 Snell 2002: 34, 48.
35 Snell 2002: 35, 48.
36 Snell 2002: 48.

scotch whiskey (which was already in free circulation in France) into Belgium in the absence a certificate of origin issued by the custom authorities of the exporting country (i.e. the United Kingdom).[37] In contrast to an importer importing goods directly from the producer state, Dassonville had to obtain the necessary certificate of authenticity "with great difficulty".[38] Consequently, the Court classified the national rule in question as an MEQR.[39] The category of 'measures having equivalent effect' was first defined in *Dassonville* as follows:

> All trading rules enacted by Member States which are capable of hindering, directly or indirectly, actually or potentially, intra-community trade are to be considered as measures having an effect equivalent to quantitative restrictions.[40]

At first, the *Dassonville* formula seemed like a promising and helpful solution: "Dassonville is an example of how bold judicial legislation by the Court has transformed a spartan legal principle into a vital, flexible doctrine wide application".[41] The all-encompassing approach to defining MEQRs, presented in *Dassonville*, was successful at prohibiting measures even in the absence of actual evidence of their restrictive effect as well as at promoting the management and regulation of the EU economy by the institutions of the European Union.[42]

However, soon the perception of *Dassonville* shifted to that of "a dangerous and misleading myth".[43] On a global level, the *Dassonville* formula failed to address the inherent tensions surrounding the interpretation of Article 34 TFEU.[44] Firstly, any interpretation of Article 34 TFEU should safeguard the common market by taking into consideration the extent of the *economic* impact of any national rule and curtailing the Member States' ability to distort competition by "formally or materially [discriminating] between imports and exports".[45] Secondly, the construction and the smooth functioning of the common market ought to be considered in conjunction with other Treaty objectives, and not in isolation.[46] Thirdly, it is advisable that any interpretation of Article 34 TFEU respects the principle of subsidiarity when assessing national measures whose economic effects hinder trade generally, so that only those with the most substantial impact on imports suffer prohibition.[47] The Court in *Dassonville* paid no regard to such considerations.

37 *Dassonville*, Case 8–74: paragraphs 1–4.
38 *Dassonville*, Case 8–74, paragraphs 4 and 9.
39 *Dassonville*, Case 8–74, paragraph 9.
40 *Dassonville*, Case 8–74: paragraph 5.
41 Chriss 1995: 153–154.
42 Chalmers 1993: 275.
43 Chalmers 1993: 269.
44 Chalmers 1993: 274.
45 Chalmers 1993: 270–272.
46 Chalmers 1993: 272–273.
47 Chalmers 1993: 274.

The CJEU's approach in *Dassonville* led to the adoption of a "sweeping and overly unforgiving" definition of MEQRs, especially with respect to non-discriminatory national rules.[48] The extreme extension of scope of Article 34 TFEU in this respect was made especially conspicuous when contrasted with the very specific exceptions listed in Article 36 TFEU.[49] The excessively broad definition of MEQRs could very well be viewed as the Court's attempt to extend its jurisdiction to the widest possible array of national measures through the preliminary ruling procedure.[50] This was a particularly important judicial move in the early days of the formation of the internal market – a period when the traditions associated with national protectionism were still alive and present and the national judges were relatively unfamiliar with the intricacies of EU law.[51] In other words, a broadly rendered remit of Article 34 TFEU would increase the likelihood that national protectionist measures be subjected to the scrutiny by the Court of Justice.[52] This admittedly important advantage, however, was insufficient to outweigh the numerous economic disadvantages of said approach.

To begin with, a broad interpretation to Article 34 TFEU[53] promotes greater centralisation in the EU legal order.[54] Arguably, a centralised vision for the EU could help build a more stable and predictable economy, where there is greater certainty about the regulations set in place.[55] However, a centralised EU system operates on the basis of uniformity that fails to take into consideration the specific circumstances of the economic reality in each Member State.[56] This may result in reduced efficiency, since it could stifle the regulatory competition between the national jurisdictions as well as the corresponding impulse for learning and discovery.[57] It could also discourage the democratic participation of the citizens in the political process forming that economic environment.[58] In contrast, a decentralised system would be more flexible and better equipped to keep the growing influence of the public sector in check and to monitor the potentially problematic activity of the private actors.[59] Therefore, it appears that the exceedingly broad rendition of the *Dassonville* formula is a problem of grave systemic ramifications for the EU, which would explain the CJEU's anxiety to narrow it down in later years.

Moreover, a wide definition of MEQRs under Article 34 TFEU would also have a serious adverse effect on all of the key actors in the preliminary ruling

48 Derlen & Lindholm citing Steiner & Woods 2010: 194–195.
49 Van Der Woude 1990: 58. Article 36 TFEU was formerly known as Article 30 TEC, Article 36 EEC.
50 Chalmers, Davies, & Monti 2010: 748–749.
51 Chalmers, Davies, & Monti 2010: 748–749.
52 Snell 2002: 71.
53 At the time of Snell's writing: Article 28 EEC.
54 Snell 2002: 70.
55 Snell 2002: 35.
56 Snell 2002: 36.
57 Snell 2002: 37–39.
58 Snell 2002: 39.
59 Snell 2002: 70.

procedure – the traders, the national courts, and the CJEU.[60] The national courts would be inundated with cases invoking Article 34 TFEU, which would compel them to make preliminary references to the Court and apply the proportionality test more frequently.[61] The national courts might may feel ill-prepared to do so, which could increase the resistance to EU rules and introduce greater tension in their relationship with the CJEU.[62] A sudden increase in the number of preliminary references would likely reduce the effective protection afforded to individuals by the Court of Justice, accompanied by possible delays and a diminished quality of reasoning.[63] Then, in response to criticism with respect to legitimacy, the Court would place greater reliance on broadening the platform of justifications,[64] as will be discussed in the next section of this chapter. From the perspective of the traders, this would largely lead to disappointment at the litigation result, since a greater number of national rules will be caught by that 'safety net' of justifications.[65] It is evident that the *Dassonville* formula had great destructive potential with respect to the preliminary ruling procedure.

In the light of these considerations, the CJEU became increasingly conscious of the pressing need to impose limits on its definition of MEQRs. There were even some traces of such early awareness in *Dassonville*, where the CJEU allowed for national measures against unfair practice to escape the prohibition under Article 34 TFEU, provided that there is no applicable Community regulation in the area and that the national measures are "reasonable".[66] However, this "rule of reason" could be easily viewed as "vaguely defined".[67] The CJEU fails to offer any statutory basis for this rule, additional explanation or examples from the Court's practice or even a list of criteria to assess the reasonableness of the national measures. As such, the rule is entirely open to future interpretation, which effectively defeats the purpose of having a rule at all. Thus, the CJEU's refusal to elaborate further on the exact dimensions of the "rule of reason" in *Dassonville* could be indicative of its reluctance to provide any extra support for the residual competence belonging to the Member States beyond a mere acknowledgement.[68]

It is no wonder then that the elusive attitude the Court adopted on this point led to a "troubling lack of consistency" in the CJEU's adjudication in the period after *Dassonville*, one which *Keck* ultimately attempted to resolve.[69] In the following years, the Court placed direct reliance only rarely, if ever, on *Dassonville*, preferring instead to develop alternative mechanisms, such as *Cassis de Dijon*.[70]

60 Snell 2002: 73–75.
61 Snell 2002: 73.
62 Snell 2002: 74.
63 Snell 2002: 74.
64 Snell 2002: 72, 75.
65 Snell 2002: 73.
66 *Dassonville*, Case 8–74, paragraph 6.
67 Chriss 1995: 157.
68 Chriss 1995: 157–158.
69 Chriss 1995: 158.
70 Chalmers 1993: 277–278.

The preliminary ruling of *Cassis de Dijon* (Case 120/78) was the next important milestone in the formative years of the CJEU's jurisprudence on free movement of goods. This case dealt with the import of "Cassis de Dijon", a French fruit liqueur whose alcoholic strength was insufficient to be lawfully marketed in Germany.[71] The preliminary reference concerned a possible incompatibility between Article 34 TFEU[72] and the German rule specifying the minimum alcoholic strength of spirits marketed on national level, since the latter could potentially be classified as a MEQR.[73]

The two major contributions of *Cassis de Dijon* to this area of law are the principle of ***mutual recognition*** and the concept of ***mandatory requirements***.[74] With regard to the former, the Court made it clear that "there is ... no valid reason why, provided that they have been lawfully produced and marketed in one of the Member States, alcoholic beverages should not be introduced into any other Member State".[75] Therefore, the German measure in question was considered incompatible with Article 34 TFEU.[76] The principle of mutual recognition has evolved since then to become a general principle of law, applied throughout the internal market as an embodiment of the idea of equality regardless of differences.[77] Nevertheless, the Court has imposed some limitations on the application of this principle by means of an array of "mandatory requirements": "the effectiveness of fiscal supervision, the protection of public health, the fairness of commercial transactions and the defence of the consumer".[78] The Court's adjudication became a balancing exercise on the basis of proportionality.[79] In this way, the Court essentially put forward a variation of the "rule of reason" in *Dassonville* by modifying the application of Article 34 TFEU, in order to fill in the gaps left by Article 36 TFEU.[80]

Ultimately, *Cassis de Dijon* challenged the previously established understanding of Article 34 TFEU through a displacement of discrimination as the starting point of the analysis, in favour of the inherently "restrictive nature" of a national rule.[81] *Cassis de Dijon* reframed the debate on MEQRs in terms of an assessment of its justifications based on the differentiation between ***distinctly*** and ***indistinctly*** applicable measures.[82] Nevertheless, this change in direction did little to address the actual problem – *Dassonville*'s extensive definition of MEQRs – which

71 *Cassis de Dijon*, Case 120/78: paragraphs 1–4.
72 At the time, Article 30 EEC.
73 *Cassis de Dijon*, Case 120/78: paragraph 5.
74 Chalmers, Davies, & Monti 2010: 763.
75 *Cassis de Dijon*, Case 120/78: paragraph 14.
76 *Cassis de Dijon*, Case 120/78: paragraph 14.
77 Chalmers, Davies, & Monti 2010: 763–764.
78 *Cassis de Dijon*, Case 120/78: paragraph 8.
79 Chalmers, Davies, & Monti 2010: 763.
80 Van der Woude 1990: 58.
81 Chalmers 1993: 279.
82 Derlen & Lindholm 2010: 195–196.

continued to haunt the CJEU's jurisprudence on free movement of goods.[83] In a series of subsequent cases,[84] the wide remit of the *Dassonville* formula demanded that the Court assessed the compatibility between Article 34 TFEU and a number of national measures in the area of social policy, cultural policy and social security, which mainly fall in the domain of national competences.[85] Such measures escaped scrutiny under the modified "rule of reason" (justification of mandatory requirements on the basis of proportionality).[86] It was their existence in and of itself, and not their differences in comparison to the national regulation in other Member States, that triggered the application of the rule.[87] This development illustrates that the innovations introduced by *Cassis de Dijon* were incapable of producing the desired effect, namely the containment of the unwarranted expansion of competences induced by *Dassonville*.

It was not until the case of *Torfaen* that the Court addressed the gap left by the modified "rule of reason" of *Cassis de Dijon*, namely including non-discriminatory national measures that restrict intra-community trade by virtue of their existence within the scope of the rule.[88] However, it must be noted that *Torfaen* went a step further in establishing a new test for national measures that are "equally harmful".[89] The test, developed by the Court in *Torfaen* and *Stoke-on-Trent*, entailed an exemption from the prohibition in Article 34 TFEU, subject to CJEU's assessment of the compatibility of the measure of EU law and to the national court's scrutiny under the 'intrinsic effects' standard in Article 3 of Directive 70/50 (failing that, the CJEU could assess the proportionality of the measure).[90] In this sense, it could be argued that *Torfaen* and the rest of the Sunday trading cases[91] contributed towards greater centralisation and economic freedom in the internal market.[92]

The Sunday trading cases were the last stop in the sequence of case-law on the way to *Keck*, which delivered a heavy blow to the pernicious practice of litigants' invoking Article 34 TFEU to tackle any restriction on intra-community trade.[93] However, this approach was not applied later with the necessary consist-

83 Derlen & Lindholm 2010: 196.
84 In this context, Van der Woude (1990: 59–60) discusses the following cases: *Oebel*, *Blesgen*, *Duphar*, *Cinéthèque*.
85 Van der Woude 1990: 60.
86 Van der Woude 1990: 60.
87 Van der Woude 1990: 60.
88 Van der Woude 1990: 61–62.
89 Barnard 1994: 458.
90 Barnard 1994: 458.
91 The 'Sunday trading cases' by the CJEU included *Torfaen* and *Stoke-on-Trent* (in the UK) and *Conforama* and *Marchandise* (in France and Belgium), which broadly concerned a national measure prohibiting trading on Sundays, by means of banning the provision of services to customers or by engaging staff in employment, respectively (Barnard 1994: 449–452, 454–455, 458).
92 Snell 2002: 67.
93 Barnard 1994: 459.

ency by the Court, which could be indicative of its hesitancy to continue down that path.[94] Although the Court actually stopped short of overruling *Torfaen* in *Keck*, a certain "incompatibility" between the two exists.[95]

This has been a brief overview of the key moments in the CJEU's jurisprudence on free movement of goods from the late 1970s to the early 1990s of the 20th century. The Court has selected the 'top-down' approach for the interpretation of Article 34 TFEU,[96] meaning that it started with a blanket statement of its intended effect in *Dassonville* which it gradually specified in the upcoming case-law. The Court's approach in *Dassonville* could be seen as an audacious act of judicial law-making. Like a skilled chess player, the Court established its dominance on the chess board in a single move with far-reaching strategic implications. The Court's pronouncement was strategically advantageous in that provided the setup for further adjudication in a wide range of situations.

However, the Court's definition in *Dassonville*, if taken on its own, was too abstract and all-encompassing to be practicable. Therefore, with each new ruling, the Court of Justice would revise its approach. In *Cassis de Dijon*, the CJEU attempted to conceptually reframe the entire debate on MEQRs and devise a mechanism in the form of the revised "rule of reason" to sift through the influx of preliminary references. It was not long after that the Court of Justice realised that further refinement was necessary in *Torfaen*. Despite these efforts, however, the problems created by the *Dassonville* formula persisted. Eventually, the CJEU went back to the drawing board and found the winning method of dealing with this critical situation in *Keck*.

The CJEU's interpretation of Article 34 TFEU in *Keck*

The *Keck* preliminary reference, issued by the Tribunal de Grande Instance, Strasbourg, questioned the compatibility between Article 34 TFEU[97] and the commercial practice 'resale at a loss', as defined by French national law.[98] It was held that the problem concerned only the freedom of movement of goods, and not of capital, services and persons.[99] The relevant legal category subject to prohibition in Article 34 TFEU was that of "measures having equivalent effect" (MEQRs).[100] The French commercial practice of 'resale at a loss' was generally aimed at diminishing the volume of sales, which included the sales of products of other Member States, in that this method of promotion was made unavailable to

94 Snell 2002: 67.
95 Derlen & Lindholm 2017: 264–265.
96 At the time, Article 30 EEC.
97 At the time, Article 30 EEC.
98 *Keck*, Joined cases C-267/91 and C-268/91: paragraphs 1–4.
99 *Keck*, Joined cases C-267/91 and C-268/91: paragraphs 6, 10.
100 *Keck*, Joined cases C-267/91 and C-268/91: paragraph 11.

traders.[101] Naturally, the question arose as to whether 'resale at a loss' could be classified as a MEQR for the purposes of Article 34 TFEU.[102]

In response, the Court of Justice clarified that, following *Cassis de Dijon*, the term MEQRs could be applied to

> obstacles to free movement of goods which are the consequence of applying, to goods coming from other Member States where they are lawfully manufactured and marketed, rules that lay down requirements to be met by such goods (such as those relating to designation, form, size, weight, composition, presentation, labelling, packaging).[103]

The Court then proceeded to invent the category of "certain selling arrangements", to contrast with "rules that lay down requirements".[104] The CJEU asserted that the category of selling arrangements fell outside the remit of Article 34 TFEU, since it was not "by nature such as to prevent [the access of products by another Member State] to the market or to impede access any more than it impedes the access of domestic product".[105] This step of its reasoning process remained unsupported by specific examples of case-law, though the Court acknowledged that its decision goes "contrary to what has previously been decided".[106] Consequently, the CJEU held that the French rules on 'resale at a loss' remained unaffected by Article 34 TFEU.

The Court of Justice's preliminary ruling of *Keck* marked a dramatic change to its problem-solving approach in this area of EU law. Thus far, all of the Court's efforts had been directed at elaborating on the discriminatory effect, the restrictive nature or the grounds for justification of MEQRs. In other words, the CJEU was preoccupied with exploring the *properties* of MEQRs, and not the *meaning* of the term. To return to the first definition of MEQRs in *Dassonville*:

> All *trading rules* enacted by Member States which *are capable of* ... are to be considered as measures having an effect equivalent to quantitative restrictions.
>
> (emphasis added) (*Dassonville*, Case 8–74: paragraph 5)

The CJEU was solely interested in defining MEQRs in terms of their properties (capabilities), which later constrained its analysis in the case-law to follow. Naturally, some indication of the actual *meaning* of the term itself was given in the form of "trading rules". However, the phrase "all trading rules" is replaced in several subsequent rulings with "all rules" or "all measures".[107]

101 *Keck*, Joined cases C-267/91 and C-268/91: paragraph 13.
102 *Keck*, Joined cases C-267/91 and C-268/91: paragraphs 13–14.
103 *Keck*, Joined cases C-267/91 and C-268/91: paragraph 15.
104 *Keck*, Joined cases C-267/91 and C-268/91: paragraph 16.
105 *Keck*, Joined cases C-267/91 and C-268/91: paragraph 17.
106 *Keck*, Joined cases C-267/91 and C-268/91: paragraph 16.
107 Chalmers, Davies, & Monti 2010: 748.

The careless treatment of terminology is a testament to the Court's generally dismissive attitude with regards to the issue of establishing the *meaning* of the term MEQRs.

It was not until *Keck* that the Court developed a keen awareness of the value of terminological accuracy with respect to the interpretation of Article 34 TFEU. In *Keck*, the Court created the category of 'selling arrangements' and placed it firmly outside the scope of Article 34 TFEU. It might be argued that the concept of 'selling arrangements' should be abandoned as a mere "a red herring", since it serves no other real purpose than to indicate that not all market interventions necessarily impede market access.[108] Its sole reason for existence appeared to be to serve as a counterpoint to 'rules that lay down requirements', which were considered MEQRs within this provision. As a result, the CJEU was accused of drawing an "excessively formalistic" distinction between 'rules that lay down requirements' and 'selling arrangements', which contrasted sharply with its "effects-based approach" to the definition of MEQRs.[109] On the surface, it would appear that the Court of Justice invented these categories in a random, but necessary, act of judicial activism.

However, there is certainly evidence to support a claim that the Court of Justice's solution in *Keck* had more substance and staying power than initially thought. Since the adjustment to the Court of Justice's approach in *Keck*, "a heavy and consistent reliance on the *Dassonville* judgment" has been observed, which makes it "clearly still good law".[110] Furthermore, the category of 'selling arrangements' has survived the initial backlash, to enjoy a fairly positive treatment from the Court itself in the subsequent years:

> [At the time of writing in 2012], this concept has been used by the CJEU on 14 occasions to exclude a variety of non-discriminatory national measures from the scope of art. 34 TFEU. These measures include: rules governing product pricing, retail trading hours and conditions, advertising, doorstep selling, and itinerant sales. To date, the CJEU has firmly rejected attempts to apply the selling arrangement criterion in the case law on workers, persons, services and capital.[111]

It is certainly encouraging to see that the CJEU is confident in the effective application of 'selling arrangements' to a variety of factual situations pertaining to the free movement of goods. Every new decision is an implicit affirmation of the actual practicability of the distinction drawn in *Keck*. Could this be the result of the Court's firm commitment to upholding *Keck* or is there something more to this story that has escaped our notice?

108 Weatherill 1996: 896.
109 Horsley 2012: 745.
110 Derlen & Lindholm 2017: 268.
111 Horsley 2012: 744.

It must be acknowledged that the Court's reluctance to extend the platform of 'selling arrangements' to cover free movement with respect to the remaining fundamental freedoms could very well be indicative of an underlying sense of insecurity about the ability of the outcome in *Keck* to withstand the pressure of scrutiny that comes with exposure to other areas of EU law. The Court seems be unsure about initiating further discussions on the meaning and purpose of the notion of 'selling arrangements', since presumably this might expose the term's artificial and hollow character. After all, there is a noticeable lack of normative justification for the distinction draw in *Keck* – the Court failed to invoke any statutory provisions, case-law or even general principles of EU law in support. As seen above, the CJEU's chosen strategy perhaps could be described as quickly building a portfolio of cases where 'selling arrangements' were applied, in the hope of entrenching said category in EU law.

By drawing the distinction in *Keck*, the Court achieved what it had set out to do – devising a workable mechanism for sifting through preliminary references invoking Article 34 TFEU without discarding the *Dassonville* definition of MEQRs. Indeed, *Keck* realised a shift towards a more decentralised system, thus abandoning the economic freedom model in the process.[112] Furthermore, the subsequent consistent and formalistic application of the *Keck* criteria by the Court of Justice guaranteed certain predictability in the area of law dealing with Article 34 TFEU.[113]

This success could perhaps be attributed to the fact that *Keck*, in stark contrast to *Dassonville*, was much more faithful to the direction, in which the CJEU jurisprudence was heading at the time.[114] A narrow interpretation of Article 34 TFEU was in line with the principle of subsidiarity, to which the Treaties of Maastricht and Amsterdam had paid particular respect.[115] Further, the CJEU had been showing signs of reluctance to engage in judicial activism, placing an emphasis on the "need of market maintenance, not market building".[116] At the same time, the EU legislature was more interested in promoting mutual recognition and minimum harmonisation, rather than total harmonisation, as a prelude to greater decentralisation.[117] Based on this characterisation of the constitutional climate at the time, the Court of Justice's stance in *Keck* is unsurprising.

It could be argued that it was the *fact* of the distinction in *Keck*, rather than its normative foundation, that mattered to the CJEU. It is interesting to note that Gerard Conway recognised the presence of ambiguity in the term "measures having equivalent effect" in Article 34 TFEU:

> [In *Cassis de Dijon*], the ECJ did not seek to recover the original intention of the Member States ... as to the meaning of what was an ambiguous

112 Snell 2002: 80.
113 Snell 2002: 81.
114 Snell 2002: 76–78.
115 Snell 2002: 76.
116 Snell 2002: 77.
117 Snell 2002: 77.

> provision. In the faces of ambiguity, more or less restrained approaches are always possible. The judgment adopts the widest possible interpretation of 'measures having an effect equivalent to quantitative restrictions', whereas it could have confined it to directly or indirectly discriminatory rules, and have left it to the Member States to fashion a broader rule.[118]

However, it is puzzling that Conway had a correct intuition about the ambiguous language of Article 34 TFEU and its effect but failed to identify the connection with the terminological distinction drawn in *Keck*, its exact location (the noun 'measures') and finally abandoned this line of reasoning without elaborating on that point further. According to Conway, the CJEU demonstrated "extra-textual, consequentialist", and "creative" reasoning in *Keck*, since "there is no textual basis for singling out trading arrangements in this way".[119] Conway also viewed *Keck* as a preliminary ruling "motivated by a desire to avoid a conflict of norms with national law" due to the scope of *Dassonville*, but it ultimately failed to perform this task well, since the CJEU "glossed over the articulation of conflict and its implicit demand for a careful normative unpacking of choice".[120] Further, Conway criticises the Court of Justice for prioritising the common market as the constitutional value of the highest significance, without paying due regard to the effect of the "common market overreach" on the competences of the Member States.[121]

On the whole, it would seem Conway underestimated and even misunderstood the true potential of ambiguity in Article 34 TFEU and its capacity to influence the CJEU's decision-making in *Keck*. The CJEU's strategic use of ambiguity resolution came about *because* the CJEU was cognizant of the limitations associated with Member State competence as well as the normative implications of its judicial choice in this respect. In this sense, the CJEU made use of the conflict-avoidance possibilities that come with interpreting the ambiguous Treaty text. The results of the multilingual analysis, displayed below, will put forward a more specific, accurate, and comprehensive account of the workings of ambiguity in the term "measures having equivalent effect" in Article 34 TFEU.

Linguistic analysis

The multilingual analysis was conducted on the basis of selected language versions of Article 34 TFEU, in order to verify the hypothesis that noun "measure" in the term "measures having equivalent effect" is a source of ambiguity (polysemy). Further, it will demonstrate that the Court's distinction between 'selling arrangements' and 'rules that lay down requirements' matches the two

118 Conway 2012: 41.
119 Conway 2012: 41.
120 Conway 2012: 271.
121 Conway 2012: 271–272.

interpretations of this ambiguous term – 'requirement' and 'arrangement'. The outcome of the multilingual analysis will help ascertain that the semantic meaning that the legislator instilled in the term "measures having equivalent effect" (MEQRs) in Article 34 TFEU corresponds to the CJEU's pragmatic interpretation. In a constitutional context, this evidence will provide rebuttal to accusations in judicial activism with respect to the Court's reasoning in *Keck*. The findings of the multilingual analysis could be seen in Appendix B in this book.

The results of the multilingual analysis showed that the English version of the noun "measure" is characterised by polysemy: a measure could be understood as "[a] legislative enactment proposed or adopted"[122] (Paraphrase 1) or "a way of achieving something, or a method for dealing with a situation"[123] (Paraphrase 2). The majority of language versions – the Germanic, Greek, and Bulgarian language versions – have all selected a similar term. The Romance and Polish language versions have opted for terms that clearly include in their definition the option of "step"/"plan"/"means" of achieving something. It is significant that French, the language of the case, is included in this group. On the basis of these findings, it was ascertained that the semantic meaning of the term "measure" encompasses both readings – rules with normative implications *and* solutions based on practical circumstances. This suggests that the term "measure" in Article 34 TFEU is indeed ambiguous.

However, the mere fact that the term "measure" is ambiguous and yields the aforementioned readings is not sufficient to conclude that the Court is engaging in the resolution of ambiguity in making a distinction between *selling arrangements* (paragraphs 16 of *Keck*) and *rules that lay down requirements* (paragraph 15 of *Keck*). There must be a semantic correspondence between the two paraphrases above and these two terms. Therefore, the nouns "arrangement" and "requirement", which belong to these terms respectively, were subjected to multilingual analysis, in order to obtain more information about their semantic meaning. Naturally, these terms appear on the pages of the preliminary ruling of *Keck*, and not in the text of any legislative provision, meaning that the multilingual analysis is applied to a selection of its official translations.

It further became clear that the semantic meaning of the term "requirement" matches Paraphrase 1 of the ambiguous term "measure". In all cases, the "requirement" was associated with some variation of legal terminology which normally carries normative implications, such as "stipulations"/"terms"/"provi sions"/"regulations"/"requirements", etc. The translation to "conditions" was equally widespread, which hints at the obligatory and binding character of the rules in question.

Further, the findings confirm that the semantic meaning of the term "arrangement" corresponds to Paraphrase 2 of the ambiguous term "measure". This

122 Oxford English Dictionary: www.oed.com/view/Entry/115506?rskey=GdLRPU&result=1&isAdvanced=false#eid last accessed on 15 July 2019.

123 Cambridge Dictionary: https://dictionary.cambridge.org/dictionary/english/measure last accessed on 15 July 2019.

could certainly be the case, seeing as the majority of the translations (North Germanic, Romance, and Greek) appear to indicate that an "arrangement" is to be understood as "form"/"shape"/"mode". The French and English definition emphasise that an "arrangement" contributes towards achieving a certain goal. The English translation expressly confirms the connection with "measure".

Within this pool of translations, there is a group that relies on terms that shares the same Latin root: *modus* (measure, manner).[124] As a result, the Spanish translation adheres to "mode or form", the German translation allows for a possible use of the term in a legal context – "provision … condition" and the French translation makes reference to both "mode" and "clause". It is important to note that the German and French terms for "arrangement" are decidedly dissimilar to those used for "requirement", therefore it is safe to say that they should have a different normative effect. This raises the question if the connection to *modus* carries any special legal connotations. To find an answer to this question, let us consider the derivatives of *modus* in English. The English noun "modality" could be understood as

> [t]hose aspects of a thing which relate to its mode, or manner or state of being, as distinct from its substance or identity; the non-essential aspect or attributes of a concept or entity. Also: a particular quality or attribute denoting the mode or manner of being of something.[125]

At the same time, in English the adjective "modal" is defined in a legal context as "containing provisions defining the manner in which it is to take effect".[126] Thus, it appears that *modus* describes the particular manner of execution, whether situated in a legal context or not. This means that *modus* does not contribute with any additional legal meaning of its own to the formation of the German (*die Modalität*) and French (*modalités*) legal concepts. Rather, the association with *modus* simply reinforces the idea that the core meaning of these terms is about manner of execution. Therefore, it is unlikely that the German *Modalität* and French translations are indicative of a substantial deviation from the trend established by the majority of the translations, namely conformity with Paraphrase 2.

Thus, it is established that the nouns 'requirement' and 'arrangement' match the semantic meaning of Paraphrase 1 and Paraphrase 2 of the ambiguous (polysemous) noun 'measure', respectively. Therefore, it is highly likely that, in drawing the distinction between 'selling arrangements' and 'rules that lay down requirements' in *Keck*, the CJEU was in fact resolving the ambiguity in the term 'measures having equivalent effect' in Article 34 TFEU. As a result, the Court

124 Merriam Webster Dictionary: www.merriam-webster.com/dictionary/modus last accessed on 17.07.2019.

125 Oxford Dictionary: www.oed.com/view/Entry/120571?redirectedFrom=modality#eid last accessed on 17.07.2019.

126 Oxford Dictionary: www.oed.com/view/Entry/120568#eid36505084 last accessed on 17.07.2019.

of Justice gave preference to Paraphrase 1 ('requirement') in interpreting the ambiguous (polysemous) noun 'measure'. In this way, the Court left Paraphrase 2 ('arrangement') outside the remit of Article 34 TFEU.

The strategic implications of the CJEU's resolution of ambiguity in *Keck*

Characterising *Keck* as an act of judicial restraint

The CJEU's acts of judicial law-making that are unsupported by sufficient elaboration as to their origins, purpose and content by the Court of Justice run the risk of triggering accusations in judicial activism. This was the case with the distinction between 'selling arrangements' and 'rules that lay down requirements' in *Keck*. However, Pollicino[127] warns against making that automatic assumption, since the judicial function normally includes not only judicial interpretation or analysis, but also judicial law-making.[128] This naturally leads to the conclusion that:

> judicial law-making in general, and European judicial creativity in particular is a necessary implication of the judiciary function, very different from legislative power and present not only in activist judgments but also in the Court's approach to self-restraint.[129]

In this sense, the Court's decisions ought to be evaluated not in terms of "whether law has been applied or created, but rather what the Community's *telos* is".[130] The *telos* of the EU legal order is framed by Pollicino[131] as the Court's choice to ensure through its decision-making the observance of the general principles of EU law and the main integration objective – "to lay the foundations of an ever-closer union among the peoples of Europe".[132] By choosing to resolve the ambiguity in Article 34 TFEU in favour of Paraphrase 1 ("rules that lay down requirements") in *Keck*, the Court removes a serious impediment in the way of the integration process, namely the excessively wide scope of the legal solution in *Dassonville*. As a result, the Court facilitated the implementation of EU law, although it achieved a *reduction*, rather than an expansion, of EU competences. In a nutshell, it is perfectly possible that the CJEU could engage in judicial law-making, to exercise judicial restraint, as is the case in *Keck*.

127 Pollicino 2004: 286.
128 The logic here is similar to that of Andreas Grimmel who advocates against the presumption that the CJEU's legal interpretation necessarily amounts to judicial activism in all cases of expansion of EU competence (Grimmel 2012: 534).
129 Pollicino 2004: 292.
130 Pollicino 2004: 289.
131 Pollicino 2004: 286–287, 289–290.
132 Joint proclamations of the signatories, the Treaty of Rome (25 March 1957).

Let us now characterise the brand of judicial restraint on display in *Keck*. In the EU legal order, the doctrine of judicial restraint could be realised on two separate levels: "systemic restraint, which relates to the competences and jurisdiction of national and supranational authorities respectively, on the one hand, and normative elements relating to the determination of the content of the provisions on the other".[133] The sharp division between the two is confusing and difficult to justify, since in practice the Court achieves the former through the latter, as was the case in *Keck*. However, this description of the workings of judicial restraint is valuable, since contains an implicit acknowledgement of the far-reaching systemic ramifications of the Court's preferred interpretation of an ambiguous term in the Treaty text.

It might be argued that the CJEU's decision-making in *Keck* could be characterised as ***judicial minimalism***, as an expression of judicial restraint. When engaging in the practice of judicial minimalism, judges generally tend to "avoid broad rulings and theoretical ambition", while showing a preference for "shallow rather than deep" and "narrow rather than wide" approach to the process of adjudication.[134] Sunstein explains that this method of reasoning entails "incompletely theorized agreements", which constitute "hollow" theories which "must be filled, and have not yet been filled with some kind of specification".[135] In this context, the smooth running of a system on a constitutional level is facilitated by means of conflict avoidance, thus ensuring agreement between the actors even in the absence of clarity as to their meaning.[136] Within this framework, *silence* is attributed significant value:

> Silence – on something that may prove false, obtuse, or excessively contentious – can help minimize conflict, allow the present to learn from the future, and save a great deal of time and expense. What is said and resolved may be no more important than what is left out.[137]

Thus, "incompletely theorized agreements" serve the function of achieving social stability, shared respect for differences in opinion, a lower political price paid for long-standing cases of disagreement and greater potential for adaptability to social change over time.[138]

In *Keck*, the Court emphasises the *fact* of the distinction between 'selling arrangements' and 'rules that lay down requirements', without providing sufficient and concrete justification for it. Having drawn said categories in broad strokes, the Court refuses to elaborate on their individual definitions. The CJEU provides no clues to aid our understanding of 'selling arrangements'. Granted,

133 Guðmundsdóttir 2015: 712.
134 Sunstein 2008: 825–826.
135 Sunstein 2008: 828.
136 Sunstein 2008: 828.
137 Sunstein 2008: 832.
138 Sunstein 2008: 832–833.

the Court clarifies that 'rules that lay down requirements' pertain to the following features of goods: "designation, form, size, weight, composition, presentation, labelling, packaging".[139] However, this list is rather unhelpful when it comes to devising a working mechanism of distinguishing between the two categories. It is not even clear whether this is an exhaustive list or not. Moreover, the Court was unable to provide examples of previous case-law or trade practice to illustrate the difference between the two categories. The Court of Justice also keeps its silence with respect to a possible typology of "measures having equivalent effect" and how 'rules that lay down requirements' fit within that frame. All of these features of the legal problem are essential for effective adjudication, and not merely hypothetical issues, which means their absence reinforces the impression of strategic judicial behaviour in the form of judicial minimalism.

The fundamental tenets of judicial minimalism could be applied to adjudication in the EU legal order. To this end, Daniel Sarmiento distinguishes between 'universal' and 'individual' preliminary rulings.[140] The former category creates generalised principles and broadly applicable guidelines for the referring court as well as for the EU legal community at large, whereas the latter category forges a rule that is contained within the specific circumstances of the case at hand.[141] Further, Sarmiento draws a line between 'argumentative' and 'decisional' minimalism.[142] If the Court of Justice demonstrates excessive brevity and provides insufficient justification for its decision, then this would be a case of 'argumentative minimalism'.[143] Should the CJEU resort to 'decisional' minimalism, it could issue a 'completely silent' judgment or a 'partially silent' judgment that leaves interpretative discretion either to the national courts, or to the national legislator.[144]

Having Sarmiento's classification in mind, *Keck* seems to be an example of judicial minimalism in a 'universal' preliminary ruling, since the categories of *selling arrangements* and *rules that lay down requirements* are essentially left open to interpretation in subsequent case-law. There is no evidence of the tell-tale signs of 'individual' preliminary rulings – expressions such as "'in the specific circumstances of the present case', 'in those precise circumstances', or 'taking into account all of the individual factors in the relevant case'".[145] Although the Court mentions „in these circumstances"[146] in *Keck*, there is a notable absence of the emphatic adjectives ("specific", "precise", "individual") contained in all of the aforementioned examples by Sarmiento. Indeed, the Court made an express

139 *Keck*, Joined cases C-267/91 and C-268/91, 1993: paragraph 15.
140 Sarmiento 2012: 19.
141 Sarmiento 2012: 19–20.
142 Sarmiento 2012: 20.
143 Sarmiento 2012: 20.
144 Sarmiento 2012: 21–22.
145 Sarmiento 2012: 20.
146 *Keck*, Joined cases C-267/91 and C-268/91: paragraph 10.

statement of purpose about the universal character of *Keck*, which indicates that *Keck* is intended as a crucial turning point to an emerging trend:

> In view of the increasing tendency of traders to invoke Article 30 of the Treaty[147] as a means of challenging any rules whose effect is to limit their commercial freedom even where such rules are not aimed at products from other Member States, the Court considers it necessary to re-examine and clarify its case-law on this matter.[148]

In addition, as discussed above, the Court's reasoning in *Keck* is seriously deficient when it comes to providing justification and explanations for the decision made. Therefore, there is a strong case to be made for the judicial behaviour demonstrated in *Keck* being classified as 'argumentative minimalism'.

More importantly, *Keck* could also fit the profile of 'decisional minimalism' accompanied by 'partial silence', since it ultimately results in a limitation to EU competences. In *Keck*, the Court of Justice sought to safeguard its legitimacy by excluding 'selling arrangements' from its jurisdiction and entrusting Member States and the national courts with the responsibility to regulate and adjudicate on this matter.[149] It could also be the case that, in ruling so, the CJEU was issuing a signal to the Commission that "it is ***neither within its jurisdiction nor necessary from an integrative perspective*** to introduce harmonisation legislation".[150] It could be that this judicial behaviour was intended to deliver a pre-emptive strike, in order to counteract the growing resistance by the Member States to the ongoing process of expansion of EU competences.[151] In any case, the result of *Keck* is clear – a significant and welcome limitation to EU competences.

At this point, it must be acknowledged that there is a fundamental flaw of judicial minimalism, namely that it operates on "the premise that the degree of decisions is the very thing that distinguishes right decisions from wrong".[152] Smith opposes this idea on the basis that "the measure of a phenomenon in itself carries no value significance, positive or negative".[153] It makes sense then that judicial minimalism does not concern itself with the ***meaning*** of the law, but with the ***result*** of the application of the legal rules.[154] As a result, a reliance on judicial minimalism as ***prescriptive*** guidance for adjudication could be damaging, as it creates an opportunity for highly subjective decision-making.[155] Nevertheless, Smith

147 At the time, the Court was referring to Article 30 EEC, which is equivalent to Article 34 TFEU today.
148 *Keck*, Joined cases C-267/91 and C-268/91: paragraph 14.
149 Friedbacher 1996: 238.
150 Friedbacher 1996: 239–240.
151 Friedbacher citing Hirschman, Weiler and Reich 1996: 239–240.
152 Smith 2010: 365.
153 Smith 2010: 365.
154 Smith 2010: 385.
155 Smith 2010: 388–391, 378–379.

demonstrates a willingness to accept judicial minimalism as a valid *description* of a court's strategic behaviour.[156]

If that be the case, the CJEU's judicial restraint in *Keck* might be classified as Dothan's notion of 'incrementalism' as a judicial tactic for increasing an international court's reputation.[157] 'Incrementalism' describes a situation where an international court advances a dramatic change in a legal doctrine, which is likely to provoke resistance or generate controversy, one case at a time.[158] However, *Keck* is not conceptually linked to another case the same way *Ruiz Zambrano* and *Dereci* are, but rather articulates the complete ambiguity-based legal solution on its own. In the case of *Keck*, the ambiguity-based legal solution is communicated on the pages of a single ruling, instead of over a long period of time and across several rulings. Therefore, it would be *more accurate* to say that *Keck* fits the profile of a *less demanding judgment* as part of the judicial tactic of "walking on the brink of non-compliance".[159] This classification is also considered an expression of "strategic restraint" exercised by the CJEU[160] for the purpose of counteracting the legitimacy crisis it was experiencing at the time.[161]

In any case, the preliminary ruling of *Keck* is a clear example of judicial restraint, designed to facilitate the implementation of the authority of EU law in the long term through the CJEU's strategic resolution of ambiguity. This impression is confirmed upon an examination of the alternative legal solutions available to the CJEU as well as upon a closer inspection of the Court's subsequent jurisprudence.

Alternative solutions to the legal problem in *Keck*

Let us first consider the approach proposed by Advocate General Van Gerven in his Opinion on *Keck* (1992). AG Van Gerven was convinced that the French provision on a resale at a loss could be viewed as an impediment to intra-Community trade, in the sense of *Dassonville*, notwithstanding its applicability to both national and imported goods.[162] This conclusion was reached by classifying resale at a loss as a "sales promotional method" within the meaning of *Oosthoek*[163] (Case 286/81).[164] Following that, AG Van Gerven applied the mandatory requirements test in *Cassis de Dijon*, in order to determine whether the French rules

156 Smith 2010: 383, 378–379.
157 Dothan 2014: 131–136.
158 Dothan 2014: 131–132.
159 Dothan 2014: 124.
160 Dothan 2014: 124.
161 Friedbach, 1996: 236; De Sousa, 2012b: 87.
162 Opinion of AG Van Gerven on *Keck*, 1992: paragraphs 3–4.
163 In *Oosthoek*, the Court of Justice actually uses the phrase "means of sales promotion" (Case 286/81, 1982: paragraphs 15, 18).
164 Opinion of AG Van Gerven on *Keck*, 1992: paragraph 4.

on resale at a loss conform to the fair trading and protection of consumers criteria.[165] The prohibition of resale at a loss ultimately failed the necessity test, due to being unjustifiably excessive.[166] Therefore, it was suggested that the prohibition of resale at a loss be deemed incompatible with Article 34 TFEU.[167]

It is evident that AG Van Gerven's suggested reasoning and outcome diverged significantly from the CJEU's approach. Nevertheless, AG Van Gerven agreed with the Court of Justice that the key to the legal problem lies with the correct classification of the national rules at hand. The solution presented in AG Van Gerven's Opinion on *Keck* classified the French rules on resale at a loss as a "sales promotional method". The fact of the matter is that the Court of Justice ignored the existence of a perfectly appropriate instrument for classification of the rules on resale. On this basis, one may conclude that the invention of the category of "certain selling arrangements" and its express contrast with "rules that lay down requirements" constitutes strategic judicial behaviour. Let us now examine the possible reasons why the Court preferred one of these solutions over the other.

Certainly, a reference to previous case-law, especially to *Oosthoek*, would have been a serious step towards ensuring greater consistency, which constitutes a persuasive argument in favour of 'sales promotional method'. An argument could be made that this approach would probably have had a short-lived effect, as it would have contributed very little to resolving the overarching lack of consistency in the case-law prior to *Keck*.

The preliminary ruling of *Oosthoek* concerned Dutch rules that restricted the free gift for promotional purposes that accompanies the purchase of a product, which were viewed as MEQRs and later justified under the consumer protection and fair trade criteria.[168] The restrictive effect of *Oosthoek* was realised in an advertising context, with the restriction being described in terms of deprivation of "marketing opportunities".[169] This was a very narrowly defined and concrete set of circumstances, which is unlikely to cover as much ground and generate as much interest as the much more broadly defined and opaquely worded term 'selling arrangements'. The real problem on a systemic level was that there was a notable absence of a term to serve as a systemic counterpoint to MEQRs, to curb the excessive scope of *Dassonville*. The preliminary ruling of *Keck* constituted a great opportunity in terms of strategically carving out a space for such a term in the form of 'selling arrangements'. It is improbable that *Oosthoek* could have provided a platform wide enough to launch a doctrine of great strategic and constitutional significance for the EU legal order. Therefore, it makes sense that the Court chose to subsume the term 'sales promotional method' in *Oosthoek*

165 Opinion of AG Van Gerven on *Keck*, 1992: paragraphs 6–8.
166 Opinion of AG Van Gerven on *Keck*, 1992: paragraphs 9–10.
167 At the time, Article 30 EEC. Opinion of AG Van Gerven on *Keck*, 1992: paragraph 11.
168 *Oosthoek*, Case 286/81, 1982: paragraphs 4–5, 16, 18.
169 *Oosthoek*, Case 286/81, 1982: paragraph 15.

under the category of MEQRs and refused to treat the national rules in *Keck* in the same way.

That being said, let us now consider the commentary on *Keck* by Advocate General Jacobs in his Opinion on *Leclerc-Siplec* (1994), which presents another alternative solution to the legal problem in *Keck*:

> In my view, the Court's reasoning – although not the result – in *Keck* is unsatisfactory for two reasons. First, it is inappropriate to make rigid distinctions between different categories of rules, and to apply different tests depending on the category to which particular rules belong. The severity of the restriction imposed by different rules is merely one of degree. Measures affecting selling arrangements may create extremely serious obstacles to imports.[170]

It is evident from this excerpt that AG Jacobs was highly critical of the artificial judge-made distinction between '*certain selling arrangements*' and '*rules that lay down requirements*' being used as the sole basis for deciding which treatment a national rule is afforded. Instead, AG Jacobs recommended that a purposive reading of Article 34 TFEU be taken into account when devising a new test.[171] Further, AG Jacobs expressed disapproval of discrimination being used as the starting point of the Court's analysis in *Keck*, since the problem of tackling an obstacle to intra-Community trade would remain unaffected by the mere existence of the same hindrance to trade at a national level.[172] In other words, the Member State placed at a disadvantage would find no solace in the fact that its competitors in the Member State, from which the restrictive rule originates, also find themselves in the same predicament.[173] Moreover, the acceptance of discrimination as the guiding criterion could cause the EU internal market to become fragmented, since traders will have no other option but to accommodate to different rules restricting selling arrangements in each Member State.[174] Naturally, this outcome would be undesirable, as it runs contrary to the aims and objectives of the Treaties.[175]

Thus, AG Jacobs proposed a return to the 'market access' logic which ruled the *Dassonville* and *Cassis de Dijon* jurisprudence prior to *Keck*.[176] This method is used to determine the remit of Article 34 TFEU[177] on the basis of

> the principle … that all undertakings which engage in a legitimate economic activity in a Member State should have unfettered access to the whole of

170 Opinion of AG Jacobs on *Leclerc-Siplec*, 1994: paragraph 38.
171 Opinion of AG Jacobs on *Leclerc-Siplec*, 1994: paragraph 38.
172 Opinion of AG Jacobs on *Leclerc-Siplec*, 1994: paragraph 39.
173 Opinion of AG Jacobs on *Leclerc-Siplec*, 1994: paragraph 39.
174 Opinion of AG Jacobs on *Leclerc-Siplec*, 1994: paragraph 40.
175 Opinion of AG Jacobs on *Leclerc-Siplec*, 1994: paragraph 40.
176 Opinion of AG Jacobs on *Leclerc-Siplec*, 1994: paragraph 41.
177 At the time, Article 30 EEC.

the Community market, unless there is a valid reason for denying them full access to a part of that market.[178]

In other words, this solution constitutes a *de minimis* test that seeks to ascertain whether there is a "substantial restriction on [market] access".[179] Such an approach would not differentiate between the types of measures under Article 34 TFEU, but will inquire into the *extent* of the restrictive effect a national rule renders.[180] Therefore, 'selling arrangements' will not be excluded from the scope of Article 34 TFEU by default, but the applicability of the provision would depend on the gravity of the hindrance caused by the 'selling arrangements'.[181] Finally, it is worth noting that AG Jacobs speculates that the Court of Justice abstained from adopting the 'market access' approach in *Keck*, since in practice the national courts may end up applying the test in such a way that only a limited number of national rules may be caught by the prohibition in Article 34 TFEU.[182]

The main advantage to this course of action is that the CJEU would not have to rely on highly formalistic distinctions between categories, in order to determine the scope of Article 34 TFEU. However, the accusation made of *Keck* could be levelled at the proposed return to the *Cassis de Dijon* and *Dassonville* jurisprudence: the solution "[addresses] the symptoms rather than the root cause".[183] Both approaches fail to deal with the problem of the differences in national regulation which, barring instances where discrimination is at play, would generally remain within the competences of the Member State.[184] In actual fact, the 'market access' approach makes an equally questionable contribution to the debate. If the restriction in issue makes it impossible to penetrate the host market, then the test is too narrowly defined.[185] Conversely, if the restriction solely makes it more difficult to trade in the host Member State, then the test is as hollow and as superficial as the *Dassonville* formula, since it could be applicable to literally any type of regulation.[186] The choice to base the determination on the question of how intense or remote the restrictive effect of the obstacle to trade is, rather than on the issue of understanding the nature of said impediment, would be to empty this approach of all conceptual or practical substance and commit it to the status of a mere "discursive technique or rhetorical device".[187] Thus, from a certain point of view, the 'market access' solution is equally as flawed as the CJEU's ultimate choice in *Keck*.

178 Opinion of AG Jacobs on *Leclerc-Siplec*, 1994: paragraph 41.
179 Opinion of AG Jacobs on *Leclerc-Siplec*, 1994: paragraph 42.
180 Opinion of AG Jacobs on *Leclerc-Siplec*, 1994: paragraph 45.
181 Opinion of AG Jacobs on *Leclerc-Siplec*, 1994: paragraph 45.
182 Opinion of AG Jacobs on *Leclerc-Siplec*, 1994: paragraph 42.
183 Bernard 2010: 462.
184 Bernard 2010: 462–463.
185 Bernard 2010: 463.
186 Bernard 2010: 463.
187 Bernard 2010: 463.

Finally, let us consider the question why the CJEU's actual approach to *Keck* might be preferable to both of the alternative solutions presented above. To reiterate, the Court of Justice clearly gave preference to *Keck*, in order to preserve the *Dassonville* formula and ensure consistency in the CJEU jurisprudence. The former was the bedrock of the CJEU's initial expansion of EU competence with respect to the scope of Article 34 TFEU. The notable deficiency in relation to the latter feature was the reason the Court set out to amend *Dassonville* in the first place. The solution in *Keck* provided one distinct strategic advantage, namely that it chartered a path that circumvented the need to address *Cassis de Dijon* in a determination based on *Dassonville*. In other words, the Court essentially isolated *Cassis de Dijon* from the influence of the faulty *Dassonville* formula. Could it be that the Court was operating under the presumption that there is very little to be gained by mixing *Cassis de Dijon* with *Dassonville*?

This conclusion would certainly be consistent with the Court's unwillingness to adopt AG Van Gerven's solution. In *Keck*, the Court of Justice concentrated on the meaning of 'measures having equivalent effect' as the decisive criterion of determination of the scope of Article 34 TFEU. The national rules identified as 'selling arrangements' were thus eliminated at the very first stage of the analysis, obviating the need to subject them to the *Cassis de Dijon* test of 'mandatory requirements'. As established above, the *Cassis de Dijon* test was interested in the adverse effects to import caused by the ***differences*** between the restrictive rules adopted in each Member State, whereas the logic of 'selling arrangements' demands that it is the *mere fact* that this national legislation *exists* that is offensive to import.[188] Therefore, the Court may well have been aware that it was very likely that the national rules in *Keck* may fail the 'mandatory requirements' test.[189] If that be the case, the Court of Justice would have been deprived of the strategic opportunity to address the 'legitimacy crisis' by curtailing EU competences for the benefit of the Member States.[190]

On a more abstract level, the *Dassonville* formula itself is has such a wide scope that it ends up being conceptually hollow, in that it "has little to tell us beyond the assertion that regulation is bad for the internal market".[191] In order to compensate for that blatant deficiency, the Court of Justice sought to use the principles of mutual recognition and home country control in *Cassis de Dijon* as a *substitute* for harmonisation, whereas the more prudent choice would have been to treat them as a *supplement* to harmonisation.[192] This reading would have stayed true to the realities of the internal market and it would have highlighted *Cassis de Dijon*'s unique contribution – a reassessment of the way regulation of the internal

188 Friedbacher 1996: 234–235.
189 Friedbacher 1996: 234–235.
190 Friedbacher 1996: 235.
191 Bernard 2010: 462.
192 Bernard 2010: 462.

market is structured.[193] The preliminary ruling in *Keck* thus lessened the pressure on *Cassis de Dijon* to accommodate for the problematic *Dassonville* formula.

Ultimately, the CJEU's strategic resolution of ambiguity in *Keck* was but one of the available options for solving the legal problem at the centre of the case. AG Van Gerven offered a low risk – low reward solution, which would have ensured consistency in CJEU's case-law in the short term. Nevertheless, the CJEU was evidently more interested in ensuring consistency in the long run and on a systemic scale. AG Jacobs put forward a more radical solution, promising a fundamental change in approach, but was in fact unsatisfactory in that it amounted to a similarly formalistic outcome. The Court of Justice's actual solution was successful in severing the link between *Dassonville* and *Cassis de Dijon*, which exposed the Court's main concern – tackling the legitimacy crisis and reducing the damage done by *Dassonville*. By means of strategically resolving ambiguity in Article 34 TFEU, the CJEU could deal with the inherent flaws in *Dassonville* and the ongoing 'legitimacy crisis', without interfering with the otherwise successful formula of *Cassis de Dijon*.

The challenges posed by the CJEU's case-law after Keck

It has been more than twenty years since the Court of Justice issued the preliminary ruling of *Keck*. Since then, the CJEU has established the market access approach as the norm. However, this shift in trajectory was executed gradually, with the *Keck* distinction demonstrating a high degree of adaptability.

The early rulings of *Hünermund* and *Leclerc-Siplec* "unthinkingly" followed in *Keck*'s footsteps, in that the CJEU readily assumed that if a national provision was deemed a 'selling arrangement', it was automatically exempted from the remit of Article 34 TFEU.[194] During the next period, the role of 'selling arrangements' was discussed by the Court in the context of national rules with a discriminatory restrictive effect, resulting in a total prevention to market access or different degrees of hindering market access.[195] Judging from the Court's reasoning in the later cases of *De Agostini*, *Heimdienst*, and *DocMorris*, it soon transpired that 'selling arrangements' could constitute a violation of Article 34 TFEU, in the absence of justification under *Cassis de Dijon*, in much the same way as 'rules that lay down requirements', the only difference being the burden of proof and the presumptions adopted as a starting point of the assessment.[196] At that stage, there was a noticeable lack of consistency in the Court of Justice's treatment of similar factual situations as well as a sudden change in its understanding of the presumption of legality in relation to selling arrangements (*Ker-Optika*).[197]

193 Bernard 2010: 461, 463.
194 Barnard 2013: 132.
195 Barnard 2013: 134–138.
196 Barnard 2013: 138.
197 Barnard 2013: 140–141.

Since then, inquiries into the meaning of the *Keck* terminological distinction were largely set aside. It was not until the CJEU had had a chance to accumulate case-law to illustrate the different practical applications of 'selling arrangements'[198] that the issue of meaning re-emerged. Thus, the Court of Justice finally found the confidence to issue the following definition:

> The Court subsequently found provisions concerning *inter alia* the place and times of sale of certain products and advertising of those products as well as certain marketing methods to be provisions governing selling arrangements within the meaning of *Keck and Mithouard*.[199]

It is evident from the above pronouncement that, in the pragmatic context of EU law, the term 'selling arrangements' pertains to the manner of execution, the method of achieving the sale of a particular product by adjusting the circumstances in which it is sold.[200] This interpretation ties in well with its semantic meaning as a paraphrase of the ambiguity found in Article 34 TFEU.

Throughout this period in the CJEU jurisprudence on Article 34 TFEU, the *Keck* distinction continued to inform the Court's reasoning in the majority of cases.[201] It soon became clear, especially in the *Heimdienst* and *Gourmet* rulings, that the *Keck* formula possessed the necessary flexibility to adapt to the particular circumstances of the case.[202] Nevertheless, the ability of *Keck* to deliver on its initial promise of greater legal certainty in this area of law was questionable.[203] There were also instances where the *Keck* solution was "sidestepped" – in cases where the *Keck* formula was accepted, but the emphasis has shifted to effect of the rule against the factual background of the case (e.g. *De Agostini*, *DocMorris*, *Gourmet*, *Mars*) or no mention was made of the *Keck* formula at all in an assessment of the restrictive effect of measures on intra-Community trade (e.g. *Franzén*).[204] Therefore, the beginnings of a transition towards a new market access approach were slowly becoming evident, though not explicitly acknowledged.[205]

It was not until the *Commission v Italy* (2009) ruling that the *Keck* distinction truly lost its position as the chief guiding criterion on the interpretation of Article 34 TFEU to the market access test. This was achieved on account of two significant amendments to the Court of Justice's position. First, the CJEU was finally prepared to let go of the presumption that selling arrangements are incapable of impeding intra-Community trade by virtue of their exclusion from the scope of

198 For a more detailed account of the CJEU's case-law on 'selling arrangements' in the time period between *Keck* and *Karner*, see Barnard (2013: 129–130).
199 *Karner*, Case C-71/02, 2004: paragraph 38.
200 Barnard 2013: 130.
201 Tryfonidou 2007: 176.
202 Koutrakos 2001: 396–398.
203 Koutrakos 2001: 400.
204 Tryfonidou 2007: 176–178.
205 Tryfonidou 2007: 178–179.

Article 34 TFEU, which meant the claimant was now required to shoulder the burden of proof, thus disposing of the only remaining difference between 'certain selling arrangements' and 'rules that lay down requirements'.[206] The abandonment of the categorisation-based *Keck* solution was executed in a hushed manner that nonetheless brooked no discussion.[207] The removal of this distinction effectively meant that *Keck* was no longer the *sole* or *reigning* legal standard in the area of free movement of goods in EU law.[208] Despite this dramatic change, there is no conclusive answer as to whether *Keck* is *completely replaced* by a single market access test, since this depends on whether paragraph 37 of *Commission v Italy (2009)* is given a narrow or a broad interpretation.[209]

Second, the Court of Justice revised the concept of 'market access', effectively restoring it to its pre-*Keck* condition and relying on a "common sense approach" to broadly assess the restrictive effect on the experience of the consumer.[210] The CJEU's decision to move away from the discrimination logic appears to have created a test that is both practically applicable and beneficial to legal certainty.[211] It could also shield Article 34 TFEU from misuse as a shortcut to unrestrained negative integration and from providing insufficient regulation of commercial activity in each Member State, which would have been the case with the earlier interpretation of 'market access'.[212] The initial understanding of 'market access' was based on an "intuitive" approach, which was characterised with a high level of arbitrariness.[213] Furthermore, the CJEU's decision-making in *Commission v Italy (2009)* and *Mickelsson and Roos* seems to have achieved a formidable feat – striking balance with respect to the distribution of competences between the CJEU and the Member States as well as between the CJEU and the EU legislature.[214] Finally, the Court of Justice's new approach, displayed in these cases, could be extended to free movement of persons, which is a distinct advantage over the Court's solution in *Keck*.[215]

Nevertheless, it must be pointed out that "even if more effects-oriented and normatively responsive than *Keck*, market access still suffers from being normatively underdetermined".[216] The concept of 'market access' arguably suffers

206 Lianos 2015: 238.
207 Lianos 2015: 238.
208 Lianos 2015: 238.
209 Spaventa 2009: 921–923. It is interesting to note that Spaventa's description (2009: 921–923) of the two parallel interpretations of the phrase "[a]ny other measure" in paragraph 37 of *Commission v Italy (2009)* could be indicative of the CJEU engaging in the strategic production of ambiguity. However, this is a peripheral issue to the problems discussed in this chapter.
210 Lianos 2015: 238.
211 Wenneras & Moen 2010: 399.
212 Wenneras & Moen 2010: 399.
213 Spaventa 2009: 923.
214 Wenneras & Moen 2010: 400.
215 Spaventa 2009: 924.
216 De Sousa 2012b: 84.

from a lack of normative substance, which means it is incapable of producing the necessary instrument to draw distinctions between measures that hinder economic activity and those that impede the freedom of economic intra-Community movement.[217] It may also mislead the CJEU to place an emphasis on discrimination on grounds of nationality as the cause for the occurrence of a hindrance to market access, as in *Ker-Optika*.[218] Although that may well be the case, the conventional understanding of market access dictates that the finding of an obstacle to market access is dependent on empirically establishing the "actual effects" of the restriction (De Sousa, 2012b: 85). These considerations led De Sousa to conclude that "[market access] is thus better seen as a refinement of *Keck*, and not as a challenge to its normative foundations".[219]

Conclusion

The *Keck* preliminary ruling emerged as an urgent and necessary solution to the problems caused by the excessively wide remit of the *Dassonville* formula. Although the resultant substantial reduction in EU competences when it comes to the interpretation of Article 34 TFEU, has been met with approval, the means of achieving this advantageous end have not enjoyed such success. The CJEU's formalistic distinction between 'rules that lay down requirements' and 'selling arrangements' has been condemned for its alleged hollowness and artificiality. The lack of sufficient elaboration on the normative content of these categories and the need for their differentiation has also given rise to suspicions of judicial activism.

The linguistic and legal analysis in this chapter proved that the distinction the CJEU made in *Keck* is actually supported by the legislative text of Article 34 TFEU as a legitimate interpretation. By means of multilingual analysis of a selection of language versions of the relevant Treaty text, it has been shown that the noun 'measure' in the term 'measures having equivalent effect' in Article 34 TFEU is ambiguous. As a matter of polysemy, it could be interpreted either as 'requirement' (in the sense of a legal rule or condition) or as 'arrangement' (in the sense of method of execution, means of achieving something). The official translations of the noun 'requirement' in the term 'rules that lay down requirements'[220] and the noun 'arrangement' in the term 'selling arrangements' have also undergone multilingual analysis, which confirmed they match the semantic meaning of the interpretations of 'measure'. Judging from the CJEU's later definition of the term 'selling arrangements' in *Karner*, which emerged as a result from the Court's pragmatic application of the term in a string of case-law, it could be concluded that the Court uses this term in accordance with the semantic

217 De Sousa 2012b: 85.
218 De Sousa 2012b: 85.
219 De Sousa 2012b: 84.
220 *Keck*, Joined cases C-267/91 and C-268/91: paragraph 15.

meaning identified in *Keck*. Therefore, the distinction drawn in *Keck* constituted an act of resolution of the ambiguity found in Article 34 TFEU.

With respect to the strategic value of the CJEU's ambiguity resolution in *Keck*, it was established that this solution was preferable to the alternative solutions proposed by AG Van Gerven and AG Jacobs. By making the strategic choice to draw the distinction between 'selling arrangements' and 'rules that lay down requirements', the Court was aiming to achieve long-term consistency in its case-law on MEQRs in Article 34 TFEU, while curtailing any detrimental effect the deficiencies in *Dassonville* might have on the winning formula of *Cassis de Dijon*. An overview of the treatment the ambiguity-based legal solution in *Keck* received in the subsequent CJEU jurisprudence on Article 34 TFEU reveals that it showed adaptability to the demands of different factual scenarios. The CJEU was clearly committed to upholding its status as the main criterion for interpretation of Article 34 TFEU, at least until the return to the pre-*Keck* market access logic. The cases of *Commission v Italy (2009)* and *Mickelsson and Roos* executed a doctrinal shift, which sought to remedy the problems associated with the *Keck* solution. Admittedly, *Keck* failed to deliver greater consistency and legal certainty in the long run on its own, but a collaboration with the 'market access' logic may be a step in the right direction.

The question then naturally arises: was it all for nothing then, if *Keck*'s groundbreaking ascent led to its inevitable descent? It was suggested that the initial concept of 'market access', as suggested by AG Jacobs in his Opinion on *Leclerc-Siplec*, would have been equally flawed. Therefore, it is fair to say that the CJEU's implementation of Dothan's judicial tactic of a less demanding judgment as part of the judicial tactic of "walking on the brink of non-compliance" eventually paid off in terms of mitigating the looming legitimacy crisis. The Court's ambiguity-based solution in *Keck* was capable of effectively curbing EU competences in favour of the Member States in one fell swoop. More importantly, it was also sufficiently flexible to sustain the momentum of that initial act of judicial restraint in the long run.

4 Judicial Activism in Retrospect?

The CJEU's Strategic Resolution of Ambiguity in *Ruiz Zambrano* (Case C-34/09) and *Dereci* (C-256/11)

Introduction

Both in *Melloni* and *Akerberg Fransson*, the outcome of the CJEU's judicial activism became evident immediately. As a result of the Court's strategic resolution of ambiguity, EU competences were expanded within the pages of a single ruling. However, a strategic act of ambiguity resolution could also reveal itself to be judicial activism with the passage of time. This is the case with the CJEU's interpretation of the parameters of EU citizenship in the preliminary rulings of *Ruiz Zambrano* and *Dereci*, which could only be recognised as judicial activism in retrospect, if the Court's subsequent jurisprudence is taken into account.

The CJEU is lauded as the chief architect of the legal doctrine of EU citizenship, as it transformed the roughly sketched blueprint first presented by the EU legislator in the Treaty of Maastricht (and later revised in the Treaty of Amsterdam) into a reality. In the early days following its enactment, EU citizenship was perceived as "the perfect means to placate the rampant legitimacy crisis in the EU".[1] Further, EU citizenship was viewed as "an instrument to legitimize the deepening of the integration project",[2] which would be made possible by granting EU citizens access to new opportunities for pursuing their aspirations.[3] In this sense, EU citizenship was imagined as a symbol of a more profound *individual* level of political and social involvement underpinning the present-day evolution of the promise of "an ever-closer union among the peoples of Europe".[4]

However, the seemingly bright future of EU citizenship was soon tainted by disillusionment. It quickly became apparent that "the initial risk inherent to EU citizenship [is that it] might after all be seen as a misnomer, an empty shell whose denomination gave rise to expectations it could not hold".[5] The central issue was that the EU legislator had failed to attach to the concept of EU citizenship

1 Besson & Utzinger 2008: 185.
2 De Witte 2011: 90.
3 De Witte 2011: 92.
4 Joint proclamations of the signatories, the Treaty of Rome (25 March 1957)
5 Besson & Utzinger 2007: 575.

DOI: 10.4324/9781003294870-10

a satisfactory set of entitlements.[6] This means that EU citizenship fell short when compared to national citizenship, which endows the individual with a wide range of rights by virtue of national law.[7] This idea is summarised in Kochenov's concise and insistent inquiry: "The right to have *what* rights?"[8]

It comes as no surprise then that the potential for constitutional impact EU citizenship could have is generally underestimated:

> Union citizenship should reflect rather than dictate which ties and forms of solidarity bind 'us Europeans' ... It seems that for the time being, Union citizenship will remain what it is – a conveyor of cosmopolitan rights, a demand of procedural justice, and a normative intuition.[9]

This criticism seems to resonate with the Court's proclamation that "citizenship of the Union ... is not intended to extend the scope *ratione materiae* of the Treaty also to internal situations which have no link with Community law".[10] By this account, EU citizenship is relegated to a secondary position of a follower, rather than a trend-setter, in the integration-through-law process in the EU. Due to its normative 'hollowness', the capacity for independence of the doctrine of EU citizenship is generally perceived as questionable.

The underlying cause for these inherent flaws in its doctrinal design is that EU citizenship is indebted to the key economic freedoms – to freedom of movement (Article 45 TFEU) and to freedom of establishment (Article 49 TFEU) for providing a solid legal and ideational foundation for its conception. While the history of the right to live and work at any location in the EU – the rights at the very heart of EU citizenship – dates all the way back to the Treaty of Paris (1952), EU citizenship received a formal recognition for the first time in the Treaty of Maastricht (1993) as the natural consequence of a political agenda for greater integration combined with the possibility of endowing an individual with EU rights directly.[11] Naturally, this origin story has left its mark on the legal regime governing EU citizenship: "[a]lmost every substantive judgment on EU citizenship to date has related ... actually or potentially, directly or indirectly to free movement and residence rights".[12]

Although the status of EU citizen is granted simply by virtue of holding the nationality of an EU Member State (Article 20 TFEU), the logic of economic freedoms seems to underpin the CJEU's reasoning in adjudicating on access to the entitlements stemming from EU citizenship in contentious situations. To be more specific, in constructing the doctrine of EU citizenship, the CJEU seems

6 Besson & Utzinger 2007: 574.
7 Eleftheriadis 2014: 785–786.
8 Kochenov 2013a: 512.
9 De Witte 2011: 108.
10 Uecker Jacquet, Joined cases C-64/96 and C-65/96, 1997: paragraph 23.
11 Maas 2014: 800.
12 Nic Shuibhne 2010: 1612.

to have relied on adopting the structural components, methods, and a wide array of concepts endemic to the internal market jurisprudence, all of which had the distinct advantage of already being deeply ingrained in EU law.[13] Accordingly, any violation of the rights of an EU citizen was reimagined as an instance of discrimination, an obstacle, or an unjustified and disproportionate restriction.[14] This strategy was particularly well-suited for fostering greater "narrative coherence" in the CJEU's jurisprudence and for ensuring the doctrine of EU citizenship in the EU legal order was accepted with relative ease and speed, due to a sense of familiarity with the concepts and methods used.[15] There might be reason to believe that EU citizenship might have had an even more substantial contribution, since it has enriched the CJEU's adjudication with "a – legitimate – *material* dimension".[16] Nevertheless, this advantage could be merely attributed to a constitutional reading of the main source of motivation – promoting freedom of movement and residence rights.[17] Ultimately, despite its purportedly vital significance for the EU legal order, the doctrine of EU citizenship ended up being allocated a mere ancillary role to its counterparts – economic fundamental freedoms.[18]

However, this may not necessarily be the case in present times. EU citizenship has undergone an intense period of transformation, unlocked by the groundbreaking preliminary ruling of *Ruiz Zambrano*, which led to a substantial increase in its constitutional significance. *Ruiz Zambrano* is a highly influential ruling in the entire CJEU jurisprudence on EU citizenship that secured a place among the 'top 10' cases with the highest hub and authority scores in Šadl and Hink's empirical study.[19] The outcome of *Ruiz Zambrano* appears to constitute "an interesting twist"[20] in the CJEU's jurisprudence on family reunification rights with respect to EU citizenship.

In 2011, when the preliminary reference of *Ruiz Zambrano* was still pending resolution, Niahm Nic Shuibhne[21] predicted that EU citizenship would present the greatest challenge to the two essential requirements in free movement law: a cross-border link and reverse discrimination. Nevertheless, 'market citizenship' would be well-equipped in both conceptual and formal terms to survive the *Ruiz Zambrano* crisis, due to "the *ambiguous* Treaty language defining the EU internal market and the scope of the free movement of persons" (emphasis added).[22] The following chapter will demonstrate how the Court *indeed* resorted to ambiguity resolution of Article 20(2)(a) TFEU to solve the *Ruiz Zambrano* conundrum.

13 Penot 2012: 16.
14 Penot 2012: 16.
15 Penot 2012: 16.
16 Nic Shuibhne 2010: 1612–1613.
17 Nic Shuibhne 2010: 1613.
18 Penot 2012: 16.
19 Šadl & Hink 2014: 567.
20 Nic Shuibhne 2010: 1615.
21 Nic Shuibhne 2010: 1616.
22 Nic Shuibhne 2010: 1616.

In the light of the following analysis, Niamh Nic Shuibhne's prediction could be credited with almost prophetic accuracy.[23]

The need to utilise the full potential of EU citizenship to promote constitutional change, without being hindered by the inherent flaws in its design, will necessarily inform the reasoning of the CJEU and its decision to strategically use ambiguity resolution in *Ruiz Zambrano*. In *Ruiz Zambrano*, the CJEU proposed an innovative interpretation of Article 20(2)(a) TFEU, the full text of which is as follows:

> [Citizens of the Union] shall have … the right to move and reside freely within the territory of the Member States.

The CJEU's act of strategic resolution of the ambiguity contained in Article 20(2)(a) TFEU was initially committed in *Ruiz Zambrano* and later confirmed in *Dereci*. Although the principle of deprivation of 'the genuine enjoyment of the substance of the rights' makes its first appearance in *Ruiz Zambrano*, it was then further specified in *Dereci*. The new test is fully brought to fruition and reaches a level of sufficient clarity in *Dereci*. In other words, there is an extremely close bond[24] between *Ruiz Zambrano* and *Dereci*, which makes it necessary to be well-acquainted with both, before the sample of ambiguity is examined.

This chapter will show that the expression "*within the territory of the Member States*" in Article 20(2)(a) TFEU is ambiguous, giving rise to two alternative interpretations. On the one hand, it could be given a distributive reading, namely "within the territory of [*each* of] the Member States" (Paraphrase 1). On the other hand, it could be given a collective reading, namely "within the territory of [*all* of] the Member States' (Paraphrase 2). The former could be understood as 'any combination of the territories of at least two Member States' (Paraphrase 1), while the latter denotes 'the total sum of the territories of the Member States' (Paraphrase 2).

The CJEU's strategic resolution of ambiguity allowed the Court to circumvent the inherent flaws in the design of EU citizenship, while allowing it to reach its full potential by outgrowing its association with economic freedoms without the need to place reliance in fundamental rights. As it will be seen by the end of this chapter, the CJEU applied the ambiguity-based solution at the centre of its reasoning in *Ruiz Zambrano/Dereci* at first cautiously as a matter of judicial restraint, and then proceeded to engage in judicial activism in its subsequent case-law on its basis. This formula, based on the strategic resolution of ambiguity,

23 Although Nic Shuibhne likely intended to refer to the free movement of workers, the point still stands, since the wording of Article 45(3)(b) TFEU shares a very close resemblance with that of Article 20(2)(a) TFEU.

24 In the *Dereci* preliminary ruling, *Ruiz Zambrano* is cited a total of eight times (paragraphs 40, 53, 62, 64, 65, 30, 31, 32); *McCarthy* is cited a total of six times (paragraphs 50, 54, 55, 60, 61, 63); *Metock* is cited a total of three times (paragraphs 50, 56, 60).

enjoyed great longevity and was eventually instrumental in executing an expansion of EU competences in *Chavez-Vilchez* (Case C-133/15).

Let us begin with a brief case summary of the preliminary ruling of *Ruiz Zambrano* (Case C-34/09). A third-country national, Mr Zambrano from Columbia, was denied asylum, following his application to the Belgian Government.[25] Mr Zambrano was a father to two minor children who were in possession of EU citizenship, by virtue of having been born on the territory of Belgium.[26] Mr Zambrano resisted the residence category to which the Belgian Government allocated him, as such a classification would deprive him of certain entitlements.[27] Mr Zambrano claimed that his right of residence stems directly from the EU Treaty or that at the very least his right of residence is granted by association, as a parent to EU citizens who are minor children that are financially dependent on him.[28]

In the preliminary reference, *Tribunal du travail de Bruxelles* (Employment Tribunal, Brussels) sought to establish whether Article 18 TFEU (now repealed), Article 20 TFEU, and Article 21 TFEU,[29] on their own or in combination with each other, guarantee that an EU citizen would be entitled to a right of residence in the territory of the Member State of which they hold a nationality, regardless of the fact that they had not exercised their right to free movement in the past.[30] Furthermore, the Belgian Employment Tribunal was interested to clarify whether that infant's parent (a third-country national), on whom the infant (an EU citizen) was financially dependent, would be entitled to a secondary right of residence, along with the work permit exemption and unemployment benefits stemming thereof.[31]

Ultimately, the Court relied on its earlier affirmation that "citizenship of the Union is intended to be the fundamental status of nationals of the Member States" by making reference to a plethora of cases, including *Garcia Avello*, *Zhu and Chen*, and *Rottmann*.[32] On the basis of *Rottmann*, the CEJU proceeded to state that:

> In those circumstances, Article 20 TFEU precludes national measures which have the effect of depriving citizens of the Union of the genuine enjoyment

25 *Ruiz Zambrano*, Case C-34/09: paragraph 14–15.
26 *Ruiz Zambrano*, Case C-34/09: paragraphs 19, 22.
27 *Ruiz Zambrano*, Case C-34/09: paragraph 33–34.
28 *Ruiz Zambrano*, Case C-34/09: paragraph 34.
29 Article 12 EC (repealed) corresponds to Article 18 TFEU; Article 17 EC corresponds to Article 20 TFEU; Article 18 EC corresponds to Article 21 TFEU (Tables of Equivalences Referred to in Article 5 of the Treaty of Lisbon. Official Journal of the European Union, 17 December 2007, C-306/208. Available at: https://eur-lex.europa.eu/resource.html?uri=cellar:8d1c14fc-6be7-4d4e-8416-f28cfc7b3b60.0006.01/DOC_17&format=PDF last accessed 4 December 2018).
30 *Ruiz Zambrano*, Case C-34/09: paragraph 35.
31 *Ruiz Zambrano*, Case C-34/09: paragraph 35.
32 *Ruiz Zambrano*, Case C-34/09: paragraph 41.

of the substance of the rights conferred by virtue of their status as citizens of the Union.[33]

This principle led the Court to conclude that a refusal to grant a right of residence (and a work permit) to Mr Ruiz Zambrano would result in a situation where his minor children would be deprived of the "genuine enjoyment of the substance the rights" they enjoy as EU citizens.[34] Under such circumstances, the children would have no other choice but to leave the territory of the Union along with their parent, since they were financially dependent on him.[35]

The reasoning in *Ruiz Zambrano* is particularly significant in a broader, constitutional context. The outcome of the case depends on whether or not a cross-border link could be established. In the absence of such, this would be considered a purely internal situation and thus would fall outside the scope of EU law. *Ruiz Zambrano* implied that a cross-border link need not be established when an individual wishes to claim the entitlements and protection stemming from their status as an EU citizen. In other words, an individual need not have exercised their right to freedom of movement to take advantage of their EU citizenship. *Ruiz Zambrano* marks the decisive moment when the CJEU terminates the reliance of EU citizenship on the internal market logic, along with the inescapable association with fundamental freedoms, and affirms its status as an autonomous source of rights.[36]

Now let us proceed with a case summary of *Dereci* (Case C-256/11). The five applicants in the main proceedings in *Dereci* (Case C-256/11) were all third-country nationals resident in Austria.[37] The applicants wished to live with their family members[38] who were EU citizens resident in Austria, while enjoying the status of citizens of that Member State.[39] All applicants suffered from the Austrian Ministry of Home Affairs's (*Bundesministerium für Inneres*) rejection of their application for residence authorisation, which in four of the instances was also accompanied by an expulsion order and individual removal orders from Austria.[40] Crucially, the EU citizens had not previously exercised their right to free movement, which became the reason why the *Bundesministerium für Inneres* considered the applicants ineligible for the protection of the regime under Directive 2004/38 available to the family members of EU citizens.[41]

33 *Ruiz Zambrano*, Case C-34/09: paragraph 42.
34 *Ruiz Zambrano*, Case C-32/09: paragraphs 43–45.
35 *Ruiz Zambrano*, Case C-32/09: paragraphs 44.
36 Kochenov & Plender 2012: 387–388.
37 *Dereci*, Case C-256/11: paragraph 2.
38 In terms of the type of familial relationship concerned, the applicants were either the spouse or a direct descendant over the age of 21 of an EU citizen (*Dereci*, Case C-256/11: paragraph 51).
39 *Dereci*, Case C-256/11: paragraph 22.
40 *Dereci*, Case C-256/11: paragraphs 2, 27.
41 *Dereci*, Case C-256/11: paragraph 29. The applicants were also denied protection under Article 8 ECHR (*Dereci*, Case C-256/11: paragraphs 29).

The Austrian *Verwaltungsgerichthof* made a reference to the CJEU in the hope of establishing if

> the refusal of the Bundesministerium für Inneres to grant the applicants in the main proceedings a right of residence may be interpreted as leading, for their family members who are Union citizens, to a denial of the genuine enjoyment of the substance of the rights conferred on them by virtue of their status as citizens of the Union.[42]

Regardless of the fact that the referring court chose to tailor its questions to the specific circumstances of each applicant,[43] it is evident that the interpretation of Article 20 TFEU is at the very heart of the dispute in every scenario.[44] The referring court made the connection with the case of *Ruiz Zambrano* explicit,[45] though in its view the case was to be distinguished from *Ruiz Zambrano*, on the basis that there was a lack of risk that the EU citizens in question could be "deprived of their means of subsistence" in *Dereci*.[46]

The Court started with expressing agreement with the inapplicability of Directive 2004/38 in the present case.[47] The Court then refused to catalogue the case as a purely internal situation, simply because the EU citizens had not exercised their right to free movement.[48] Following that, the CJEU retraced the steps of its earlier reasoning in *Ruiz Zambrano* leading to its groundbreaking resolution.[49] Most notably, the Court clarified the *Ruiz Zambrano* principle with the following statement:

> It follows that the criterion relating to the denial of the genuine enjoyment of the substance of the rights conferred by virtue of European Union citizen status refers to situations in which the Union citizen has, in fact, to leave not only the territory of the Member State of which he is a national but also *the territory of the Union as a whole*.[50]
>
> (emphasis added)

This made it perfectly clear that the most important ingredient in the *Ruiz Zambrano* reasoning was that the deprivation of the substance of rights one

42 *Dereci*, Case C-256/11: paragraph 33
43 The differences between the individual situations of applicants were explicitly acknowledged: whether their entry in Austria was lawful or not; their present place of residence; the nature of their familial links to the EU citizen; whether the third-country national is maintained by the EU citizen (*Dereci*, Case C-256/11: paragraph 23).
44 *Dereci*, Case C-256/11: paragraph 35.
45 *Dereci*, Case C-256/11: paragraphs 30–32.
46 *Dereci*, Case C-256/11: paragraph 32.
47 *Dereci*, Case C-256/11: paragraph 52–58.
48 *Dereci*, Case C-256/11: paragraph 61.
49 *Dereci*, Case C-256/11: paragraphs 62–65.
50 *Dereci*, Case C-256/11: paragraph 66.

enjoys because of their status as an EU citizen occurs as a result of having to leave the territory of the entire Union. The CJEU also ruled that simple economic convenience or the mere desire to keep the whole family together in the EU would be insufficient to invoke the protection of the Treaty provision.[51]

The Court then considered the potential of the right to respect to private and family life, enshrined in Article 7 CFREU,[52] to act as an alternative source of protection for the applicants in the main proceedings, which is preconditioned on satisfying the requirements for the field of application of EU law in Article 51(1) CFREU and Article 51(2) CFREU.[53] Finally, the CJEU clarified that a Member State could refuse to grant a residence permit to a third-country national in the present circumstances, but only if such a refusal does not lead to a deprivation of "the genuine enjoyment of the substance of the rights" stemming from their status as EU citizens, which is a decision left to the referring court to make.[54]

Dereci complements *Ruiz Zambrano* in that it tackles an issue the earlier case failed to resolve, in that the CJEU's reasoning in *Dereci* effectively circumvents the need for referring to fundamental rights as a means for establishing a "deprivation effect".[55] Instead, a finding of 'deprivation effect' places reliance on the plain fact of the expulsion of the individual from "the territory of the Union as a whole".[56] This decision on part of the CJEU dispenses with the "need for the ECJ to answer the delicate question concerning fundamental rights".[57] In the alternative scenario, the CJEU would have risked accusations of an unsanctioned expansion of the substantive scope of application of EU law, in violation of Article 6(1) TEU as well as Article 51(2) of the Charter of Fundamental Rights of the EU.[58] Ultimately, the CJEU's decision-making in this instance could be interpreted as a "judicial strategy" designed to evade an outright declaration excluding the possibility of relying on the Charter in the main proceedings.[59] In this sense, the CJEU's decision in *Dereci* was arguably dictated by concerns for the vertical division of competences between the Member States and the Union.[60]

Moreover, in a broader constitutional context, it might be that the development of EU citizenship reflects the progress made with respect to solidarity, belonging and integration within the EU community.[61] In this sense, the CJEU's preferred choice of interpretation in *Dereci* is arguably the clearest articulation (and perhaps the most literal illustration), of the novel vision of the European

51 *Dereci*, Case C-256/11: paragraph 68.
52 The Court also clarifies that Article 7 CFREU corresponds to Article 8(1) ECHR (*Dereci*, Case C-256/11: paragraph 70).
53 *Dereci*, Case C-256/11: paragraph 71–72.
54 *Dereci*, Case C-256/11: paragraph 74.
55 Lenaerts 2015: 4–5.
56 *Dereci*, Case C-256/11: paragraph 66.
57 Lenaerts 2015: 5.
58 Lenaerts 2015: 5.
59 Adam & van Elsuwege 2012: 184.
60 Adam & van Elsuwege 2012: 177.
61 De Witte 2011: 108.

Union in the series of case-law that began with *Ruiz Zambrano*. The Court of Justice implicitly recognised a trend "towards a less geographical notion of Europe and towards a new construe whereby Europe is regarded as a common space of rights and common values".[62] There is a direct link between the normative dimensions of this space and the language of the Treaty:

> [t]he reference to 'the territory of the Union' is a central reference in the judgment. This reference is not only the metaphor which designates the sum of the physical territories of the member states. It is a normative reference which refers to a new common space, a space of distribution of rights and common values ... To reside in Europe means not only to be physically located in its territory but also to be granted a number of rights and ultimately to be under the protection of certain values of personal welfare and moral security.[63]

Thus, the Court's priority seems clear – to overcome the resistance towards making this novel vision a reality.

The following linguistic and legal analysis aims to reveal how the act of ambiguity resolution, first formulated in *Ruiz Zambrano* and further specified in *Dereci*, allowed the Court of Justice to facilitate the implementation of the authority of EU law. In issuing these preliminary rulings, the Court was conscious of the inherent flaws in the design of EU citizenship as well as its enormous potential for outgrowing its economic freedoms origins and promoting constitutional change. At the same time, the Court was acutely aware of the dangers that come with addressing the issue of the relationship between fundamental rights and EU citizenship. Given these competing considerations, the CJEU was driven to seek creative adjudicative solutions that yield more strategic advantages than disadvantages. Ambiguity resolution appears to have won the Court's favour in this regard, initially marking the beginning of a long period of judicial restraint, but also eventually opening the door for judicial activism down the line.

Linguistic Analysis

Let us now examine closely the provision the CJEU interpreted in *Ruiz Zambrano* and *Dereci*, namely Article 20(2)(a)TFEU (ex Article 17 TEC):

> [Citizens of the Union] shall have ... the right to move and reside freely within the territory of the Member States.

It is argued that the expression "*within the territory of the Member States*" is ambiguous, leading to the emergence of two alternative interpretations. If given

62 Stasinopoulos 2011: 92.
63 Azoulai 2011: E – 34–35.

a distributive reading, the expression could be interpreted as 'within the territory of [*each* of] the Member States' (Paraphrase 1). If given a collective reading, the expression could be interpreted as 'within the territory of [*all* of] the Member States' (Paraphrase 2). Paraphrase 1 could be understood as 'any combination of the territories of at least two Member States', while Paraphrase 2 denotes 'the total sum of the territories of the Member States'.

Semantic Analysis of the Ambiguity in Article 20(2)(a) TFEU

The concepts of *collectivity* and *distributivity* of the noun phrase are central to the example at hand. To reiterate, these categories could be defined as follows:

> In general, the collective reading of a plural noun phrase is one where the objects in the set associated with the noun phrase ... are treated as a unit, or an aggregate object; the distributive is one where it is not the case that any two distinct members of the denotation of the noun phrase are treated as a unit, or an aggregate object.[64]

The following Case Study will reaffirm and expand on the idea of "collective-distributive ambiguity"[65] presented in the chapter on the *Melloni* preliminary ruling, where the distributivity-collectivity parallels stemming from ambiguity, arising out of plural noun phrases were discussed.[66] Here it is worth noting that Gregory Scontras and Noah D. Goodman also claim that plural predications giving rise to distributivity-collectivity parallels may be seen as a source of ambiguity.[67] Given that Brendan S. Gillon seems inclined to view *distributivity* as a mere negation of collectivity, it would be useful for the purposes of this chapter to supplement our knowledge of the term with Lucas Champollion's definition: "the application of a predicate to the members or subsets of a set, or to the parts of an entity".[68]

Let us now consider a helpful example of collectivity-distributivity parallels in the sentence "*The suitcases are heavy*".[69] Roger Schwarzschild[70] contends that, depending on the context, this statement might be understood in one of the following ways:

(1) "Each of the suitcases is heavy". (*Context*: the emphasis falls on the weight of the individual suitcase, especially if each one is carried by a different passenger.)

64 Gillon 1992: 615.
65 Aone 1991: 32–33.
66 Gillon 1987: 443–444, 199, 215–216.
67 Scontras & Goodman, 2017.
68 Champollion 2010: 70.
69 Schwarzschild 1993: 228–229.
70 Schwarzschild 1993, 228–229.

(2) "The total weight of the suitcases is great". (*Context*: the emphasis falls on the weight of the total pile of suitcases, presumably because it will be transported by porters.)

Consequently, the context evokes a distributive reading in the first instance *and* a collective reading in the second.[71] Thus, it appears that the interpretation of a plural noun phrase coupled with the determiner *the* ("the suitcases") can be given a distributive or a collective construal, depending on the context.

The issue of the nature of the predicate used is fundamental to the collectivity-distributivity parallels. As previously mentioned in the *Melloni* chapter, David R. Dowty claims that predicates could be broadly classified as distributive,[72] collective,[73] or ambiguous,[74] with the latter kind evoking both distributive and collective readings at the same time.[75] The predicate "to be" (in the sense of "to weigh") in Schwarzschild's example above could easily succumb to such parallel interpretations. However, the question arises if the same could be said of the predicate in the wording of Article 20(2)(a) TFEU – "to have a right (to move and reside freely)"?

Yoad Winter builds up on that Dowty's well-known classification by drawing a line "between meanings of natural language expressions that range over atomic entities and meanings that range over sets of such entities".[76] Accordingly, Winter proposes a distinction based on semantic number between *atom predicates* and *set predicates*[77] and illustrates this principle in the following manner:

(1) All the/No/At least two/Many students/committees PRED.
(2) Every/No/More than one/Many a student/committee PRED.[78]

In the case of atom predicates, plural noun phrases[79] could easily be combined with *each* and *all* quantifiers, without undermining their acceptability or the semantic equivalence of the sentence.[80] In the case of the set predicates, there is a palpable difference in the acceptability or the truth-conditions of the sentences.[81] Winter gives examples to further clarify the difference between atom predicates and set predicates.[82]

71 Schwarzschild 1993: 228–229.
72 For example: "be asleep, walk, be pregnant".
73 For example: "gather", "be a couple", "be numerous".
74 For example: "build a house", "carry the piano upstairs".
75 Dowty 1987: 98.
76 Winter 2002: 494.
77 Winter 2002: 494, 497–498. Winter (2002: 497–499) also proposes a third category – *mixed predicates*, but they are often end up being reduced to *atom predicates*.
78 Winter 2002: 497. "PRED" here signifies a predicate, which could be a noun, adjective or a verb, such as "be a good team" or "be a vegetarian" (Winter, 2002: 497).
79 The suitable plural noun phrases must be uninflected for number (Winter, 2002: 494).
80 Winter 2002: 497–498.
81 Winter 2002: 497–498.
82 Winter (2002: 498) explains that examples of atom predicates could be "sleep", "be a good team", "weigh 1 kg", "write a book", "student(s)", "committee(s)", etc., while instances of set predicates could be "meet", "be similar", "write a book together", "colleague(s)", etc.

On a semantic level, the use of *all* and *each/every* in formulating the proposed paraphrases above is noteworthy, seeing as these quantifiers correspond to a collective and a distributive reading, respectively. Particularly with respect to definite plurals, the quantifier *all* is said to conclusively indicate a state of totality.[83] Further, it might be that *all* is universally applicable, in that it seems to be capable of exerting a "maximising effect" on collective and distributive predicates alike.[84] In contrast, the quantifiers *every/each* are strictly associated with distributive predicates.[85] Seeing as the *all* qualifier is strictly allocated to the realm of collectivity and the *each/every* qualifiers belong to that of distributivity, total equivalence cannot be established between the two paraphrases.

Pragmatic Analysis of the Ambiguity in Article 20(2)(a) TFEU

On face value, it appears that there is no significant difference between the two interpretations of Article 20(2)(a) TFEU, since they both seem to indicate a situation where the right in question can be exercised in *any Member State on an exhaustive list of 27 Member States.*[86] However, upon closer inspection, one notices that Paraphrase 1 could easily refer to "within the territory of [one of the Member States]" (Paraphrase 1.1.), "within the territory of [two of the Member States]" (Paraphrase 1.2.) or "within the territory of [more than two but less than twenty-seven of the Member States]" (Paraphrase 1.3.). At the same time, Paraphrase 2 denotes "within the territory of [twenty-seven of the Member States]".[87]

From a pragmatic point of view, these options refer to different sizes of total surface area and different (groups of) sovereign states with their respective national jurisdictions. The significance of this finding increases further in the light of the fact that "the right to move and reside freely" necessarily entails an element of *movement*, which raises issues pertaining to the point of departure, the final destination and other general parameters of the journey. It is reasonable to conclude that a normative characterisation of the physical act of movement demands a certain degree of specificity about exactly *which* borders are being crossed. Thus, a superficial reading of Article 20(2)(a) TFEU without an appreciation of the ambiguity contained therein might lead to decidedly divergent pragmatic and normative results.

83 Brisson 2003: 129–130.
84 Brisson 2003: 130–131.
85 Brisson 2003: 130–131.
86 There are a total of 27 Member States in the EU, at the time of writing (15.02.2022).
87 In the light of the wide array of possibilities contained in Paraphrase 1, one might be tempted to conclude that this is actually a case of vagueness, and not of ambiguity. However, Paraphrase 1 and Paraphrase 2 are positioned as alternatives to each other, without the need to pay mind to the different versions of Paraphrase 1. Each of the versions of Paraphrase 1 could be contrasted with Paraphrase 2 in its own right, when viewed from the perspective of physical movement across borders. Therefore, vagueness fails to accurately reflect the complexity of the situation.

Judging from its treatment of the Treaty provision in *Ruiz Zambrano* and *Dereci*, the CJEU seems to be acutely aware of this requirement. In *Ruiz Zambrano*, the CJEU equates "the territory of the Member States" to "the territory of the Union".[88] In *Dereci*,[89] the Court explicitly contrasts two situations, based on a logic that closely follows the semantic intuition that informs the collectivity-distributivity parallel giving rise to ambiguity in linguistic theory. In one scenario, the legal rule demands that the EU citizens physically move from the territory of the Member State of which they are a national to that of another (the logic of *distributivity*). In the alternative, EU citizens need not cross the border between two Member States to exercise this right, as long as they remain within the outer borders that encompass the entire territory of the Union (the logic of *collectivity*). This conclusion is further supported by the CJEU's curious addition of the expression "as a whole" to the phrase "the territory of the Union" in *Dereci*,[90] which is normally associated with *collectivity*.

In other words, the CJEU directly contrasts these two situations, while giving a clear indication of the concrete pragmatic distinction between them. It is also worth noting here that such a complete congruity between the semantic and the pragmatic (normative) implications of a sample of ambiguity is rare to observe and therefore all the more precious to analyse. More importantly perhaps, this interplay has left an indelible mark on the development of the concepts behind the designations.

At this stage, Friederike Moltmann's theory of parts and wholes with respect to distributivity phenomena[91] might be helpful to consider. In particular, one of its fundamental building blocks – "the notion of an integrated whole" – could allow us to gain a more profound understanding of the linguistic implications of CJEU's proclamation pertaining to an EU citizen's exercising the right to move and reside freely within "the territory of the Union as a whole":[92]

> The notion of an integrated whole is important in two quite different ways. First, integrity generally gives unity to an individual: it makes an entity count as a single object rather than as a collection of its parts. Second … integrity in a situation[93] influences what counts as the parts of an entity in that situation.[94]

This is where the expression "as a whole" comes into play. This classification given to "as a whole" by Moltmann[95] likens it to phrases such as "as a group" and

88 *Ruiz Zambrano*, Case C-34/09: paragraph 44.
89 *Dereci*, Case C-256/11: paragraph 66.
90 *Dereci*, Case C-256/11: paragraph 66.
91 Moltmann 1997: 40.
92 *Dereci*, Case C-256/11: paragraph 66.
93 Moltmann clarifies the term: "by a situation I mean simply a way of specifying an entity with properties that may include only accidental properties and of specifying an entity possibly only partially with the properties it in fact has" (Moltmann 2005: 600).
94 Moltmann 2005: 613.
95 Moltmann 1997: 69–70.

"together" and means the function ascribed to it would be to present the entity as "an integrated whole", and not to emphasise its constitutive parts.[96] In other words, "the distributive reading of a predicate is impossible, if the argument is modified by *as a whole*".[97] Therefore, it could be argued that the addition of the phrase "as a whole" commits the expression "the territory of the Union" to collectivity, as opposed to distributivity. This finding reinforces the impression that the CJEU is interested in distinguishing between a collective and a distributive interpretation of Article 20(2)(a) TFEU in *Dereci* (and in *Ruiz Zambrano*, by association).

Moreover, the connection between the plural noun phrase "the Member States" and the term "the European Union" should be investigated more closely. Chris Barker defines 'a term' as: "any noun phrase which is interpreted as a definite descriptor, including some nonsingular noun phrases"[98] and distinguishes between 'group terms', 'plural terms', and 'conjoined terms'.[99] Based on Barker's examples,[100] it seems that "the European Union" would qualify as a *group term* and "the Member States" – as *a plural term*. In this context, group terms exhibit a semantic and syntactic behaviour that is different from plurals and conjunctions, when it comes to extensional contexts and entailments.[101] Nevertheless, the CJEU pays no heed to these semantic and syntactic differences. The Court seems intent on asserting the pragmatic equivalence between the terms, most likely for strategic purposes.

Furthermore, Barker's *group term* is strongly reminiscent of Winter's[102] category of "*group atom*", which Winter illustrates with the following example sentences:[103]

(1) The members of the organizing committee met.
(2) All the members of the organizing committee met.
(3) The organizing committee met.

Winter[104] suggests that the equivalence between (1) and (2) is not necessarily guaranteed, since (1) could still be true even in the absence of some of the members. Rather, (1) is more likely to be equated with (3).[105] If that be the case, *the members of the organizing committee* will be deemed a "group atom", which

96 Moltmann 1997: 69–70.
97 Moltmann 1997: 70.
98 Barker 1992: 71.
99 Barker 1992: 71.
100 Barker offers relevant examples of group terms (e.g. "the committee", "the group", "the list of reasons"), plural terms (e.g. "the men", "those people", "the members of the group") and conjoined terms (e.g. "Bill and John", "the men and the women", "the chairman and the secretary") (Barker, 1992: 71).
101 Barker 1992: 71.
102 Winter 2002: 504.
103 Winter 2002: 504.
104 Winter 2002: 504.
105 Winter 2002: 504.

signifies *the organizing committee* itself.[106] Similarly, Godehard Link asserts that there is a distinction to be made between "the committee" and "the collection of [the committee's] members"[107] as well as between "the cards" and "the deck of cards".[108] Furthermore, Link points to the following pertinent example about the dividing line to be drawn in pragmatic terms between the plural terms "the children" and "all the children":

> It seems to be that in *all the children built the raft* it is claimed that every child took part in the action, whereas in *the children built the raft* it is only said that the children somehow managed to build the raft collectively without presupposing an active role in the action for every single child.[109]

The important takeaway here is that the plural term "the Member States" does not necessarily denote "all (of) the Member States". In other words, "all the Member States" constitutes but one of the possible interpretations of "the Member States". Accordingly, "the European Union" seems to be more accurately matched to "the Member States", and not "all (of) the Member States", as the former is the broader category.

Based on these findings, the breakdown of readings detailed above seems plausible in semantic terms. This would explain the high degree of flexibility the CJEU has exhibited when it comes to interpreting Article 20(2)(a) TFEU. In the pragmatic and normative context of the EU legal order, the CJEU affirmed the equivalence to "the territory of the Member States" to "the territory of the Union as a whole" (Paraphrase 2) in *Ruiz Zambrano* and *Dereci*, after a long period of seemingly equating it to Paraphrase 1.2 ("within the territory of [two of the Member States]") and Paraphrase 1.3 ("within the territory of [more than two but less than twenty-seven of the Member States]"). Looking at the big picture, the connection between these findings and the CJEU's shift in understanding when it comes to defining the normative dimensions of the physical act of *movement*, compared to its stance prior to *Ruiz Zambrano*, is easily discernible. Paraphrase 1.2. and Paraphrase 1.3. seem to refer to the internal borders that exist between neighbouring Member States, whereas Paraphrase 2 is only concerned with the external borders of the EU. This pragmatic distinction appears to be rooted in the normative interaction between fragmentation and unification, which seems to have been the underlying rationale for defining the internal market as "an area without internal frontiers" (Article 26 TFEU [ex Article 14 TEC])[110].

106 Winter 2002: 504.
107 Link 2002: 128.
108 Link citing Blau 2002: 129.
109 Link 2002: 133.
110 Kochenov and Van Elsuwege make the connection between the outcome in *Ruiz Zambrano* and Article 26 TFEU (Van Elsuwege & Kochenov 2011: 451).

Legal Analysis

Article 20(2)(a) TFEU as the Source of Ambiguity

The discovery of ambiguity in Article 20(2)(a) TFEU is hardly surprising, given the unusual circumstances surrounding the conception and evolution of this doctrine. The legislative history of the EU citizenship provisions is rather unconventional, in that the established order of law-making is reversed: the *predating* CJEU jurisprudence was essentially codified in the Treaty of Maastricht, later to serve as the foundation of the currently operative Part II TFEU.[111] This attempt at codification arguably failed to portray the CJEU's jurisprudence with sufficient specificity, leading to the "perpetuation of a number of unwritten assumptions" which play a decisive role in the Court's adjudication, but were nevertheless left outside the remit of the Treaty of Maastricht.[112] This incongruity allegedly caused the rising tension between the text of the Treaties as it appeared on the page and the Court's actual understanding of EU citizenship,[113] which persists to date. Ultimately, the legacy of this unusual chain of events is a set of Treaty provisions on EU citizenship where "the recourse to any restrictive language has been dismissed by the drafters".[114] As a result, the CJEU was given an extraordinary amount of interpretative freedom to shape and mould the concept of EU citizenship, thus utilising the "capacity for mutation, growth and plasticity" of EU law.[115]

At face value, this seems like a great opportunity for the Court to further advance its activist agenda. In reality, the CJEU appears to be anxious to avoid provoking the ire of 'the masters of the treaty'. The Court's top priority in this volatile situation seems to be to seek consensus and to encourage the national courts to engage in the preliminary reference procedure by ensuring the dialogue remains open, amicable, and co-operative.[116] That is precisely why the CJEU opted to generally exercise judicial restraint, while adopting the "stone-by-stone" approach to building its case-law in the field of EU citizenship.[117] This method suggests that the Court developed an innovative doctrine or principle of constitutional law in a gradual and cautious fashion, on a case-by-case basis.[118] Nevertheless, this approach severely backfired, in that the CJEU let the circumstances of the individual cases dictate its decision-making, which gave rise to accusations of "fact-based judicial activism".[119] More importantly, the heavy

111 Kochenov & Plender 2012: 370–371.
112 Kochenov & Plender 2012: 372–373.
113 Kochenov & Plender 2012: 372–373.
114 Kochenov & Plender 2012: 372, 375.
115 Kochenov & Plender 2012: 388.
116 Lenaerts 2015: 1, 9.
117 Lenaerts 2015: 1.
118 Lenaerts 2015: 1, 9.
119 Everson 2014: 967.

reliance on the material facts inevitably had a detrimental effect on coherence with respect to legal concepts and consistency.[120]

Despite its best efforts, the CJEU ultimately failed to deliver on perhaps the most fundamental aspect of the legislator's original promise – creating a *coherent* concept of EU citizenship.[121] This confirms the intuition that "the incoherence of EU citizenship is internal, it is not the result [of] its mismatch with other EU law doctrines".[122]According to Šadl and Hink's empirical study of the CJEU's jurisprudence, "'precedent' in European citizenship case-law exerts weak gravitational force [, with the cases being] held together by specific repeated formulations, meaning judicial rhetoric, rather than the rationale of cases".[123] In the end, it appears that the legal developments in the area "do not reflect the building of a coherent doctrine on the basis of an underlying (unifying) principle".[124] More importantly, Šadl and Hink concluded that: "the Court uses the rhetoric of non-discrimination and fundamental status to systematically eschew the confrontation with the division of competence between the EU and the Member states".[125]

In a nutshell, the CJEU's jurisprudence on EU citizenship rests on the unstable foundation of Treaty provisions that are drafted in far too abstract and broad terms. Regardless of its cautious approach to adjudication, the Court is exposed to accusations of 'fact-based judicial activism' and overall lack of coherence in building the doctrine of EU citizenship. These circumstances generate an acute demand for creative and innovative solutions, which the Court would strive to implement strategically within the scope of the singularly relaxed relevant legislative provisions. The combination between all of these factors makes EU citizenship an area of EU law-making that is particularly conducive to the emergence of ambiguity.

Ruiz Zambrano *as a Departure from the CJEU's Traditional Approach in the Area of EU Citizenship*

The CJEU's ambiguity-based solution in *Ruiz Zambrano* and *Dereci* defied expectations and dramatically changed the trajectory of the Court's jurisprudence until then. The logic of a 'cross-border element'/'purely internal situation' in EU law and the concept of 'reverse discrimination' had heretofore played a pivotal role in adjudication on EU citizenship.

The 'cross-border element'/'purely internal situation' logic

In the EU legal order, the universal pattern for eligibility criteria for entering the scope of fundamental freedoms could arguably be summarised as follows:

120 Everson 2014: 967, 972.
121 Besson & Utzinger 2007: 574.
122 Eleftheriadis 2014: 783.
123 Šadl & Hink 2014: 565.
124 Šadl & Hink 2014: 565.
125 Šadl & Hink 2014: 560.

(1) "the existence of a cross-border element"; (2) "the economic aim of the exercise of the free movement right", and (3) "the existence of a specific hindrance to the pursuit of cross-border movement with an economic aim".[126] In the absence of a cross-border element that attracts the applicability of EU law, a situation is typically deemed to be wholly internal (purely internal) and thus, governed by the domestic law of the relevant Member State. The rule originates from the *Saunders*[127] preliminary ruling, where the CJEU held that: "[t]he provisions of the Treaty on freedom of movement for workers cannot therefore be applied to situations which are wholly internal to a Member State, in other words, where there is no factor connecting them to any of the situations envisaged by Community law".[128] Thus, the cross-border element and the 'purely internal situation' rule are two sides of the same coin.

This criterion has been hugely influential in determining the scope of EU law and, therefore, the jurisdiction of the CJEU, on both a procedural and a substantive level. With respect to 'the purely internal situation' being used as a means for filtering out preliminary references to the Court, it seems that the decision is made with respect to admissibility (a procedural matter), rather than in relation to jurisdiction (a substantive matter).[129] In the context of the current discussion, it seems to be the case that the jurisdiction of the Court in a substantive sense is at stake.[130] Further, it would seem that lately a situation is more likely to be eligible to fall within the remit of fundamental freedoms than to be considered 'purely internal' – a trend, which one might attribute to the more flexible interpretation of the cross-border element based on the facts of the case and the broader definition applied to restrictions to freedom of movement.[131] The outcomes of *Ruiz Zambrano* and *Dereci* appear to fall in line with this trend.

The standard of a 'purely internal situation' has attracted criticism on account of being an "oversimplification" and "a rather confusing influence".[132] Its definition could also be viewed as being devoid of actual substance and practical relevance.[133] This impression is confirmed when one considers the meaning of the phrase 'purely internal situations' up close and breaks it down to its constitutive elements.[134] The adjective 'internal' seems to have gradually lost its concrete

126 De Sousa 2011: 154. De Sousa concedes that the structure he proposes resembles the one suggested by Alina Tryfonidou (De Sousa 2011: 154, footnote [14])

127 The Queen v Vera Ann Saunders, Judgment of the Court of 28 March 1979, Case 175/78, ECLI identifier: ECLI:EU:C:1979:88.

128 *Saunders*, Case 175/78, paragraph 11.

129 Krommendijk 2017: 1366–1368.

130 In her Opinion on *Ruiz Zambrano*, AG Sharpston disagreed with the Member States that submitted observations and the Commission classify the situation as purely internal, which means the EU provisions on citizenship rights were not activated (AG Sharpston, 2010: paragraph 91–92). Evidently, the Court agreed with AG Sharpston.

131 Sanchez 2018: 10–11.

132 Sanchez 2018: 22–23.

133 Sanchez 2018: 25.

134 Sanchez 2018: 23.

meaning in a geographical and territorial context and has transformed into a "conceptual metaphor" that alludes to 'potential' effect as the central criterion for the scope of fundamental freedoms.[135] Furthermore, the adverbs 'purely' and 'wholly' frame the debate in terms of absolutes, which leaves room for an arbitrary classification of any situation that cannot be so labelled and thus imperils the consistent application of the standard.[136] Last but not least, the use of the noun "situation" is problematic, as it places an emphasis on the factual details of the case and leaves out any guidance as to the application of the legal rule and its respective procedure.[137] Therefore, it is doubtful whether the '*purely internal situation*' rule could effectively function as the benchmark for the scope of EU law with respect to fundamental freedoms. In the light of the arbitrariness inherent in the '*purely internal situation*' test, it is no wonder that the Court had reservations about allowing this standard free rein over EU citizenship, which is itself already a doctrine susceptible to incoherence due to its extraordinary legislative beginnings and relatively recent conception.

Nevertheless, it could be argued that the rejection of the *cross-border element* standard and the acceptance of a reliance on the status of EU citizenship in and of itself could open the floodgates to a "limitless" expansion of EU competences.[138] The threshold for being included in the personal scope of application of EU law by virtue of being an EU citizen is already very low – an individual need simply be a citizen of an EU Member State.[139] In comparison, the reward is very high – the status of an EU citizen grants access to a wide array of EU freedoms and EU fundamental rights protection.[140] A proposition such as this is too attractive to be left without some measure of protection from potential abuse.

It is not surprising then that the CJEU is in no haste to sever ties with the old test completely. Naturally, in its decision not to overthrow the reigning standard, the CJEU might be guided purely by its inability to craft an acceptable substitute for the time being. After all, adjudication on a case-by-case basis is constrained by the specific circumstances of the factual scenario. However, could it be that the 'cross-border element' test is capable of yielding benefits beyond mere familiarity and convenience? It might be that movement and economic freedom need not necessarily be equated.[141] If that be the case, this requirement actually has a favourable effect on democracy, since it encourages mobility between the EU Member States.[142] This could result in a positive reinforcement of the image of the EU as a home to a number of modern liberal democracies.[143] Furthermore,

135 Sanchez 2018: 23.
136 Sanchez 2018: 23–24.
137 Sanchez 2018: 24–25.
138 O'Leary 2012: 50–51.
139 O'Leary 2012: 50.
140 O'Leary 2012: 50.
141 Silveira & McKenny Engström 2016: 152.
142 Silveira & McKenny Engström 2016: 152.
143 Silveira & McKenny Engström 2016: 152.

it stresses the tremendous contribution EU citizenship has for engaging and empowering the individual as a key actor in improving interstate relations within the European community – a characteristic that makes it decidedly dissimilar from national citizenship.[144]

It seems that, despite its dubious merits, the 'purely internal situation'/'cross-border element' requirement will be difficult to set aside. Any alternative proposition must have a high chance of success, as it will be entrusted with guarding the gates to a wealth of entitlements EU citizens enjoy and would have the potential to wreak havoc with the distribution of competences. This is a high standard that the Court's ambiguity-based solution in *Ruiz Zambrano* and *Dereci* will eventually prove to be capable of satisfying.

The concept of 'reverse discrimination'

Another obstacle in the way of the CJEU's innovative vision for EU citizenship, which the Court was able to overcome (or rather, circumvent) through its ambiguity-based reasoning in *Ruiz Zambrano/Dereci*, is the prospect of reverse discrimination. *Reverse discrimination* denotes a situation where, as a result of the application of EU law, citizens from other Member States in any given host Member State are treated more favourably than the host Member State's own citizens.[145] Naturally, discrimination on grounds of nationality would offend the principle of equality. This phenomenon could be seen as the result of an overlap between national and supranational spheres of competence, with their dissimilar values and objectives.[146]

More specifically, reverse discrimination signifies a misalignment between the national and supranational rules where EU law exercises restraint in regulating an issue only on a transnational level, while leaving the domestic aspects in the hands of the Member States.[147] This might occur accidentally or deliberately, with the latter scenario gaining particular relevance with respect to the distinction between static and mobile EU citizens in family reunification cases with third-country nationals.[148]

In *Ruiz Zambrano*, *Tribunal du travail de Bruxelles* (Employment Tribunal, Brussels) explicitly sought clarification on the relationship between Article 18 TFEU and reverse discrimination. AG Sharspton included it in the inventory of legal issues to address, albeit with the proviso that it may become "redundant" if the Court chooses to recognise a 'free-standing right of residence' under Article 21 TFEU.[149] In the actual preliminary ruling, the Court conveniently 'forgot' about the existence of the problem. Given that up to that point the Court had entrusted the Member States with the matter of reverse discrimination, revisiting

144 Silveira & McKenny Engström 2016: 152.
145 Cannizzaro 1997: 29; Hanf 2011: 30.
146 Cannizzaro 1997: 29.
147 Hanf 2011: 34.
148 Hanf 2011: 34.
149 Opinion of AG Sharpston, 30 September 2010: paragraph 124.

the notion would have necessarily entailed a pronouncement on the delimitation of competences. Nevertheless, AG Sharpston relied on *Carpenter*, *Zhu and Chen*, and *Metock* to demonstrate that "continuing to apply that traditional, hands-off approach is capable of generating results that are curiously random".[150]

Therefore, it is reasonable to assume that the Court was wary of interfering with the status quo with respect to reverse discrimination, especially if it was not strictly necessary. It could be argued that the CJEU's articulation of its reasoning in *Ruiz Zambrano* made no demands on reverse discrimination, as it essentially eliminated the need to address the classic division between mobile and static EU citizens. In this sense, the Court's ingenious solution had a similar effect to that of AG Sharpston's, in that it helped circumvent an area of great controversy and left the delicate balance already achieved there undisturbed. This is one distinct advantage of the ambiguity-based solution that the Court ultimately put forward in *Ruiz Zambrano* and *Dereci*.

The CJEU's Strategic Resolution of Ambiguity in Ruiz Zambrano *and* Dereci

Rottmann *as the predecessor to* Ruiz Zambrano/Dereci

Despite the risks, the erosion of the 'cross-border element' standard was a necessary prerequisite for the growth of the EU citizenship doctrine. In fact, before *Ruiz Zambrano*, the CJEU took the first decisive step in this direction in *Rottmann*. The case of *Rottmann* posed the question whether, subject to the principle of proportionality, it was for EU law (Article 17 EC) to preclude a Member State from withdrawing its nationality, acquired by naturalisation, from an individual that obtained it by deception.[151] The *Rottmann* scenario is uncharacteristic in that it exemplifies a role reversal: "the nationality of the member states becomes dependent on the fortunes of Union citizenship", so it is no wonder that the result it yielded is equally extraordinary.[152] Despite responding to that question in the negative,[153] the Court confirmed, following *Micheletti* among others, that the Member State "must have due regard to" EU law in making this determination.[154] Curiously enough, the Court also held that the case fell within the scope of EU law "by reason of its nature and its consequences",[155] without making any reference to *a cross-border element*.

Given the high stakes, the outcome of *Rottmann* was generally viewed as a "predictable and logical" step, especially in continuation of *Micheletti*.[156] It made sense in the light of the fact that to rule otherwise would be tantamount to

150 Opinion of AG Sharpston, 30 September 2010: paragraph 135–138.
151 *Rottmann*, Case C-135/08: paragraph 35.
152 D'Oliveira 2011: 141.
153 *Rottmann*, Case C-135/08: paragraph 59.
154 *Rottmann*, Case C-135/08, paragraph 41, 45, 47.
155 *Rottmann*, Case C-135/08: paragraph 42.
156 Kochenov 2013b: 116.

letting the Member States become the sole arbiters of who could become an EU citizen, even at the expense of breaching key EU principles.[157] Still, the CJEU is to be commended for opting for a more unconventional approach to problem-solving than what might appear to be the case at face value. By adopting the more convenient and relatively low-risk solution offered by AG Maduro,[158] the Court would have produced arbitrariness and more incoherence by introducing two divergent statuses of EU citizenship – one of cross-border situations, where the Member States would be obliged to take EU law into consideration on matters of nationality, and another of purely internal situations, beyond the reach of EU law and subjugated to the Member State nationality laws.[159] Thankfully, the Court managed to avoid "the dead-end of cross-border logic".[160]

Nevertheless, as a direct consequence of *Rottmann*, the CJEU has guaranteed "a potentially infinite enlargement" of the scope of EU law.[161] The outcome in *Rottmann* aggravated fears the Member States have harboured for a long time, namely that the advancement of EU citizenship might turn out to be a prelude to loss of their control over national citizenship. Unlike more traditional forms of citizenship, EU citizenship is grounded not in birthright or residential rights in the EU, but rather in Member State nationality.[162] This unusual origins story makes the control an EU Member State holds over an individual's ability to acquire or lose EU citizenship vulnerable to the transnational phenomenon of freedom of movement in the EU.[163] After all, the definition, scope and application of the traditional decisive criterion on EU citizenship, *the cross-border element*, are firmly entrusted to the CJEU. This seems to be the reason why the Member States have experienced anxiety about being forced to relinquish control over the conditions surrounding their national citizenship under the growing influence of EU citizenship since its very inception in Article 8(2) of the Maastricht Treaty, to the point where they felt the need to include a Declaration[164] therein on the preservation of their prerogative in this respect.[165]

157 Kochenov 2013: 116.

158 AG Maduro argues that without exercising his right to free movement, Mr Rottmann would not have obtained German citizenship in the first instance: "Although it was in accordance with the conditions laid down by national law that [Mr Rottmann] acquired the status of German national and lost that of Austrian national, it was therefore only after exercising a fundamental freedom conferred on him by Community law. According to settled caselaw, situations involving the exercise of the fundamental freedoms guaranteed by the Treaty, in particular those involving the freedom to move and reside within the territory of the Member States, as conferred by Article 18 EC, cannot be regarded as internal situations which have no factor linking them with Community law" (Opinion of Advocate General Maduro on *Rottmann*, 30 September 2009, paragraph 11).

159 Kochenov 2011: 79–80.

160 Kochenov 2011: 80.

161 Kochenov 2013b: 120.

162 Baubock 2014: 757.

163 Baubock 2014: 757.

164 Declaration No. 2: "Declaration on nationality of a Member State", Treaty of Maastricht of 7 February 1992

165 De Groot & Luk 2014: 822.

Ultimately, the development of the doctrine of EU citizenship in the direction indicated in *Rottmann* led to "an exponential growth of the scope of EU law", beyond a mere interference with the Member State nationalities.[166] By reassessing the 'purely internal situation' criterion, EU citizenship was capable of expanding the scope *ratione personae* of EU law to cover all EU citizens, regardless of their ability to establish a cross-border link by residing in a Member State other than their own.[167] In effect, this approach resulted in enlarging the domain of fundamental freedoms.[168] The *ratione materiae* of EU law is equally affected by this development, since the CJEU has taken great liberties in classifying as 'cross-border' the situations in *Zhu and Chen*, *Schempp*, and *Garcia Avello*.[169]

Thus, the combined effect of *Rottmann* and *Ruiz Zambrano* sufficed to introduce a noteworthy exception to the 'cross-border element' standard. A common ground between the cases of *Rottmann* and *Ruiz Zambrano* is that they both pertain to "the effectiveness of Union citizenship", since the entire "concept of EU citizenship" is at stake, and not a single right contained therein.[170] Both rulings precluded interference with the essence of EU citizenship through national measures – *Rottmann* protected the loss (and acquisition) of EU citizenship, while *Ruiz Zambrano* safeguarded the 'genuine enjoyment of the substance of rights' stemming therefrom.[171] Thus, *Ruiz Zambrano* was capable of providing "a more logically coherent" method of unlocking the applicability of EU law–directly showing that the Court is shielding the rights of EU citizens from undue interference exercised by the Member States, rather than taking pains to establish a transfer over some internal border.[172] The compatibility between the two tests is predicated on the fact that, in constructing the new standard, the Court makes no attempt to modify the core values of the Union or to undermine the principle of conferral.[173] It is also important to note here that, perhaps mindful of the tremendous constitutional significance of the revision of the standard, *Ruiz Zambrano* sets a very high threshold for activating the exception – "a character of crisis, of last resort situations".[174]

To sum up, no full displacement of the 'cross-border element' standard is to be observed in the aftermath of the arguably controversial *Ruiz Zambrano*. It is simply a case of the further refinement and specification of the cross-border logic by introducing a type of exceptional situation that constitutes its inviolable core.

166 Kochenov 2013b: 119, 121.
167 Kochenov 2013b: 112, 119.
168 Kochenov 2013b: 112, 119.
169 Kochenov 2013b: 120.
170 Nowak 2011: 695.
171 Nic Shuibhne 2012: 365.
172 Van Elsuwege & Kochenov 2011: 451.
173 Van Elsuwege & Kochenov 2011: 451.
174 Nic Shuibhne 2012: 365–366.

The CJEU's strategic resolution of ambiguity in Ruiz Zambrano/Dereci

To appreciate the full impact of the CJEU's ambiguity-based reasoning in *Ruiz Zambrano/Dereci*, one needs to consider whether the Court could have taken a different turn at this crossroads for the evolution of EU citizenship. Attorney General Sharpston's Opinion is particularly helpful in this respect, as it offers a "rearrangement" of the issues pinpointed by the referring court:

(1) the specifics of the distinction between Articles 20 and 21 TFEU and the economic freedoms enshrined in Article 45 TFEU and Article 49 TFEU;
(2) the significance of the fundamental right to family life with respect to delimiting the scope of Article 20 and 21 TFEU, and
(3) the function of Article 18 TFEU in the context of reverse discrimination as a result of the effect of EU citizenship provisions. [175]

AG Sharpston's Opinion sheds light onto the immense *potential* the ECJ's ruling of *Ruiz Zambrano* had for changing the course of the case-law on EU citizenship. The CJEU was presented with the tempting opportunity to revolutionise its jurisprudence in a variety of ways in one fell swoop. However, true to its generally incremental approach to adjudication in this area of EU law, the Court restricted itself to solely ruling on essential matters that are indispensable for the resolution of the case at hand. Thus, the CJEU sagely steered clear of the problematic interaction with fundamental rights and the conundrum of reverse discrimination. Seeing as the Court later revisited the former issue in *Dereci*, it seems that the Court did not abdicate its responsibility to make a decision, but strategically postponed the making of that decision. A simple comparison between the depth and breadth of issues that the Court could have resolved in an activist manner in *Ruiz Zambrano* and the issue it confined itself to resolving speaks of judicial restraint at this stage. Is this impression confirmed when one considers the alternative solutions to the *Ruiz Zambrano* conundrum?

An argument based on the prospect of future exercise of the right to free movement could have been made in *Ruiz Zambrano* (and in *Rottmann*).[176] The Court could have ruled that the Ruiz Zambrano children could exercise their right to free movement effectively only after turning the required legal age to return to the EU on their own.[177] However, such an outcome would have been inconsistent with the previous case-law, where the possibility of future movement was real and concrete, and not merely "hypothetical" (*Bosman*; *Lehtonen c.f. Moser*; *Kremzow*) and the removal of the national measure was the only precondition to realising this goal (*Graf*).[178] The comparison with free movement in *Garcia Avello* is also unhelpful, as the EU citizens in *Kremzow*, *Moser*, *Graf*

175 Opinion of AG Sharpston, 30 September 2010: paragraphs 45–53
176 Nowak 2011: 693.
177 Nowak 2011: 693.
178 Nowak 2011: 693.

and *Ruiz Zambrano* were not focused on the link with one Member State, but were potentially going to prospectively exercise the right to free movement in the "abstract", to any other EU Member State.[179] The Court of Justice favoured coherence in this instance and abstained from following this path. Evidently, this approach would have had only limited success.[180]

At this stage, one is reminded of the ingenious solution recommended by AG Sharpston in answer to the *Ruiz Zambrano* conundrum – a recognition of a "free standing right of residence" in Article 21 TFEU.[181] The solution proposed by AG Sharpston, namely recognising an autonomous right of residence for static citizens of the EU, could have had unforeseeable long-term constitutional ramifications.[182] It remains unclear whether EU citizens could challenge any limitations to that right and on what basis as well as the consequences for the remit of EU fundamental rights and for the problem of the limitations of competences stemming therefrom.[183] It is plain to see why "such a blanket extension of the material scope of EU law" would be rejected by the Court.[184] Nevertheless, in the aftermath of the preliminary ruling of *McCarthy* (Case C-434/09), one gains a newfound appreciation of AG Sharpston's proposition.

To begin with, let us review the facts of the case. Mrs McCarthy was a Union citizen by virtue of holding a dual UK and Irish nationality, but she lived in the UK her whole life.[185] She was married to a Jamaican national, who applied for a residence permit and a residence document as a spouse to an EU citizen, whose application was ultimately rejected by the UK Secretary of State.[186] The applicant sought to secure a right of residence for Mr McCarthy under Directive 2004/38, which is why the UK Supreme Court sought clarification on Articles 3, 16 and 7 of Directive 2004/38 in its preliminary reference to the CJEU.[187]

The CJEU deftly repositioned the legal issue to focus on Article 21 TFEU and emphasised the fact that Mrs McCarthy had never exercised her right of free movement, despite holding dual nationality.[188] Finally, the Court expressly distinguished the case from *Ruiz Zambrano* on the grounds that there was no obligation for Mrs McCarthy to leave the territory of the Union, which means there was no interference with her 'genuine enjoyment of the substance of rights' stemming from her status as EU citizen.[189] Curiously enough, the Court also drew a

179 Nowak 2011: 694.
180 Nowak 2011: 693.
181 Opinion of AG Sharpston, Case C-34/09, 2010: paragraph 101.
182 Nowak 2011: 692.
183 Nowak 2011: 692.
184 Nowak 2011: 692.
185 *McCarthy*, C-434/09: paragraph 14–16.
186 *McCarthy*, C-434/09: paragraphs 14–17, 20.
187 *McCarthy*, C-434/09: paragraph 21, 23.
188 *McCarthy*, C-434/09: paragraph 26.
189 *McCarthy*, C-434/09: paragraphs 49–50, 53.

distinction between Mrs McCarthy's situation and the one in *Garcia Avello*.[190] On this basis, Article 21 TFEU was rendered inapplicable.[191]

Perhaps the most significant aspect of the Court's reasoning was the relationship between the *Ruiz Zambrano* solution and the statutory requirement under Article 21 TFEU. The two tests are positioned as alternatives to each other, which is evident from the use of the conjunction *or*:

> no element of the situation of Mrs McCarthy, as described by the national court, indicates that the national measure at issue in the main proceedings has the effect of depriving her of the genuine enjoyment of the substance of the rights associated with her status as a Union citizen, or of impeding the exercise of her right to move and reside freely within the territory of the Member States, in accordance with Article 21 TFEU.[192]

Nevertheless, in the aftermath of paragraph 49 of *McCarthy*, it would appear that AG Sharpston was correct in her intuition: Article 21 TFEU *is* capable of governing situations where the EU citizen had not previously exercised their right to free movement, although Court was disinclined to resort to this solution in *Ruiz Zambrano*.[193] However, following the Court's refusal to engage with the right to family life yet again, the principle might now be devoid of substance with respect to residency.[194]

The outcome of *McCarthy* indicates that the Court is determined to normalise the use of the *Ruiz Zambrano* formula in its EU citizenship jurisprudence.[195] The CJEU's attempt to retrospectively revisit its reasoning in *Garcia Avello* with the improved logic of *Ruiz Zambrano* was likely intended to suggest this new approach was commonly applied in the past, albeit implicitly.[196] In doing so, the Court was implicitly admitting the scope of 'cross-border situations' was too widely drawn to be able to convincingly and conclusively determine the material scope of EU law.[197]

Moreover, according to the Court's reasoning in paragraph 49 above, there are two possibilities of circumventing the 'cross-border element' requirement – the *Ruiz Zambrano* solution under Article 20 TFEU or the right to residence under Article 21 TFEU – but Mrs McCarthy's case satisfied neither. Therefore, the message the Court sent to Mrs McCarthy was plain and simple: to avoid separation from her family, she should exercise her right to freedom of movement and physically *move* across Member State borders.[198] This is a tremendous hurdle

190 *McCarthy*, C-434/09: paragraphs 51.
191 *McCarthy*, C-434/09: paragraph 56.
192 *McCarthy*, C-434/09: paragraph 49.
193 Lansbergen & Miller 2011: 297–298.
194 Lansbergen & Miller 2011: 297–298.
195 Kochenov 2011: 91.
196 Kochenov 2011: 88–89.
197 Kochenov 2011: 89.
198 Kochenov 2013a: 510–511.

to overcome in the specific circumstances of Mrs. McCarthy's situation.[199] This only serves to show the extremes to which the Court is prepared to go, in order to execute the vision for EU citizenship it articulated in *Ruiz Zambrano*.

At the same time, *McCarthy* could be said to be representative of "a more wide-scaled and sustained recent shift from *predominantly* rights-opening to *predominantly* rights-curbing assessments of citizenship rights".[200] The Court of Justice seems to be willing to make arbitrary and unwarranted distinctions between different classes of applicants, in order to reinforce the *exceptionality* of the *Ruiz Zambrano* scenario.[201] If the Court of Justice continues down that path, it may develop an excessive preoccupation with the facts of the preliminary references, not unlike a court of lower instance but in the absence of in-depth knowledge of the factual circumstances, which will result in the CJEU crafting "a bizarrely over-detailed matrix of primary Union law".[202]

This scenario brings to mind the requirement that a CJEU legal argument must be "universalisable" to be considered acceptable as a good justificatory reason and escape accusations of judicial activism.[203] Seeing as *Ruiz Zambrano* was deemed inapplicable in both *McCarthy* and *Dereci* on different grounds and regardless of the similarity in their factual circumstances, it may be safe to conclude that the *Ruiz Zambrano* formula ('the genuine enjoyment of the substance of the rights') is unable to satisfy this requirement.[204]

McCarthy is a preliminary ruling that sends mixed signals regarding its attitude towards *Ruiz Zambrano*: "the result of the decision in *McCarthy* arguably both simultaneously purports to affirm the principle in *Ruiz Zambrano* and yet in essence completely undermines it".[205] The fault seems to lie with *Ruiz Zambrano*'s bewildering *exceptionality* which could very well be the product of strategic manoeuvring on part of the Court. It was established that the tension in *McCarthy* comes from the combination between *Ruiz Zambrano* and Article 21 TFEU. Perhaps the incongruity between the outcomes of *Ruiz Zambrano* and *McCarthy* would not exist, had *Ruiz Zambrano* been decided according to AG Sharpston's proposition in the first place? The CJEU's treatment of *Gacia Avello* stands as compelling evidence in this regard. AG Sharpston uses *Garcia Avello* to substantiate her conclusion that "the 'right to reside' is a free-standing right, rather than a right that is linked by some legal umbilical cord to the right to move".[206] At the same time, the Court of Justice detected a discrepancy between *Garcia Avello* and *Ruiz Zambrano*, which it was anxious to retrospectively rem-

199 Shirley McCarthy v. Secretary of State for the Home Department [2008] EWCA Civ 641, paragraph 8, p. 176. Kochenov 2013a: 510–511.
200 Nic Shuibhne 2015: 902.
201 Nic Shuibhne, 2015: 368–369; O'Leary, 2012: 65–66.
202 Nic Shuibhne 2015: 371.
203 Šadl 2013: 206.
204 Šadl 2013: 227.
205 Lansbergen & Miller 2011: 298.
206 Opinion of AG Sharpston, Case C-34/09: paragraph 84.

edy in *McCarthy*.[207] It thus becomes clear that *Ruiz Zambrano* could be seen as an exceptional detour in the Court's jurisprudence that fits neither with its predecessor *Garcia Avello*, nor with its successor *McCarthy*.

In the end, *Ruiz Zambrano*'s *exceptionality* proved to be a double-edged sword. On the one hand, it sets the *Ruiz Zambrano* test apart as a powerful strategic tool for reserving special treatment for otherwise similar factual situations in the Court of Justice arsenal. On the other hand, it prevents the CJEU's ambiguity-based solution in *Ruiz Zambrano* from crystalising into a 'universalisable' legal rule that supplements in a meaningful way the rest of the CJEU jurisprudence. Therefore, AG Sharpston's solution would have produced mixed results.

Nevertheless, the ultimate resolution in *Ruiz Zambrano* could not escape criticism, either. Urška Šadl set out to concretise the objectionable aspects of the Court's decision-making in *Ruiz Zambrano*.[208] To begin with, Šadl justifies her distaste for coherence as the traditional basis for assessment of the legitimacy of the Court's decision-making by exposing an inherent flaw therein – its "formal and open-ended character".[209] That is why Šadl decided to redirect her attention to *persuasiveness* as the guiding criterion in the assessment which means that a deficiency in the persuasiveness of the Court's reasoning is a more accurate description of the root cause for accusations of judicial activism.[210] Šadl then proceeded to deliver a compelling analysis on the Court's failings in terms of persuasiveness, which exposed *Ruiz Zambrano* as "poorly reasoned" due to its dependence on citations as authority, the superfluous repeated and circular use of references and the *ad hoc* reliance on social propositions.[211] Finally, she asserted that "[w]hat holds the cases, which are cited in support of the Court's argument, together, is language (the Court's rhetoric)".[212]

In the light of Šadl's conclusion, the "elliptical" nature of the CJEU's reasoning in *Ruiz Zambrano*[213] becomes even more conspicuous and meaningful. Although the Court based the prohibition of forceful expulsion from the territory of the Union on the need to guarantee the 'genuine enjoyment of the substance of rights attaching to the status of European Union citizen', the CJEU omitted to clarify what precisely constitutes the substance of these rights.[214] Thus, it

207 Kochenov 2011: 88–89.
208 Šadl 2013: 206–208.
209 Šadl 2013: 208.
210 Šadl 2013: 206, 208.
211 Šadl 2013: 208, 229.
212 Šadl 2013: 229. This is a conclusion Šadl reiterates in her empirical analysis of CJEU case-law in the area of EU citizenship, jointly conducted with Hink (Šadl & Hink, 2014: 565). There a distinction is made between judicial rhetoric and rationale: "The rationale will usually be a matter of principle, which will have true gravitational force. It will constrain judicial decision making. Judicial rhetoric, on the contrary, will be confined to the wording (rhetoric) of the decision. It will not constrain judges and it will not have justificatory force" (Šadl & Hink, 2014: 555).
213 Raucea 2013: 2032.
214 Raucea 2013: 2032.

would seem that at any given moment in time the picture the Court paints is one step away from completion, which is consistent with the underlying philosophy behind the Court's 'stone-by-stone' approach.[215] It appears that, in one and the same breath, the Court introduces greater clarity as to the meaning of Article 20 TFEU, while generating more uncertainty by inventing curious language formulations of its own.

The Strategic Implications of the CJEU's Resolution of Ambiguity in Ruiz Zambrano and Dereci

At its very heart, the *Ruiz Zambrano* scenario concerns the nature of the relationship between EU citizenship and EU fundamental rights. For a long while the CJEU acquiesced in proposing a feasible plan for dealing with this problem of great constitutional magnitude. Two competing explanations for the Court's inactivity and hesitance could be identified, depending on how one could characterise the interaction between the two categories.

To begin with, an argument could be made to the effect that these two areas of EU law are tightly interwoven, to the point where "if Union citizenship is to be taken seriously, it cannot be completely separated from fundamental rights questions".[216] EU citizenship and fundamental rights seem to be united in a mutually advantageous alliance in their pursuit of the same goal – suspending the distance between the individual and the Union.[217]

If one subscribes to this interpretation of the relationship between EU citizenship and fundamental rights, Von Bogdandy et al.[218] propose a novel reading of the *Ruiz Zambrano* formula – "the genuine enjoyment of the substance of the rights" conferred upon the individual by virtue of their status as an EU citizen. In particular, an interpretation in the spirit of a "'reverse' *Solange*" is suggested:

> beyond the scope of Article 51(1) CFREU Member States remain autonomous in fundamental rights protection *as long as* it can be presumed that they ensure the essence of fundamental rights enshrined in Article 2 TEU.[219]

This approach is seen as advantageous, as it shows respect for the principle of pluralism, as prescribed by Article 4(2) TEU, and it promises safe passage between "the *Scylla* of a dysfunctional Union and the *Charybdis* of suffocating national constitutional identities".[220]

The proposition of a "reverse" *Solange* seems like a plausible explanation for the Court's behaviour thus far. It sits well with the priorities presented in

215 Lenaerts 2015.
216 Von Bogdandy et al. 2012: 506.
217 Von Bogdandy et al. 2012: 506.
218 Von Bogdandy et al. 2012.
219 Von Bogdandy et al. 2012: 491.
220 Von Bogdandy et al. 2012: 491, 519.

Micheletti and *Rottmann*, the predecessors to *Ruiz Zambrano*. As for its successors, if the *Ruiz Zambrano* ambiguity-based solution was designed to protect the inviolable core of EU fundamental rights protection against interference on part of the Member States, its heretofore bizarre *exceptionality* suddenly makes sense. It is no longer seen as an inherent flaw, precluding it from cohering with the rest of its surrounding case-law, but rather as a symbol of its special, elevated status.

In addition, the Court is by no means unfamiliar with the "reverse" *Solange* approach, as demonstrated by the fact that it adopted a very similar line of reasoning when interpreting Article 53 TFEU in the *Melloni* preliminary ruling[221]. There the Court was once again faced with a balancing act between fundamental freedoms and a constitutional element of great significance (mutual trust), which the Court had to perform while safeguarding at all costs "the primacy, unity and effectiveness of EU law".[222] Similarly, the *Ruiz Zambrano* exception aims to protect "the effectiveness of citizenship of the Union".[223] It is worth noting here that the CJEU's decision-making *Melloni* constituted a strategic resolution of ambiguity, as discussed earlier in this book. It seems that a pattern in the Court's problem-solving emerges between *Ruiz Zambrano* and *Melloni* – the Court seems to favour the strategic resolution of ambiguity found in Treaty provisions in situations where a line must be drawn for the protection of core components of the constitutional makeup of the EU legal order from Member State interference.

However, the "reverse" *Solange* approach seems to be designed as a defence mechanism of protection of core EU constitutional values. It is reserved for those situations where the CJEU is 'cornered' by circumstance and has no choice but to set hard limits for the protection of the fundamental tenets of the EU legal order. In this sense, the Court of Justice's ensuing offensive action, spearheaded by the preliminary ruling of *Chavez-Vilchez*, comes as a surprise.

Now let us take as a starting point the belief that EU citizenship and fundamental rights belong to "two formally and systematically differentiated legal regimes that have been built upon divergent rationales".[224] Their incompatibility is predicated on the fact that EU citizenship promotes a sense of exclusivity, while fundamental rights are meant to enhance inclusivity.[225] By virtue of Article 20(1) TFEU, EU citizenship is a category strictly reserved for those holding

221 Schima 2015: 1116–1117; Anagnostaras 2017: 2017: 252. "It is true that Article 53 of the Charter confirms that, where an EU legal act calls for national implementing measures, national authorities and courts remain free to apply national standards of protection of fundamental rights, provided that the level of protection provided for by the Charter, as interpreted by the Court, and the primacy, unity and effectiveness of EU law are not thereby compromised" (*Melloni*, Case C-399/11: paragraph 60).

222 *Melloni*, Case C-399/11: paragraph 60.

223 *Rendon Marin*, Case C165/14: paragraph 74.

224 Sanchez 2014: 465.

225 Sanchez 2013: 147: Brink 2019: 31.

the nationality of an EU Member State, which results in clearly drawn division lines, indicative of exclusivity.[226] Thus, third-country nationals cannot invoke EU Treaty provisions, but must rely either on secondary legislation or on agreements with non-EU countries, or on both, in order to show that their situation falls within the remit of EU law.[227] At the same time, the Charter applies universally in situations where provisions of EU law or acts of EU institutions operate, regardless of the nationality or citizenship of the individuals involved, which speaks of inclusivity.[228] Thus, the tension between the exclusivity of EU citizenship rules and the inclusivity of fundamental rights protection causes a noticeable lack of coherence in the status allocated to EU citizens and that of third-country nationals.[229] For this reason, regardless of the fact that the fusion between the two categories could help boost the legitimacy of the EU, a union between the two would be ill-advised.[230]

If that be the case, it makes sense to assume then that the CJEU would be anxious to avoid a situation where it would have to make the impossible choice between the two areas of EU law. A declaration of clear preference is no doubt constitutionally costly, since it creates more problems than it solves. Firstly, it exposes the Court to the danger of *severe* accusations of judicial activism, if the reasons given in support are unpersuasive or insufficient, seeing as the issue is of utmost constitutional importance. Secondly, even if the Court manages to convincingly justify the choice made, its room for manoeuvring in the future will be significantly reduced. The factual circumstances and the legal issues of the groundbreaking judgment will set a standard, any deviation from which would demand even more elaborate justification from the CJEU. This could potentially result in a 'domino effect' of fundamental constitutional issues emerging on the horizon and demanding urgent resolution. Evidently, the Court would be interested holding this possibility at bay until a future moment in time when: (a) committing to a solution is truly unavoidable, meaning that the strategic loss would be greater if the problem is left unresolved yet again, or (b) when it sees a window of opportunity for a strategic gain that outweighs the risks of delivering a solution.

The Court's behaviour in *Ruiz Zambrano* indicates that the Court recognises the difficulty in reconciling EU citizenship and fundamental rights and has chosen to ignore the problem outright. AG Sharpston suggests a plausible explanation for the Court's unwillingness to engage on that point:

> Making the application of EU fundamental rights dependent solely on the existence of exclusive or shared EU competence would involve introducing

226 Wiesbrock 2012: 67.
227 Wiesbrock 2012: 68.
228 Sánchez 2013: 147.
229 Sánchez 2013: 147.
230 Brink 2019: 31.

> an overtly federal element into the structure of the EU's legal and political system.[231]
>
> I therefore conclude that ... the fundamental right to family life under EU law could not be invoked as a free-standing right, independently of any other link with EU law.[232]
>
> In proposing that answer, I am accepting that the Court should not, in the present case, overtly anticipate change. I do suggest, however, that (sooner rather than later) the Court will have to choose between keeping pace with an evolving situation or lagging behind legislative and political developments that have already taken place. At some point, the Court is likely to have to deal with a case – one suspects, a reference from a national court – that requires it to confront the question of whether the Union is not now on the cusp of constitutional change ... Answering that question can be put off for the moment, but probably not for all that much longer.[233]

It is evident that AG Sharpston is sympathetic to the Court's predicament and mindful of the hindrances standing in the way of its resolution. Nevertheless, she presented a fairly accurate overall assessment of the situation – the Court cannot postpone the inevitable forever. If that is indeed the case, and the inescapable resolution is on the cards, why stall constitutional progress? The most plausible conclusion is that the Court wishes to conduct this revolution *on its own terms and at its own pace*. This is where incrementalism comes into play, to maximise acceptability and minimise risk. This is precisely why *Ruiz Zambrano* has to be read in conjunction with *Dereci*.

The outcome of *Dereci* fell in line with the Court's principal findings in *Ruiz Zambrano*. The 'substance of the rights' originating from the status of EU citizenship continued to be defined in terms of negation, which means it was associated with a *preclusion* from expulsion from the territory of the Union and a *prevention* from total deprivation.[234] No guidelines are issued and no description is given by the Court on the actual contents of the term.[235] More importantly, the Court of Justice seemed treat fundamental rights protection as an afterthought, rather than an essential supplement, to its central line of reasoning:

> That finding is, admittedly, without prejudice to the question, whether, on the basis of other criteria, inter alia, by virtue of the right to protection of family life, a right of residence cannot be refused. However, that question

231 Opinion of Advocate General Sharpston: *Ruiz Zambrano*, 30 September 2010: paragraph 172.

232 Opinion of Advocate General Sharpston: *Ruiz Zambrano*, 30 September 2010: paragraph 176.

233 Opinion of AG Sharpston, 30 September 2010: paragraph 177.

234 Raucea 2013: 2036.

235 Raucea 2013: 2036.

> must be tackled in the framework of provisions on the protection of fundamental rights which are applicable in each case.[236]

This dismissive attitude, coupled with the fact that the Court took care to articulate even more clearly its vision of "the territory of the Union as a whole",[237] confirmed the impression of the Court's utter reluctance to make any serious effort to engage with the issue of fundamental rights at that point in time. The Court afforded no substantial deviation from this line of action in *Rendon Marin*.[238] It was not until the preliminary ruling of *Chavez-Vilchez* that the Court of Justice reconsidered its stance and switched from 'defence' to 'offence' mode.

In *Chavez-Vilchez*, the Court was invited to pronounce itself on the interpretation of Article 20 TFEU in eight disputes in the main proceedings, where applications for social assistance and child benefits were made to the Netherlands authorities by the mothers (third-country nationals) of one or more children of Netherlands nationality.[239] The fathers of the children, also of Netherlands nationality, acknowledged paternity but lived separately from their children and their mothers.[240] The applications were rejected, since the applicants did not have a right of residency.[241]

The Higher Administrative Court of the Netherlands (*Centrale Raad van Beroep*) sought clarification on the effects of *Ruiz Zambrano* and *Dereci*, since it recognised the need to consider whether the children would be forced to leave the territory of the Union as a whole, if their mothers were denied the right to residence.[242] In particular, it was interested whether, despite being third-country nationals, the mothers of EU citizens can derive a right of residence on the basis of Article 20 TFEU.[243] Further, it wanted to know what significance was to be attributed to the father staying on the territory of the Netherlands or the EU as a whole.[244] The referring court was also concerned with the relevance of the extent of dependence on the parent and the distribution of responsibility between the parents.[245]

The CJEU held that it was indeed the case that the children would suffer "a deprivation of the genuine enjoyment of the substance of the rights", if the mothers were expelled from the territory of the Union as a whole.[246] To make an

236 *Dereci*, Case C-256/11: paragraph 69.
237 *Dereci*, Case C-256/11: paragraph 66.
238 The CJEU needs to conduct its assessment "in the light of the principle of proportionality, of the child's best interests and of the fundamental rights whose observance the Court ensures" (*Rendon Marin*, Case C165/14, 2016: paragraph 85).
239 *Chavez-Vilchez*, Case C-133/15: paragraph 20.
240 *Chavez-Vilchez*, Case C-133/15: paragraph 20.
241 *Chavez-Vilchez*, Case C-133/15: paragraph 29.
242 *Chavez-Vilchez*, Case C-133/15: paragraph 33.
243 *Chavez-Vilchez*, Case C-133/15: paragraph 32.
244 *Chavez-Vilchez*, Case C-133/15: paragraph 34.
245 *Chavez-Vilchez*, Case C-133/15: paragraph 39.
246 *Chavez-Vilchez*, Case C-133/15: paragraph 65.

assessment of the risk of such expulsion, the competent national authorities must ascertain the extent of dependency on the third-country national parent by

> [taking] account of the right to respect for family life, as stated in Article 7 of the Charter of Fundamental Rights of the European Union, that article requiring to be read in conjunction with the obligation to take into consideration the best interests of the child, recognised in Article 24(2) of that charter.[247]

Further, the willingness or ability of the other parent to become the primary carer for the child is "a relevant factor, but it is not in itself a sufficient ground" to assess the risk of being forced to leave the territory of the Union as a whole.[248] The Court of Justice then proceeded to enumerate what concrete circumstances must be taken into consideration when making that assessment "in the best interests of the child".[249]

Setting aside the Court's helpful clarifications on the parameters of the parent-child relationship of dependency, *Chavez-Vilchez* is particularly noteworthy because it constituted an open acknowledgement that the referring court must "take into account" EU fundamental rights when ruling on situations of the *Ruiz Zambrano* type. This unequivocally confirms the impression shared by commentators and Advocate Generals alike that fundamental rights protection was a real and operative concern in the CJEU's decision-making all along. The Court kept its pronouncement as concise as possible by making no reference to the ECHR or the ECtHR's relevant case-law, any other instruments on the protection of human rights or any of its own jurisprudence.[250] An explanation regarding its sudden departure from its approach in *Dereci* (at paragraph 69: "without prejudice to") and in the follow-up case of *O and S* (paragraph 59), where the Court seemed to have treated the applicability of Article 20 TFEU and the CFREU as distinctly separate, would have been a welcome addition to its reasoning.[251]

In the aftermath of *Chavez-Vilchez*,[252] the state of the law is therefore left unclear with respect to the hierarchy of considerations at play in the CJEU's reasoning. *Dereci* dictated that the fundamental rights protection is ***a mere addition*** to the debate surrounding a potential breach of Article 20 TFEU.[253] The

247 *Chavez-Vilchez*, Case C-133/15: paragraph 70.
248 *Chavez-Vilchez*, Case C-133/15: paragraph 71.
249 *Chavez-Vilchez*, Case C-133/15: paragraph 71.
250 Van Eijken & Phoa 2018: 957–958.
251 Van Eijken & Phoa 2018: 957–958.
252 The subsequent Grand Chamber preliminary ruling of *KA* (Case C-82/16, 2018: paragraph 71) confirmed and referred to *Chavez-Vilchez* on that point: "the competent authorities must take account of the right to respect for family life, as stated in Article 7 of the Charter, that article requiring to be read in conjunction with the obligation to take into consideration the best interests of the child, recognised in Article 24(2) of the Charter".
253 Van Eijken & Phoa 2018: 958–959.

outcome in *Chavez-Vilchez* seems to imply that a violation of the right to family life, in context of preserving the child's best interests, is *a constitutive element* of a potential breach of Article 20 TFEU.[254] The latter possibility suggests that the applicability of the Charter is the decisive factor in the determination, which brings the following major constitutional problems in its wake: (a) affirming EU citizenship as an "autonomous source of rights" under Article 20 TFEU undermines the 'purely internal situation' standard, and (b) in the light of the interpretation of Article 51(1) TFEU, this may constitute an encroachment on Member State competences.[255]

Thus, the argument to be discerned from CJEU's reasoning in *Chavez-Vilchez* appears to be "circular": "rights applying within the scope of the Treaty serve to determine that scope".[256] In so ruling, the Court seems to show little to no regard for Article 6(1) TEU, Article 51(1) TFEU and Article 51(2) TFEU.[257] This move on part of the Court has the effect of removing the last obstacles in the way of a potential enlargement of the scope of fundamental freedoms.[258] Finally, with respect to the effects of *Ruiz Zambrano* it could be argued that "the right to family life has the potential to push the application of *Ruiz Zambrano* from an exception to a rule with significant consequences for national immigration regimes".[259]

Thus, the Court of Justice proved EU citizenship had the capacity to act as a means for expanding the scope of the Charter, and consequently of EU competences, to cover areas previously conceived as 'purely internal situations'.[260] The CJEU achieved this goal through alternating its steps between retraction and advancement, in a series of strategic moves to be traced in the *Ruiz Zambrano* string of case-law.[261] As a result, Kochenov's appraisal of the potential of EU citizenship for changing the EU constitutional landscape appears to be correct: "any economic engagement within the Internal Market does not necessarily play a role in shaping the material scope of EU law: EU citizenship does the trick".[262]

Ultimately, *Chavez-Vilchez* demonstrates the unbridled full power of *Ruiz Zambrano*. Even though the CJEU consistently emphasised the exceptionality of *Ruiz Zambrano*, it persistently and gradually affirmed its authority by applying the test to a variety of situations that would otherwise fall outside the scope of EU law. It was irrelevant whether the *Ruiz Zambrano* standard was *actually* satisfied on the facts of these cases; what mattered was enforcing it as a well-established

254 Van Eijken & Phoa 2018: 958–959.

255 Van Eijken & Phoa 2018: 958–959. Perhaps it is also worth mentioning that there exists a milder interpretation of the Court's behaviour in *Chavez-Vilchez*, to the effect that it could be that the Court of Justice merely recommended conducting a "Charter-compliant" assessment (Van Eijken & Phoa 2018: 959).

256 Snell 2018: 476.

257 Snell 2018: 476.

258 Snell 2018: 476.

259 Snell 2018: 476.

260 Torres Perez 2017: 1087.

261 Torres Perez 2017: 1088.

262 Kochenov 2013b: 120.

legal rule through continuous use. In hindsight, it appears the CJEU was simply biding its time before an appropriate case (i.e. *Chavez-Vilchez*) comes along – one that would merit forsaking any pretence of judicial restraint and employing judicial activism instead.

Conclusion

As the CJEU set out to transform EU citizenship and fulfil the grandiose promise of this legal doctrine's inception, all the odds were stacked up against the Court. EU citizenship suffered from a chronic lack of substance and a seemingly incurable dependence on its economic origins. If the Court of Justice were to succeed in this endeavour, it had to find a way to conceal the former and overcome the latter weakness.

To this end, the Court of Justice initially chose an incremental approach for implementation of the authority of EU law,[263] while being prepared to face the consequences of the inevitable coherence deficit it could cause. The peril of upsetting the delicate balance of competences protected by the 'purely internal situation' standard was too great; the dangers of treading into fundamental rights territory in the case-law regarding third-country nationals were too real. The chances of success seemed decidedly slim.

Indeed, as the CJEU issued one ruling after another in a quick succession and its rhetoric became more elaborate, it soon became apparent that the problems with coherence were more severe than previously anticipated. Nevertheless, the CJEU soldiered on with the application of its *Ruiz Zambrano* formula with great conviction, even in situations where it did not belong. It insisted on its exceptionality, yet invoked it universally. In the process, the Court wilfully overlooked chances for clarification, turned a blind eye to controversial problems in urgent need of solution, and withheld concrete responses to the referring court's perceptive questions, all in the hope that the *Ruiz Zambrano* solution will live to see another day. With *Chavez-Vilchez*, the Court of Justice received the long-awaited reward for its effort – *Ruiz Zambrano* had not only survived; it had prospered.

To what does the CJEU's reasoning in *Ruiz Zambrano* owe its resilience? The answer is hidden in plain sight – in Article 20(2)(a) TFEU. The *Ruiz Zambrano* solution, clarified by *Dereci*, was *not* based on mere rhetoric, which one can only suppose denotes an incoherent cluster of elaborate, obscure, and incomprehensible arguments by the Court. Indeed, the roots of the *Ruiz Zambrano* solution run much deeper – to the legislative text itself. The CJEU's strategic resolution of the ambiguity found in Article 20(2)(a) TFEU offered two equally plausible interpretations of the provision, in both linguistic and legal terms. In the absence of any conclusive indication as to the legislator's intent on that point, the Court was left with the liberty to resolve the ambiguity in a strategically advantageous manner, which would ultimately facilitate the implementation of the authority

263 Dothan 2014: 131–136.

of EU law. Although the Court initially showed judicial restraint in using the *Ruiz Zambrano* formula, it soon became clear that it was equally well-suited for judicial activism.

Ambiguity resolution was the preferred solution to two other options in the arsenal of the Court of Justice's problem-solving methods – the future exercise of fundamental freedoms and the acknowledgement of a free-standing right of residence under Article 21(1) TFEU. Both strategies proved to be faulty upon closer scrutiny. It is interesting to observe, however, that AG Sharpston's proposal of a free-standing right of residence could actually be seen as an act of ambiguity resolution[264] in its own right. AG Sharpston observes that the "right to move and reside freely within the territory of the Member States" could be given different interpretations:

> Is it a combined right? (the right to "move-and-reside")? A sequential right ("the right to move and, having moved at some stage in the past, to reside")? Or two independent rights
> ("the right to move" and "the right to reside")?[265]

AG Sharpston ultimately resolved the ambiguity in favour of the latter interpretation. The strong possibility that AG Sharpston also resorted to ambiguity resolution, in order to provide an appropriate solution to *Ruiz Zambrano* serves as compelling evidence that the CJEU might have been engaging in the same practice, albeit with respect to a different part of the same sample of text. Further, the considerations that constrained AG Sharpston's reasoning – especially the awareness of the ramifications on a systemic constitutional level for the EU legal order – appear to be much the same as those informing the Court's decision-making. It seems that ambiguity resolution, in one shape or another, was the most prudent course of action in *Ruiz Zambrano*.

The CJEU's variation of ambiguity resolution seemed to be superior to that of AG Sharpston, in that it afforded the Court the necessary leeway to deal with the exceptionality of *Ruiz Zambrano* in *Chavez-Vilchez*, in a manner that resulted in a "reverse" *Solange* declaration (at the very least) or an expansion of EU competences (at most). In the former case, the CJEU gained assurance for the safe and unproblematic implementation of the authority of EU law. In the latter scenario, the Court of Justice secured a powerful means of expanding the *ratione materiae* of EU law through fundamental rights in the face of the transformed doctrine of EU citizenship, which ultimately facilitates the implementation of the authority of EU law. Both pathways fit the judicial tactic of "walking on the brink of non-compliance".[266]

264 Here the ambiguity arises by virtue of the conjunction "and" (Adams & Kaye 2006: 1172) as well as the adverb "freely", which both contribute to a distributive and collective reading.
265 Opinion of AG Sharpston, 30 September 2010: paragraph 80.
266 Dothan 2014: 117–122.

Ultimately, ambiguity resolution ensured that the *Ruiz Zambrano* ambiguity-based solution had the flexibility and staying power to endure the internal and external pressures that accompanied the evolution of EU citizenship. While it would be premature to conclude that the new version of EU citizenship consequently lived up to its promise, the result is certainly a vast improvement in comparison to the dire prospects of success the CJEU's endeavours initially had.

Part 3

Ambiguity as a Desirable Systemic Feature

Ambiguity as a Desirable Systemic Feature of the EU Legal Order

This book set out to establish the strategic value of ambiguity for the authority of EU law, based on examples of the CJEU's strategic resolution or strategic production of ambiguity, as seen in some of its leading preliminary rulings in the area of fundamental rights, freedom of movement, and EU citizenship. The outcome of the linguistic and legal analysis of each of these Case Studies proved that ambiguity was the implicit driving force behind the CJEU's reasoning, which ultimately created an opportunity for the Court to realise its strategic vision for the expansion or restriction of EU competences. Thus, the strategic production or strategic resolution of ambiguity established itself a particularly valuable technique in the arsenal of the CJEU and is particularly well-suited to resolving high-stakes scenarios that demand the weighing of constitutional considerations against each other.

Ambiguity in EU law has been traditionally seen as a strategic opportunity for the CJEU to invariably engage in judicial activism. In the rare instances where an alternative function for ambiguity has been contemplated, it has been suggested that, if mitigated by teleological and meta-teleological interpretation, ambiguity be used for the purposes of judicial restraint, which would promote greater coherence and acceptability in the EU legal order. The findings from the four Case Studies presented in this book demonstrated that neither of these competing visions of ambiguity accurately and completely describe the strategic value of ambiguity for the authority of EU law. Although the majority of the Case Studies favoured the former, there is one ruling that illustrated the latter idea. Indeed, ambiguity in EU law assists the Court of Justice in implementing the authority of EU law through judicial activism as well as judicial restraint. Thus, this book proposes an alternative theory for the strategic value of the authority of EU law. The following concluding chapter will present the outcomes of the investigation as well as some guidelines as to the type of case and type of situation in which this phenomenon is likely to be found as well as the strategic advantages and disadvantages of this judicial technique compared to alternative approaches to resolving the legal issue at the heart of the relevant case.

DOI: 10.4324/9781003294870-12

Ambiguity as a Strategic Opportunity for Judicial Activism?

To begin with, let us check the veracity and accuracy of the popular view that ambiguity is merely as an instrument that the Court wilfully exploits for the expansion of EU competences, in a gradual transition "from a *horizontal* and *bilateral* to a *vertical* and *multilateral* relationship"[1] between the CJEU and the national courts. Doubtlessly, the CJEU's strategic resolution of ambiguity in *Melloni* and its strategic production of ambiguity in *Åkerberg Fransson* resulted in an immediate and significant extension of the scope of the Charter of Fundamental rights. In the case of *Ruiz Zambrano/Dereci*, the CJEU's activist goal of expanding the *ratione materiae* of EU law through fundamental rights by transforming of the doctrine of EU citizenship under Article 20(2)(a) TFEU became clear at a later stage, following a short period of judicial incrementalism. All three Case Studies demonstrated that ambiguity could indeed enable the implementation of the authority of EU law through acts of judicial activism, whether imminently or with delayed effect.

Furthermore, it is important to note that the selection of examples contains cases of ambiguity resolution as well as *ambiguity production*. This finding demonstrates that the Court of Justice is not only taking strategic advantage of ambiguity embedded in the Treaty text by the EU legislator (*Melloni*, *Ruiz Zambrano/Dereci*), but is also *actively creating opportunities* for itself to exploit ambiguity for the purposes of judicial activism by producing ambiguity and then resolving it in the same ruling (*Åkerberg Fransson*). Seen from this perspective, the CJEU's judicial activism seems even more grave and inexcusable.

However, a closer examination of the Court of Justice's strategic acts of ambiguity resolution and ambiguity production reveals that there may be mitigating circumstances for its activist decision-making. These extenuating circumstances are not external to this discussion, but stem from the inherent properties of ambiguity.

Firstly, in the *Melloni* Case Study (Type 1), the Court of Justice was left with little to no guidance by the legislator as to that particular aspect of the interpretation of Article 53 CFREU. The issue of the primacy of EU law was of such overwhelming constitutional significance, that it might have been "entirely open and left ambiguous, perhaps consciously" by the EU legislator.[2] Therefore, the CJEU had no choice but to engage in extreme meta-teleological interpretation, so as to be able to adjudicate in an effective manner. At the same time, the CJEU was at full liberty to make a choice of interpretation which would be supported by the legislative text either way. On the crossroads between 'system-maintenance through acceptability'[3] and 'system-building through concepts',[4] the CJEU opted for the latter, which revealed its true strategic priorities when it comes to

1 Craig & De Burca 2011: 482.
2 Besselink 2014: 1181.
3 Paunio 2013: 157, 191, 176.
4 Leczykiewicz 2008: 782–785.

its approach to the implementation of EU law. It might be argued that the CJEU was concerned with affirming the young and vulnerable doctrine of mutual trust through the language and rhetoric of the principle of primacy, which already had a strong foothold in EU law. However, such a systemic necessity is highly unlikely to be an excuse for judicial activism that ultimately had a detrimental effect on acceptability.

Secondly, in *Ruiz Zambrano/Dereci* (Type 1), the Court of Justice was invited to adjudicate on Article 20(2)(a) TFEU. The problem the CJEU was grappling with from the start was assuaging the effect of the 'empty shell' syndrome from which the doctrine of EU citizenship was suffering[5] since its very conception by the EU legislator. This substantive hollowness made EU citizenship dependent on internal market logic and precluded it from achieving conceptual autonomy. The Treaty provisions on EU citizenship are notoriously broadly drafted, since they essentially codified the predating CJEU case-law on the matter, albeit not in a particularly faithful manner.[6] This circumstance gave the CJEU immense interpretative freedom.[7] The ensuing tension between the legislative text and the Court's understanding continued to haunt the Court's jurisprudence on EU citizenship. As a result, the doctrine of EU citizenship was plagued by a serious inherent coherence deficit.[8] The Court's strategic resolution of ambiguity in *Ruiz Zambrano* and its clarification in *Dereci* was an attempt to halt the domino effect of incoherent interpretations triggered by the EU legislator's recklessly non-committal attitude to defining the substance of EU citizenship, which started as early as the Treaty of Maastricht. The strategic resolution of ambiguity in *Ruiz Zambrano/Dereci* was particularly helpful in ensuring a coherent transition from the old approach in *Rottmann*, while allowing the Court of Justice to propel the doctrine of EU citizenship forward on its way to conceptual autonomy without the need to base that progress on fundamental rights protection. Mindful of the future, the Court proceeded in an incremental manner, until it was prepared to make a decisive step in *Chavez-Vilchez*. Having built a solid foundation of case-law in support of the *Ruiz Zambrano/Dereci* approach, the Court finally felt secure enough to engage in judicial activism in *Chavez-Vilchez* in a more overt and unapologetic fashion. However, this time the doctrine of EU citizenship *independently and on its own* took the credit for the expansion of EU competences, proving that the CJEU's strategic resolution of ambiguity paid off in the end.

In the *Ruiz Zambrano/Dereci* as well as in the *Melloni* examples (Type 1), one could observe a pattern: by adopting an extremely lenient drafting approach due to exceptional circumstances, the EU legislator leaves a window of opportunity in the form of ambiguity in the Treaty text, of which the Court of Justice

5 Besson & Utzinger 2007: 575.
6 Kochenov & Plender 2012: 370–375.
7 Kochenov & Plender 2012: 370–375.
8 Besson & Utzinger 2007: 574; Sadl & Hink 2014: 565; Eleftheriadis 2014: 783.

takes strategic advantage by means of ambiguity resolution. The results in both instances are evident: a substantial expansion of EU competences. However, it must be noted that this is not a thoughtless, wilful abuse of the mandate given by the 'masters of the treaty'. Rather, it appears to be a carefully premeditated judicial choice, made on the basis of a sober assessment of pros and cons. More importantly, it is a means of combating a certain *systemic deficit*. In *Melloni*, this was the need for effective implementation of the European Arrest Warrant despite the immaturity of the doctrine of mutual trust in the Area of Freedom, Security and Justice, whereas in *Ruiz Zambrano/Dereci*, it was the need to effectively adjudicate on EU citizenship despite its normative hollowness and the lack of coherence in the EU citizenship jurisprudence. In other words, the CJEU could be said to be exercising judicial activism through the strategic resolution of ambiguity in response to a problem left unaddressed by the EU legislator, especially in cases where there is a 'glitch in the system' that precludes the effective implementation of the authority of EU law. In both Case Studies, the CJEU's strategic resolution of ambiguity showed great enduring power and flexibility in the face of the subsequent case-law.

The Case Study of *Åkerberg Fransson* (Type 3) differs from the aforementioned examples, in that the CJEU is seen strategically producing ambiguity. In the *Åkerberg Fransson* preliminary ruling, the CJEU put forward a broad interpretation of Article 51(1) CFREU, resulting in a clear expansion of EU competences. The EU legislator was clearly determined to take every precaution in drafting the legislative text against that possibility. While in *Melloni* and *Ruiz Zabrano/Dereci*, the legislator either purposefully or negligently left room for ambiguity in the drafting of the relevant Treaty provision, in *Åkerberg Fransson* both the semantic and pragmatic meaning of the legislative text, instilled by the legislator, demanded a narrow interpretation of the term 'implementation' in Article 51(1) CFREU. Based on this evidence, one could surmise that the Court of Justice is fully capable of creating opportunities for activist strategic ambiguity resolution even where the EU legislator has ostensibly left none to be found in the EU Treaty text. However, let us not forget that, in the Explanations to the Charter, the EU legislator confusingly equated the terms 'implementation' and 'the scope of Union law'. Although the binding effect of the Explanations is debatable, the CJEU still had to take this piece of legislative guidance into account when interpreting Article 51(1) CFREU. This adjudicative dilemma was further complicated by the fact that the CJEU's preceding case-law of *Wachauf* and *ERT* drew a distinction between these two terms.

Thus, the CJEU's decision-making in *Åkerberg Fransson* had the tremendous task of settling the incompatibility between its previous jurisprudence and the Charter.[9] In response to this need, the CJEU imposed a pragmatic model of interchangeability between divergent terms, in order to establish relationships of equivalence between a set of otherwise divergent terms that would support

9 Sarmiento 2013: 1277.

its preferred interpretation. By applying multilingual analysis to these terms, it was established that the term 'applicability', invented by the CJEU in *Åkerberg Fransson*, was actually ambiguous, with 'implementation' and '(scope/field of) application' being its Paraphrases. The *Åkerberg Fransson* Case Study argues that the CJEU's production of ambiguity was aimed at allowing the CJEU to push forward the '(scope/field of) application' (broad) interpretation and expand EU competences, without actually dismissing the 'implementation' (narrow) interpretation of Article 51(1) CFREU that the legislator intended and without overruling the distinction made in its *Wachauf* and *ERT* jurisprudence.

Seen from this perspective, the CJEU's decision-making with respect to judicial activism through the strategic production of ambiguity, as seen in *Åkerberg Fransson (Type 3)*, seems to largely conform to the insight obtained from the *Melloni* and *Ruiz Zambrano/Dereci* Case Studies (Type 1). The CJEU's strategic behaviour occurs as a response a problem of systemic value –the necessity to reconcile *Wachauf* and *ERT* with the EU legislator's contradictory instructions in the legislative text of Article 51(1) and the Explanations.[10] To a lesser extent than in the Case Studies of *Melloni* and *Ruiz Zambrano/Dereci*, the EU legislator in the case at hand also gave somewhat equivocal guidance to the Court in the form of the confusing Explanations to the Charter.

However, there is one important difference between Type 1 and Type 3 examples. The Type 1 examples produced ambiguity-based legal solutions that had tremendous longevity. In the subsequent case-law, the CJEU noticeably steered clear from the legal solution it endorsed in *Åkerberg Fransson* (Type 3), showing a reluctance to use it as a foundation for further analysis or to revisit and improve it. This could be revealing of the Court's awareness of the inherent brittleness of such a legal solution.

On the basis of this evidence, it could be concluded that the idea that ambiguity in the legislative text could be exploited for the purposes of judicial activism provides a fairly accurate description of the strategic value of ambiguity for the authority of EU law. The Court of Justice is consistently using ambiguity (by means of resolution or production thereof) to implement the authority of EU law through judicial activism in the examples from Type 1 and Type 3. Where ambiguity is present in an EU Treaty provision, the Court tends to choose the paraphrase that supports an activist interpretation. Where such an opportunity is not immediately available or obvious, the Court creates one for itself by means of ambiguity production. In all of these Case Studies, the Court facilitates the implementation of the authority of EU law by advancing further autonomous concepts of EU law, meaning that the CJEU engages in 'system-building through concepts'.[11] However, there is one more example which proves that these findings fail to paint a *complete* picture of the strategic value of ambiguity for the authority of EU law: *Keck*.

10 Sarmiento 2013: 1277.
11 Leczykiewicz 2008: 782–785.

Ambiguity as a Strategic Opportunity for Judicial Restraint?

Due to the fact that this example stands alone in its category and the neighbouring category of Type 4 is left unoccupied by a Case Study, it is difficult to generalise the findings drawn from *Keck*. What could be derived from this experience instead is an *indication* of the strategic value of ambiguity in this area, which has the potential to be specified by further examples. It would seem that an example of ambiguity as an opportunity for judicial restraint is rare enough to be regarded as an exception to the rule, which confirms the impression that ambiguity generally creates strategic opportunities for judicial activism. After all, three out of four Case Studies lead to this conclusion. Nonetheless, the existence of even a single example, let alone a ruling of the tremendous constitutional impact that *Keck* has for the evolution of the EU legal order, cannot in good faith be overlooked.

If the examples from Type 1 indicated that the Court tends to be interested in the paraphrase of the ambiguity found in the legislative provision that promotes the expansion of EU competences, the Case Study from Type 2 shows that this is not always the case. In *Keck*, the CJEU interpreted the ambiguous noun 'measure' in the term 'measures having equivalent effect' from Article 34 TFEU in a *restrictive* manner, to denote 'rules that lay down requirements', and not 'selling arrangements'. In order to achieve this result, the CJEU had to invent the category of 'selling arrangements' and distinguish it from 'rules that lay down requirements'. This had been traditionally regarded as a solution unsupported by the legislative text, but multilingual analysis shows that the semantic meaning of the terms suggests that the Court put forward a *legitimate* interpretation of the legislative text. Thus, the Court of Justice's decision-making in *Keck* could now be seen as an expression of judicial restraint by virtue not only of its outcome, but also of the means the Court uses to reach this end.

Similarly to the Hypothesis 1 Case Studies, the Court's strategic resolution of ambiguity in *Keck* was enabled by the EU legislator's principally broad drafting of the Treaty provisions concerning the internal market (perhaps even leading to ambiguity), thus granting the Court tremendous interpretative freedom.[12] The Court's decision in *Keck* was understood by the Court as a correction of the trajectory of its case-law in the wake of the all-encompassing *Dassonville* formula: "[b]y contrast, contrary to what has previously been decided".[13] However, on a systemic level, it can be perceived as an attempt to solve the 'legitimacy crisis' the CJEU found itself in at the time.[14] In this respect, *Keck* again conforms to the model established by the Cases Studies of Type 1 and Type 3 earlier.

12 Weatherill 2017: 125, 127–128.
13 Joined cases C-267/91 and C-268/91: paragraph 16.
14 Friedbach 1996: 236; De Sousa 2012b: 87.

Finally, a few words are in order about the reasons why the Case Studies from Type 4 were altogether missing from the pool of examples. This book presented examples of both ambiguity production and judicial restraint, paired up with different categories. Therefore, the problem probably does not lie in either of them, taken individually, but *in the combination between the two*. Firstly, there may be an inherent incompatibility between the two. If the CJEU strategically engages in ambiguity production, this may easily provoke accusations in judicial activism, since the Court's creative output will most likely be detached from the legislative text. Secondly, if the Court's ambiguity production for some reason remains undetected, it might be problematic, since it could cause unforeseen complications in the process of building a coherent doctrine down the line. Therefore, the strategic production of ambiguity carries a *high cost* for the CJEU. In cases where it is coupled with judicial activism, it could also lead to a *high reward*, since the Court is effectively advancing the state of EU law and pushing the boundaries of EU competence further. However, where the strategic production of ambiguity is paired with judicial restraint, the reward might be perceived as *not worth the cost*, since judicial restraint effectively either keeps the scope of EU competence the same or reduces it. Judicial restraint has great systemic value for the authority of EU law in terms of balancing out judicial activism, as was the case with *Keck* being seen as a remedy for the preceding 'legitimacy crisis'. Therefore, it might just be *a matter of rarity*. A Type 4 example must be (a) a judicial restraint case, (b) a case where ambiguity is at the heart of the legal problem, and (c) a case of strategic production of ambiguity. There is not enough empirical evidence to make a definitive judgment regarding the frequency of the first two criteria, but given the Court's historical tendency towards judicial activism and the narrow set of circumstances in which ambiguity tends to be observed, the combination between (a) and (b) is probably fairly rare. Additionally, only one out of three Case Studies presented here concerns the strategic production of ambiguity, which suggests that this phenomenon tends to be seldom found among ambiguity-based examples. For all of these reasons, a Type 4 example fulfilling all three criteria is likely to be extremely rare.

Which of these visions for the strategic value of ambiguity for the authority of EU law more accurately describes reality? Given that the only Case Study on judicial restraint falls in line with the pattern established by the Case Studies on judicial activism (especially Type 1), it is most likely *no isolated incident*. In other words, there is reason to believe that *Keck* is a reliable and faithful representative of its category, and is not some solitary aberration. If all of the Case Studies unfold in a similar manner under closer scrutiny, this probably indicates that their common characteristics are not attributable to their association with *judicial activism* or *judicial restraint*, but to the presence of *ambiguity*. Therefore, the most accurate and complete vision for the strategic value of ambiguity for the authority of EU law must bring together Case Studies on both judicial activism and judicial restraint under the same overarching theory.

Ambiguity is a Desirable Systemic Feature of the EU Legal Order

The key conceptual difference between the two competing visions detailed above lies in their attitude towards ambiguity. The idea that ambiguity will invariably be exploited for the purposes of judicial activism treats ambiguity as a serious problem in need of eradication, since it facilitates the CJEU's unwarranted expansion of EU competences and undermines legal certainty. The view that ambiguity could also be used for judicial restraint also regards ambiguity as problematic, but believes its detrimental effects on legal certainty could be mitigated through the CJEU's teleological and meta-teleological reasoning in the EU legal order. Ambiguity could also create the need for more intense judicial co-operation between the CJEU and the national courts through the preliminary ruling procedure, which ultimately helps the participants in judicial dialogue establish common ground and reach agreement. This would in turn contribute towards greater acceptability and coherence in the EU legal system. How could these two diverging views be reconciled, while taking into account the evidence presented in this book?

To begin with, ambiguity *itself* must not be perceived as a problem that necessarily leads to redrawing the boundaries of competence between the CJEU and the national courts in favour of the latter, whether or not its allegedly adverse effects could be mitigated or not. The findings indicate that ambiguity could be used both for the expansion and the limitation of EU competences. Therefore, ambiguity is *indifferent* to the concrete strategic purpose with which it is resolved or produced. In this sense, ambiguity merely *creates opportunities* for the CJEU to realise its strategic intent. This function is particularly relevant to the preliminary ruling procedure, where the national courts could be induced to make a reference by their inability to understand the meaning of EU law. By seeking a clarification on a certain ambiguous legislative text, the national courts are initiating dialogue with the CJEU. In issuing a preliminary ruling, the Court of Justice resolves the ambiguity and could produce ambiguity of its own on the same occasion or a subsequent one. Thus, ambiguity could serve as fuel to a cyclical and systematic exchange that could bring the CJEU and national courts together through co-operation or draw them apart by conflict. However, ambiguity is not to be held responsible for the outcome, it merely triggers and then maintains the momentum in the process. Therefore, ambiguity should be viewed as *a desirable feature* of the EU legal system.[15]

What is the strategic value of ambiguity for the authority of EU law, if ambiguity is seen as a desirable systemic feature of the EU legal order? The Case Studies presented in this book demonstrated that ambiguity is neither an omission in the sense of a systemic failure that the CJEU would inevitably abuse for its activist agenda, nor a chance to promote greater coherence and acceptability on

15 Piantadosi, Tily, & Gibson 2012: 282.

a systemic level, if its effects are mitigated by teleological and meta-teleological reasoning.

Firstly, in defiance of the notion that ambiguity is a strategic opportunity that invariably leads to judicial activism, it was shown that ambiguity does not necessarily result in judicial activism in all instances. There is even some evidence (in *Melloni*, *Ruiz Zambrano/Dereci*, *Keck*) that the EU legislator might have purposefully left the Treaty text ambiguous, so as to reach consensus in an effective manner at the drafting stage or postpone the resolution to decide in the future on a case-by-case basis, according to the Court's discretion.

The Court of Justice often resorts to ambiguity where there is a coherence deficit to be addressed, but it is doubtful to what extent coherence is actually achieved as a result of the CJEU's treatment of ambiguity. The same is valid for Case Studies on judicial activism.[16] What is more important, however, is that the Case Study of *Keck* also failed to deliver greater coherence, which is in theory the ultimate aim of the strategic use of ambiguity for the purposes of judicial restraint. Granted, some semblance of coherence was eventually achieved, but the *Keck* legal solution had to be later supplemented with market access logic, which means this relative success cannot be fully attributed to the CJEU's strategic resolution of ambiguity in *Keck*. Finally, the outcome in *Keck* generally enjoyed acceptance by the academic community and the national courts. However, the means the Court used to achieve this end – the (undisclosed) strategic resolution of ambiguity – gave rise to accusations of judicial activism. Nevertheless, that outcome could have in theory been made possible even without the strategic resolution of ambiguity, following AG Jacob's proposed solution of *Keck*, but at a very high strategic cost. Therefore, ambiguity resolution made the achievement of acceptability *in a cost-effective manner* possible.

On the basis of these findings, it seems that the strategic value of ambiguity for the authority of EU law is that ambiguity is a desirable systemic feature of the EU legal system that ensures greater *flexibility*, so that the communicative system (the EU legal order) could be more stable and function more efficiently. This conclusion is the result of merging the ideas that ambiguity is a "desirable feature" of efficient communication[17] and ambiguity in the EU legal order could be capable of ensuring flexibility and stability as a supplement to legal certainty.[18] In this way, ambiguity allows the CJEU to engage both in 'system-building through concepts', described by Leczykiewicz,[19] and in 'system-maintenance through acceptability', envisioned by Paunio,[20] depending on the needs of the

16 It is also interesting to note that, in *Åkerberg Fransson* and *Ruiz Zambrano/Dereci*, coherence proved to be elusive in the long term. Therefore, the CJEU's strategic resolution of ambiguity is also unlikely to lead to this desirable outcome.

17 Piantadosi, Tily, & Gibson 2012: 281–282, 288–290.

18 Paunio 2013: 52–54, 157, 175–176, 191–192; Paunio & Lindroos-Hovinheimo 2010: 396–397.

19 Leczykiewicz 2008.

20 Paunio 2013.

system. By creating opportunities for '*judicial choice*'[21] to be the guiding criterion in the CJEU's decision-making, ambiguity serves as a complement to Paunio's discursive model of legal certainty, and not its antithesis, and thus contributes to greater stability of the system.[22] This overarching theory explains why the Court of Justice's strategic resolution of ambiguity in the Case Studies from Type 1 and Type 2 demonstrated remarkable endurance in the face of the challenges by subsequent case-law in *the long term*.

However, this proved not to be the case with Type 3, in the sense that details of the formula from the Type 3 example were neither revisited, nor overruled, but perhaps *sidelined* by the Court in the succeeding case-law. The origins of the ambiguity-based legal solution in the Type 1 and Type 2 examples could be traced back directly to the legislative text, thus having the benefit of a more legitimate provenance. The *Åkerberg Fransson* formula is the result of the Court's own invention of a term, which is unconnected to the Treaty provision, and a pragmatically enforced model of interchangeability, which is not semantically or pragmatically supported by the legislative text. This shows that ambiguity has strategic value not only as a long-term, but also as a *short-term*, solution in the CJEU's decision-making process on systemic problems of great constitutional significance for the authority of EU law. Having used the production of ambiguity for the strategically advantageous resolution of a certain legal problem, the Court of Justice prefers to then *isolate*, but not overrule, the legal solution articulated in the language of ambiguity. This decision has the dual effect of shielding the strategically produced ambiguity from further scrutiny and of precluding it from spreading its influence in subsequent case-law.

The Circumstances in which the CJEU Would Strategically Produce or Strategically Resolve Ambiguity

The Type of Case

The research methods, detailed in Chapter 3 of Part 1 ("A Framework for Analysis"), proved to be effective in the search for relevant examples of ambiguity in EU law. Accordingly, a set of characteristic traits of a case that is likely to contain a sample of ambiguity that is strategically significant for the implementation of the authority of EU law has now emerged. For instance, it was confirmed that such ambiguity may be found in a preliminary ruling by the CJEU, which has been decided by the Grand Chamber and which is accompanied by a great number of observations by the Member States. The initial expectation of the relevant areas of law has also been confirmed, so ambiguity of this kind is probably present in the CJEU's case-law on fundamental freedoms and the internal market, fundamental rights, EU citizenship, and the Area of Freedom, Security,

21 Pollicino 2004.
22 Paunio 2013: 53–54.

and Justice. The same goes for cases concerning Treaty provisions that deal with tasks, objectives, and principles of the Treaties. Finally, it might also be the case that such examples of ambiguity may be found in historically significant and/or controversial leading cases of EU law, which attract great academic interest.

The Type of Situation

Based on the insight gained from the selected Case Studies, one can conclude that relevant examples of ambiguity are also likely to be found in situations where there is a clash between legal doctrines of great constitutional significance with grave implications for the principle of the primacy of EU law (e.g. mutual trust and the protection of fundamental rights in *Melloni*). The same is true for cases where there is the need to negotiate the overlap between two or more areas of EU law through prioritisation, especially if this includes an underdeveloped or contentious area of EU law (*Melloni*). Moreover, ambiguity of this kind is also likely to be found in a dispute concerning the limitation of the scope of the Charter of Fundamental Rights of the EU (*Åkerberg Fransson*). Where there is interchangeable use of divergent terms by the CJEU, such ambiguity might also come into play (*Åkerberg Fransson*). A dispute surrounding the interpretation of a particular term of EU law might also revolve around this kind of ambiguity (*Åkerberg Fransson*, *Keck*). Finally, a relevant example of ambiguity might be found in an area of law where a legal rule is drafted so broadly that it impedes the effective and practicable course of the adjudication process through the preliminary ruling procedure (*Keck*) or an area of law where there is a serious coherence deficit (*Ruiz Zambrano/Dereci*).

The Advantages and Disadvantages of the CJEU's Strategic Production or Strategic Resolution of Ambiguity

Each example of ambiguity became the foundation of a legal solution that was preferred by the CJEU over any other (more traditional) methods of resolving the legal problem at hand. At this stage, it would be a useful to contemplate the strategic advantages and disadvantages of ambiguity (production or resolution) when compared to the alternative solutions available in each Case Study.

In *Keck*, it was made clear that ambiguity resolution constituted an innovative solution that had the potential for long-term consistency, unlike the more narrow and predictable solution offered by AG Van Gerven. The strategic resolution of ambiguity in *Keck* was also preferred over AG Jacobs's solution that had the advantage of innovation but was equally formalistic. As opposed to the CJEU's strategic ambiguity resolution, this method would have done nothing to isolate the praiseworthy *Cassis de Dijon* doctrine from the influence of the faulty *Dassonville* formula. Further, the CJEU could have followed through with AG Sharpston's Opinion in *Ruiz Zambrano*, but it would have produced mixed results when it comes to the strategic usefulness of the formula and it would have probably also constituted an ambiguity-based solution. Ambiguity is a solution that is largely self-contained, since it does not require the development of any additional principles or pertinent examples. All of the necessary ingredients for an interpretation that is conceptually well-rounded are already there, in the legislative text. Its flexibility and streamlined simplicity are especially appreciated in the resolution of legal problems such as *Melloni*, where every word of the Court's pronouncement could have grave implications for the principle of primacy of EU law. In contrast, ambiguity production such as the one in *Åkerberg Fransson*, requires a tremendous investment of time, energy, and forethought to execute. It could also be a rather convoluted exercise with unpredictable results.

To summarise, the strategic advantages of a legal solution based on the strategic production or strategic resolution of ambiguity, as perceived by the CJEU in comparison to alternative solutions, could be the capacity for innovation and sweeping constitutional change on a large scale and in the long term. It is also a self-contained solution of great flexibility and simplicity, with the latter advantage being only valid in cases of the strategic resolution of ambiguity. The disadvantages of the strategic production or strategic resolution of ambiguity include excessive formalism, complexity and unpredictability, with the latter two disadvantages being only valid in cases in the strategic production of ambiguity.

Conclusion

This book was written in response to the need to determine the strategic value of ambiguity for the authority of EU law. A selection of relevant examples from the CJEU's preliminary rulings with the greatest significance for the implementation of the authority of EU law was collected and systematised in a typology of examples of ambiguity within this context. Each Case Study underwent linguistic and legal analysis of ambiguity found in the EU Treaty text or in the wording of the CJEU's preliminary rulings. As a result, it was established that ambiguity was not always strategically used by the CJEU for the purposes of judicial activism (Type 1 and Type 3). Where the CJEU strategically used ambiguity for the purposes of judicial restraint (Type 2), the results were disappointing in terms of achieving greater coherence and acceptability.

Consequently, this book proposed an alternative theory that more accurately and completely describes the strategic value of ambiguity for the authority of EU law: *ambiguity is a desirable systemic feature of the EU legal system that facilitates the implementation of the authority of EU law by ensuring greater flexibility, so that the EU legal order could enjoy greater efficiency and stability.* This theory combined the ideas that ambiguity is a "desirable feature" of efficient communication[23] and ambiguity in the EU legal order is capable of ensuring flexibility and stability as a supplement to legal certainty.[24]

23 Piantadosi, Tily, & Gibson 2012: 281–282, 288–290.
24 Paunio 2013: 52–54, 157, 175–176, 191–192; Paunio & Lindroos-Hovinheimo 2010: 396–397.

Further, this book also produced a summary of the circumstances in which the strategic production or resolution of ambiguity is likely to be observed in the CJEU's preliminary rulings. Additionally, this book discussed the strategic advantages and disadvantages of ambiguity-based solutions to a given legal problem over alternative solutions, viewed from the perspective of the CJEU.

In the end, this book offered a basic, likely incomplete, account of the workings of ambiguity in EU law. Nevertheless, the scale and significance of the object of study is not such that would allow for an exhaustive and detailed record of its workings. Instead, this book offered a conceptual and analytical framework and a set of appropriate research methods that would assist further investigation into the nature of this phenomenon in the future.

Appendix A

Multilingual Analysis – *Åkerberg Fransson* (C-617/10)[1]

1. "Implementation"

West Germanic Language Family[2]

English: *implementation* – "the process of putting a decision or plan into effect; execution".[3]

German: *die Durchführung* – "carrying out/through, execution, realization; [Gesetz] implementation, implement; enforcement".[4]

North Germanic Language Family

Danish: *anvendelsen* – "employment, use, application".[5]

Swedish: *tillämpning* – "putting into action".[6]

1 An earlier version of this information has been presented in: Kartalova, Sofiya (2018). The Strategic Value of Ambiguity in Divergent Terms Used Interchangeably in the CJEU's Preliminary Rulings. iCourts Working Paper Series, No. 136/2018. Available at SSRN: https://ssrn.com/abstract=3214463 or http://dx.doi.org/10.2139/ssrn.3214463.

2 For the purposes of the study of all three terms, the main language families in the EU are West Germanic, North Germanic, Romance, Slavic/Slavonic, Uralic, Hellenic. For more information: www.britannica.com/topic/Romance-languages, last accessed on 4 April 2018; www.britannica.com/topic/Slavic-languages, last accessed on 3 April 2018; www.britannica.com/topic/Germanic-languages, last accessed on 3 April 2018; www.britannica.com/topic/Uralic-languages, last accessed on 2 June 2019; www.britannica.com/topic/Greek-language, last accessed on 2 June 2019.

3 https://en.oxforddictionaries.com/definition/implementation, last accessed on 20 March 2018.

4 Wüstefeld, Barbara (1991) Law Dictionary: Fachwörterbuch der anglo-amerikanischen Rechtssprache einschließlich wirtschaftlicher und politischer Begriffe/Technical Dictionary of the Anglo-American Legal Terminology including Commercial and Political Terms. Walter de Gruyter: Berlin, New York. p. 407

5 Magnussen, Johs. & Madsen, Otto & Vinterberg, Hermann (1954). McKay's Modern English–Swedish and Swedish–English Dictionary. New York: David McKay Company. p. 19

6 Collin, P.H. & Fisher, David & Wiman, Mikael (1990). English–Swedish Dictionary of Law. Great Britain: Peter Collin Publishing. p. 152.

Romance Language Family

***French*:** *matten en œuvre* – "implementation".[7]

***Spanish*:** *aplicación* – "enforcement to make effective; to put into execution".[8]

Slavic/Slavonic Language Family

***Polish*:** *stosowania* – "application" in the sense of "uniform application of law".[9]

***Bulgarian*:** прилагане – "applying … application; execution".[10]

Uralic Language Family

***Finnish*:** *solvetamista* (derived from *sovellus*) – "application; adaptation".[11]

Hellenic Language Family

***Greek*:** *εφαρμόζουν* (derived from the verb *εφαρμόζω*) – εφαρμόζω (v.): "to fit, apply, put into effect".[12]

2. "(Scope/field of) application"

West Germanic Language Family

***English*:** *(scope/field of) application* – "the action of putting something into operation (practical use or relevance)".[13]

***German*:** *der Anwendungsbereich* – "area (scope, field, range) of application, application range, applicability, coverage; (Gesetz, Abkommen) scope".[14]

North Germanic Language Family

***Danish*:** *anvendelsesområdet* – "sphere (field) of application; sphere of an act; application".[15]

7 https://dictionary.cambridge.org/dictionary/french-english/oeuvre?q=%C5%93uvre, last accessed on 19 March 2018.

8 Solis, Gerardo & Gasteazoro, Jr.. Raul A. (eds.) (1992). West's Spanish–English/English–Spanish Law Dictionary, St. Paul, Minn.: West Publishing Co. p. 28.

9 Bar, Ludwik (ed.) (1986). Polish–English Dictionary of Legal Terms. Polish Academy of Sciences: Institute of State and Law: Wroclaw, Warszawa, Krakow, Gdansk, Lodz. p. 111.

10 Atanassova, T. & Rankova, M. & Rousev, R. & Spassov, D. & Philipov, Vl. & Chakalov, G. (1990). Bulgarian–English Dictionary (Volume II O – Я).Sofia: Naouka I Izkustvo Publishing House, p. 734.

11 Alanne, V.S. (1968). Finnish–English General Dictionary. Werner Sönderström Osakeyhtio. p. 814.

12 Pring, J.T. (1965). The Oxford Dictionary of Modern Greek (Greek–English). Oxford University Press. p. 75.

13 https://en.oxforddictionaries.com/definition/application, last accessed on 20 March 2018.

14 Wüstefeld, Barbara (1991) Law Dictionary: Fachwörterbuch der anglo-amerikanischen Rechtssprache einschließlich wirtschaftlicher und politischer Begriffe/Technical Dictionary of the Anglo-American Legal Terminology including Commercial and Political Terms. Walter de Gruyter: Berlin, New York. p. 133.

15 Vinterberg, Hermann & Bodelsen, C.A. (1998). Dansk-Engelsk Ordbog. Gyldenhal (Gyldendalske Boghandel, Copenhagen. p. 99.

This term was included in the expression "inden for Traktatens ~ ", which in the context of the EU means "within the purview (or the scope of application)".[16]

Swedish: *tillämpningsområdet* – "putting into action"[17] (see above: the same term as the one used for "implementation").

Romance Language Family

French: *application* – "applying, application".[18]

Spanish: *aplicación* – "enforcement to make effective; to put into execution"[19] (see above: the same term as the one used for "implementation").

Slavic/Slavonic Language Family

Polish: *zastosowanie* – "application".[20]

Bulgarian: *приложно поле* – "field (sphere) of application"[21] – a collocation, comprised of an adjective and a noun:

приложен (adj.): "applied, executed".[22]

поле (n.): "a field of activity, a sphere/scope of action".[23]

Uralic Language Family

Finnish: *soveltamisaala* – "sphere (range of application (t. of adaptation) … the range within which a th. may be applied".[24]

Hellenic Language Family

Greek: *αρμοδιοτήτων* (derived from the noun *αρμοδιοτής*) – αρμοδιοτής (n.) : "competency, province".[25]

16 Vinterberg, Hermann & Bodelsen, C.A. (1998). Dansk-Engelsk Ordbog. Gyldenhal (Gyldendalske Boghandel, Copenhagen. p. 99.

17 Collin, P.H. & Fisher, David & Wiman, Mikael (1990). English–Swedish Dictionary of Law. Great Britain: Peter Collin Publishing. p. 152.

18 https://dictionary.cambridge.org/dictionary/french-english/application, last accessed on 19 March 2018.

19 Solis, Gerardo & Gasteazoro, Jr.. Raul A. (eds.) (1992). West's Spanish–English/English–Spanish Law Dictionary, St. Paul, Minn.: West Publishing Co. p. 28.

20 Bar, Ludwik (ed.) (1986). Polish–English Dictionary of Legal Terms. Polish Academy of Sciences: Institute of State and Law: Wroclaw, Warszawa, Krakow, Gdansk, Lodz. p. 154.

21 A Bulgarian native speaker would normally translate "приложно поле" to "field (sphere) of application".

22 Atanassova, T. & Rankova, M. & Rousev, R. & Spassov, D. & Philipov, Vl. & Chakalov, G. (1990). Bulgarian–English Dictionary (Volume II О – Я). Sofia: Naouka I Izkustvo Publishing House, p. 734.

23 Atanassova, T. & Rankova, M. & Rousev, R. & Spassov, D. & Philipov, Vl. & Chakalov, G. (1990). Bulgarian–English Dictionary (Volume II О – Я). Sofia: Naouka I Izkustvo Publishing House, p. 669.

24 Alanne, V.S. (1968). Finnish–English General Dictionary. Werner Sönderström Osakeyhtio. p. 814.

25 Pring, J.T. (1965). The Oxford Dictionary of Modern Greek (Greek–English). Oxford University Press. p. 27.

3. "Applicability"

West Germanic Language Family

English: *applicability* – "the quality of being relevant or appropriate"[26]

German: *die Anwendbarkeit* – "applicability; availability; practicability; usability ... ; ~ eines Gesetzes – operation of a law".[27]

North Germanic Language Family

Danish: *anvendelse* – "employment, use, application".[28]

Included in the following collocations: "finde unmiddelbar ~" ("to be directly applicable"),[29] "bestemmelserne finder ~ " ("the rules shall apply"),[30] "loven finder ikke ~på" ("this law is not applicable to ... : to invoke before the Court of Justice the inapplicability of the regulation").[31]

Swedish[32]: ***tillämplig*** – "applicable (relevant) to".[33]

Romance Language Family

French: *applicabilité* – "applicability".[34]

Spanish: *applicabilidad* (derived from the adjective *aplicable*) – "applicability".[35] *aplicable* (adj.): "applicable",[36] "that which can be or should be applied".[37]

Slavic/Slavonic Language Family

Polish: *stosowanie/zastosowanie* – "the applicability of European Union law". (stosowanie) and "the applicability of fundamental rights" (zastosowanie).

26 https://en.oxforddictionaries.com/definition/applicability, last accessed on 20 March 2018.

27 Wüstefeld, Barbara (1991) Law Dictionary: Fachwörterbuch der anglo-amerikanischen Rechtssprache einschließlich wirtschaftlicher und politischer Begriffe/Technical Dictionary of the Anglo-American Legal Terminology including Commercial and Political Terms. Walter de Gruyter: Berlin, New York. p. 132.

28 Magnussen, Johs. & Madsen, Otto & Vinterberg, Hermann (1954). McKay's Modern English–Swedish and Swedish–English Dictionary. New York: David McKay Company. p. 19.

29 Vinterberg, Hermann & Bodelsen, C.A. (1998). Dansk-Engelsk Ordbog. Gyldenhal (Gyldendalske Boghandel, Copenhagen. p. 98.

30 Vinterberg, Hermann & Bodelsen, C.A. (1998). Dansk-Engelsk Ordbog. Gyldenhal (Gyldendalske Boghandel, Copenhagen. p. 99.

31 Vinterberg, Hermann & Bodelsen, C.A. (1998). Dansk-Engelsk Ordbog. Gyldenhal (Gyldendalske Boghandel, Copenhagen. p. 99.

32 Language of the case.

33 Nöjd, Ruben & Tornberg, Astrid & Ångström, Margareta (1959). McKay's Modern English–Swedish and Swedish–English Dictionary. New York: David McKay Company. p. 187.

34 https://dictionary.cambridge.org/dictionary/french-english/applicabilite?q=applicabilit%C3%A9, last accessed on 20 March 2018

35 www.collinsdictionary.com/dictionary/spanish-english/aplicabilidad, last accessed on 19 March 2018.

36 www.collinsdictionary.com/dictionary/spanish-english/aplicable, last accessed on 19 March 2018.

37 "Que se puede o debe aplicar" https://es.oxforddictionaries.com/definition/aplicable, last accessed on 19 March 2018.

stosowanie: "application (as in: uniform application of law)".[38]

zastosowanie: "applicable/inapplicable" ("możliwy/niemożliwy do zastosowania").[39]

Note: A consultation with a Polish native speaker confirmed that the two terms seem to have the same meaning, but their use depends on context.

Bulgarian: *приложимост* – "applicability; workability".[40]

Uralic Language Family

Finnish: *sovellettavuus – soveltuvuus* (n.): "adaptability, fitness, suitability; applicability, applicableness".[41]

sovellettava (v.): "to be applied, fitted, adjusted to; applicable to; that may be applied/fitted to; fitted/adjusted to the needs of a th.".[42]

Hellenic Language Family

Greek: *δυνατότητα* (derived from adjective *δυνατός*) – δυνατός (adj.): "possible ... able".[43]

38 Bar, Ludwik (ed.) (1986). Polish–English Dictionary of Legal Terms. Polish Academy of Sciences: Institute of State and Law: Wroclaw, Warszawa, Krakow, Gdansk, Lodz. p. 111.

39 https://en.pons.com/translate?q=zastosowanie&l=enpl&in=ac_pl&lf=en, last accessed on 20 March 2018.

40 Atanassova, T. & Rankova, M. & Rousev, R. & Spassov, D. & Philipov, Vl. & Chakalov, G. (1990). Bulgarian–English Dictionary (Volume II О – Я).Sofia: Naouka I Izkustvo Publishing House, p. 735.

41 Alanne, V.S. (1968). Finnish–English General Dictionary. Werner Sönderström Osakeyhtio. p. 814.

42 Alanne, V.S. (1968). Finnish–English General Dictionary. Werner Sönderström Osakeyhtio. p. 814.

43 Pring, J.T. (1965). The Oxford Dictionary of Modern Greek (Greek–English). Oxford University Press. p. 56.

Appendix B

Multilingual Analysis – *Keck* (Joined cases C-267/91 and C-268/91)

1. The noun "measure" in the term "measures having equivalent effect to qualitative restrictions"

Note: In the interest of greater accuracy, the original version of the term is presented in its plural form, as it appears in the legal text. For the same reason, the translated version is displayed in its singular form, as it appears in the respective dictionary.

West Germanic Language Family

English: *measures* – "a way of achieving something, or a method for dealing with a situation";[1] "A legislative enactment proposed or adopted".[2]

German: *Maßnahmen* – "measure".[3]

North Germanic Language Family

Danish: *foranstaltninger* – "measure".[4]

Swedish: *åtgärder* – translation not found.[5]

Romance Language Family

French: *mesures* – "measure, step".[6]

1 Cambridge Dictionary: https://dictionary.cambridge.org/dictionary/english/measure last accessed on 15 July 2019.

2 Oxford English Dictionary: www.oed.com/view/Entry/115506?rskey=GdLRPU&result=1&isAdvanced=false#eid last accessed on 15 July 2019.

3 PONS Dictionary: https://de.pons.com/%C3%BCbersetzung?q=Ma%C3%9Fnahme&l=deen&in=ac_de&lf=de&qnac=ma%C3%9Fna last accessed on 15 July 2019.

4 The original definition in German reads: " … Maßnahme … " (translation in English done by the author). Bergstrøm-Nielsen, Henrik & Lange, Henrik & Larsen, Henry Verner (1991). *Dansk-tysk ordbog*. Munksgaards Store Ordbøger. p. 248.

5 Due to a lack of access to a Swedish–English dictionary that includes this term, the translation was not found.

6 Cambridge Dictionary: https://dictionary.cambridge.org/dictionary/french-english/mesure last accessed on 15 July 2019.

Spanish: *medidas* – “measure … a plan of action or something done”.[7]

Slavic/Slavonic Language Family
Polish: *crodki* – “resources … facilities: the means to do something … means”.[8]
Bulgarian: мерки – “measure”.[9]

Uralic Language Family
Finnish: toimenpiteet – “measure”.[10]

Hellenic Language Family
Greek: μέτρα – “measure”.[11]

2. The noun “requirement” in the term “rules that lay down requirements”.

Note: In the interest of greater accuracy, the original version of the term is presented in its plural form, as it appears in the legal text. For the same reason, the translated version is displayed in its singular form, as it appears in the respective dictionary.

West Germanic Language Family
English: *requirements* – “Something called for or demanded; a condition which must be complied with. Frequently in ***plural***”.[12]
German: *Vorschriften* – “regulation … rule … instruction … provision … requirement”.[13]

North Germanic Language Family
Danish: *betingelser* – “condition”, “precondition”, “prerequisite”, “term”[14]

7 Cambridge Dictionary: https://dictionary.cambridge.org/dictionary/spanish-english/medida last accessed on 15 July 2019.
8 Cambridge Dictionary: https://dictionary.cambridge.org/dictionary/polish-english/srodki?q=%C5%9Brodki+ last accessed on 15 July 2019.
9 Atanassova, T. & Rankova, M. & Rousev, R. & Spassov, D. & Philipov, Vl. & Chakalov, G. (1990). Bulgarian–English Dictionary (Volume I A–H). Sofia: Naouka I Izkustvo Publishing House, pp. 447–448.
10 Finnish–English Dictionary (Edlanti – Suomi Sanakirja) (1998). The Netherlands: Berlitz Publishing Company, p. 286.
11 The original definition in German reads: “ … Maßnahme … ” (translation in English done by the author) Karagiannakis, Dimitrios (1997). *PONS-Kompaktwörterbuch Neugriechisch-Deutsch*. Stuttgart: Ernst Klett Verlag GmbH. pp. 369–370.
12 Oxford English Dictionary: www.oed.com/view/Entry/163260?redirectedFrom=requirement#eid last accessed on 15 July 2019.
13 PONS Dictionary: https://de.pons.com/%C3%BCbersetzung?q=Vorschrift&l=deen&in=ac_de&lf=de&qnac=vorschrift last accessed on 15 July 2019.
14 The original definition in German reads: “ … Bedingung … Vorbedingung … Voraussetzung … Kondition … ” (translation in English done by the author). Bergstrøm-Nielsen,

Swedish: *villkor* – "condition … term[s] … stipulation … provision … circumstance[s]".[15]

Romance Language Family
French: *conditions* – "condition(s) … (plural) terms".[16]
Spanish: *requisitos* – "requirement".[17]

Slavic/Slavonic Language Family
Polish: official translation not available.[18]
Bulgarian: official translation not available.[19]

Uralic Language Family
Finnish: *edellytykset* – translation not found.[20]

Hellenic Language Family
Greek: όρους – "condition", "term".[21]

3. The noun "arrangement" in the term "selling arrangements".

West Germanic Language Family
English: *arrangement* – "a plan for how something will happen".[22]

Henrik & Lange, Henrik & Larsen, Henry Verner (1991). *Dansk-tysk ordbog.* Munksgaards Store Ordbøger. p. 93.

15 Bohman, Jan (1988). *Primas Swedish-English Dictionary.* Bokförlaget Prisma Stockholm. p. 587.

16 Collins Dictionary: www.collinsdictionary.com/dictionary/french-english/condition last accessed on 15 July 2019.
PONS Dictionary: https://en.pons.com/translate?q=condition&l=enfr&in=fr&lf=fr&qnac=#result-sig-61618324-0 last accessed on 15 July 2019.

17 Lexico Dictionary (powered by Oxford University Press and Dictionary.com): www.lexico.com/es-en/traducir/requisito last accessed on 15 July 2019.

18 There is no official translation in Polish of the *Keck* preliminary ruling available at the EUR-Lex database: https://eur-lex.europa.eu/legal-content/EN/ALL/?uri=CELEX%3A61991CJ0267 last accessed on 15 July 2019.

19 There is no official translation in Bulgarian of the *Keck* preliminary ruling available at the EUR-Lex database: https://eur-lex.europa.eu/legal-content/EN/ALL/?uri=CELEX%3A61991CJ0267 last accessed on 15 July 2019.

20 Due to a lack of access to a Finnish–English dictionary that includes this term, the translation was not found.

21 The original definition in German reads: " … Bedingung … Kondition … Terminus … " (translation in English done by the author) Karagiannakis, Dimitrios (1997). *PONS-Kompaktwörterbuch Neugriechisch-Deutsch.* Stuttgart: Ernst Klett Verlag GmbH. p. 423.

22 Cambridge Dictionary: https://dictionary.cambridge.org/dictionary/english/arrangement last accessed on 15 July 2019.

"Disposition of measures for the accomplishment of a purpose; preparations for successful performance".[23]

German: *Verkaufsmodalitäten (die Modalität)* – "provision … condition".[24]

North Germanic Language Family

Danish: *former* – "form", "shape".[25]

Swedish: *försäljningsformer* – *försäljning*: "sale";[26] *form* (noun): "form", "mould".[27]

Romance Language Family

French:[28] *modalités* – "mode",[29] "1. terms … practical details … methods … 2. (LAW) clauses".[30]

Spanish: *modalidades* – *modalidad* (noun): "mode or form of existence or manifestation of something".[31]

Slavic/Slavonic Language Family

Polish: official translation not available.[32]

Bulgarian: official translation not available.[33]

23 Oxford English Dictionary: www.oed.com/view/Entry/10968?redirectedFrom=arrangement#eid last accessed on 15 July 2019.

24 PONS Dictionary: https://de.pons.com/%C3%BCbersetzung?q=Modalit%C3%A4t&l=deen&in=ac_de&lf=de&qnac=modalit%C3%A4 last accessed on 17 July 2019.

25 The original definition in German reads: " … Form … Gestalt … " (translation in English done by the author). Bergstrøm-Nielsen, Henrik & Lange, Henrik & Larsen, Henry Verner (1991). *Dansk-tysk ordbog*. Munksgaards Store Ordbøger. p. 261.

26 The original definition in German reads: "Verkauf" (translation in English done by the author) PONS Dictionary: https://de.pons.com/%C3%BCbersetzung/schwedisch-deutsch/f%C3%B6rs%C3%A4ljning last accessed on 17 July 2019.

27 Bohman, Jan (1988). *Primas Swedish-English Dictionary*. Bokförlaget Prisma Stockholm. p. 144.

28 Language of the case (*Keck* was a preliminary reference by *Tribunal de grande instance de Strasbourg* – France).

29 Cambridge Dictionary: https://dictionary.cambridge.org/dictionary/french-english/modalite?q=modalit%C3%A9 last accessed on 15 July 2019.

30 PONS Dictionary: https://en.pons.com/translate?q=modalite&l=enfr&in=fr&lf=fr&qnac= last accessed 15 July 2019.

31 The original definition in Spanish reads: "Modo o forma de ser o de manifestarse una cosa" (translation in English done by the author). Lexico Dictionary (powered by Oxford University Press and Dictionary.com): www.lexico.com/es/definicion/modalidad last accessed on 15 July 2019.

32 There is no official translation in Polish of the *Keck* preliminary ruling available at the EUR-Lex database: https://eur-lex.europa.eu/legal-content/EN/ALL/?uri=CELEX%3A61991CJ0267 last accessed on 15 July 2019.

33 There is no official translation in Bulgarian of the *Keck* preliminary ruling available at the EUR-Lex database: https://eur-lex.europa.eu/legal-content/EN/ALL/?uri=CELEX%3A61991CJ0267 last accessed on 15 July 2019.

Uralic Language Family
Finnish: myyntijärjestelyjä – translation not found.[34]

Hellenic Language Family
Greek: μορφές – "form", "shape".[35]

34 Due to a lack of access to a Finnish–English dictionary that includes this term, the translation was not found.

35 The original definition in German reads: " … Form … Gestalt … " (translation in English done by the author) Karagiannakis, Dimitrios (1997). *PONS-Kompaktwörterbuch Neugriechisch-Deutsch*. Stuttgart: Ernst Klett Verlag GmbH. p. 378.

Bibliography

Literature: alphabetical order

Adam, Stanislas & van Elsuwege, Peter (2012). Citizenship Rights and the Federal Balance between the European Union and its Member States: Comment on *Dereci*. *European Law Review*, 37(2), 176–190.

Adams, Kenneth A. & Kaye, Alan S. (2006). Revisiting the Ambiguity of "And" and "Or" in Legal Drafting. *St John's Law Review*, 80, 1167–1198.

Aljanati, Lucie Pacho (2015). *The Court of Justice of the European Union's Case Law on Linguistic Divergences (2007–2013): Interpretation Criteria and Implications for the Translation of EU Legislation* (PhD Thesis). Autonomous University of Barcelona, University of Geneva.

Alkema, Evert A., Van der Hulle, Robert, & Van der Hulle, Rick (2015). Safeguard Rules in the European Legal Order: The Relationship between Article 53 of the European Convention of Human Rights and Article 53 of the Charter of Fundamental Rights of the European Union. *Human Rights Law Journal*, 35(1–8), 8–20.

Alter, Karen J., Helfer, Lawrence R., & Rask Madsen, Mikael (2018). International Court Authority in a Complex World. In Alter, Helfer & Rask Madsen (Eds.), *International Court Authority* (pp. 3–23). Oxford: Oxford University Press.

Alter, Karen J., Helfer, Laurence R., & Rask Madsen, Mikael (2016). How Context Shapes the Authority of International Courts. *Law and Contemporary Problems*, 79(1), 1–36.

Anagnostaras, Georgios (2016). Mutual Confidence is Not Blind Trust! Fundamental Rights Protection and the Execution of the European Arrest Warrant: *Aranyosi and Căldăraru*. *Common Market Law Review*, 53, 1675–1704.

Anagnostaras, Georgios (2017). Solange III? Fundamental Rights Protection Under The National Identity Review. *European Law Review*, 42(2), 234–253.

Anesa, Patrizia (2014). Defining Legal Vagueness: A Contradiction in Terms? *Pólemos*, 8(1), 193–209.

Aone, Chinatsu (1991). *Treatment of Plurals and Collective-Distributive Ambiguity in Natural Language Understanding*. Doctoral dissertation. Department of Linguistics. The University of Texas at Austin.

Avbelj, Matej (2017). Pluralism and Systemic Defiance in the EU. In A. Jakab & D. Kochenov (Eds.), The Enforcement of EU Law and Values: Ensuring Member States' Compliance (pp. 44–61). Oxford University Press.

Azoulai, Loïc (2011). "Euro-Bonds": The Ruiz Zambrano Judgment or the Real Invention of EU Citizenship. *Perspectives on Federalism*, 3(2), E-31–E-39. ISSN: 2036-5438.

Baaij, Coernelis J. W. (2012). Fifty Years of Multilingual Interpretation in the European Union. In Solan & Tiersma (Eds.), *The Oxford Handbook of Language and Law* (pp. 217–232). Oxford: Oxford University Press.

Bajčić, Martina (2018). Coping with Vague EU Legal Concepts. G. G. Sander et al. (Eds.), *Transnational, European, and National Labour Relations* (pp. 97–107). New York: Springer.

Baquero Cruz, Julio (2008). What's Left of the Charter? Reflections on Law and Political Mythology. *Maastricht Journal of European and Comparative Law*, 15(1), 65–75.

Barker, Chris (1992). Group Terms in English: Representing Groups as Atoms. *Journal of Semantics*, 9, 69–93.

Barnard, Catherine (1994). Sunday Trading: A Drama in Five Acts. *The Modern Law Review*, 57, 449–460.

Barnard, Catherine (2013). *The Substantive Law of the EU: The Four Freedoms.* Oxford: Oxford University Press.

Baubock, Rainer (2014). The Three Levels of Citizenship within the European Union. *German Law Journal*, 15(5), 751–764.

Bernard, Nicolas (1996). Discrimination and Free Movement in EC Law. *International and Comparative Law Quarterly*, 45(1), 82–108.

Bernard, Nicolas (2010). On the Art of Not Mixing One's Drinks: *Dassonville* and *Cassis de Dijon* Revisited. In Maduro & Azoulai (Eds.), *The Past and Future of EU Law: The Classics of EU Law Revisited on the 50th Anniversary of the Rome Treaty* (pp. 456–464). Oxford and Portland: Hart Publishing.

Bernitz, Ulf (2015). The Åkerberg Fransson Case. Ne bis in idem: Double Procedures for Tax Surcharge and Tax Offences Not Possible. In Nergelius & Kristofferson (Eds.), *Human Rights in Contemporary European Law* (pp. 191–209). Bloomsbury Publishing.

Besselink, Leonard F. M. (2014). The Parameters of Constitutional Conflict After *Melloni*. *European Current Law*, 10, 1169–1189.

Besson, Samantha & Utzinger, André (2007). Introduction: Future Challenges of EU Citizenship : Facing a Wide-Open Pandora's Box. *European Law Journal*, 13(5), 573–590.

Besson, Samantha & Utzinger, André (2008). Toward European Citizenship. *Journal of Social Philosophy*, 39(2), 185–208. DOI: 10.1111/j.1467-9833.2008.00421.x.

Bierwisch, Manfred & Schreuder, Robert (1992). From concepts to lexical terms. *Cognition*, 42, 23–60.

Billing, Vojtech (2012). Supranational Fundamental Rights or Primacy of Sovereignty? Legal Effects of the So-Called Opt-Out from the EU Charter of Fundamental Rights. *European Law Journal*, 18(2), 251–268.

Bonelli, Mateo (2018). The *Taricco* Saga and the Consolidation of Judicial Dialogue in the European Union. *Maastricht Journal of European and Comparative Law*, 25(3), 357–373.

Borowski, Martin (2018). Virtues and Vices of Two Layers of Fundamental Rights: Lessons from the Protocol on the Charter of the Fundamental Rights of the EU. *Revista Brasileira Estudos Politicos*, 117, 363–442.

Bratanić, Maja & Lončar, Maja (2016). The Myth of EU Terminology Harmonization on National and EU Level. In Šarčević (Ed.), *Language and Culture in EU Law: Multidisciplinary Perspectives* (pp. 207–218). London and New York: Routledge.

Brink, Marijn van den (2019). EU Citizenship and (Fundamental) Rights: Empirical, Normative, and Conceptual Problems. *European Law Journal*, 25(1), 21–36. https://doi.org/10.1111/eulj.12300.

Brisson, C. (2003). Plurals, ALL, and the Nonuniformity of Collective Predication. *Linguistics and Philosophy*, 26, 129–184.

Brittain, Stephen (2013). The EU Charter of Fundamental Rights and the Member States: An Originalist Analysis. *Dublin University Law Journal*, 36, 277–310.

Broberg, Morten (2017). Preliminary References as a Means of Enforcing EU Law. In Jakab & Kochenov (Eds.), *The Enforcement of EU Law and Values: Ensuring Member States' Compliance* (pp. 99–111). Oxford: Oxford University Press. DOI:10.1093/acprof:oso/9780198746560.003.0007.

Burr, Isolde (2013). Article 55 [Languages and Deposit of the Treaty] (ex-Article 53 TEU and ex-Article 314 EC). In Blanke & Mangiameli (Eds.), *The Treaty on European Union (TEU): A Commentary* (pp. 1461–1525). Heidelberg, New York, Dordrecht, London: Springer. DOI: 10.1007/978-3-642-31706-4.

Byers, Michael (2021). Still Agreeing to Disagree: International Security and Constructive Ambiguity. *Journal on the Use of Force and International Law*, 8(1), 91–114.

Cannizzaro, Enzo (1997). Producing 'Reverse Discrimination' through the Exercise of EC Competences. *Yearbook of European Law*, 17(1), 29–46.

Cao, Deborah (2007). Inter-lingual Uncertainty in Bilingual and Multilingual Law. *Journal of Pragmatics*, 39, 69–83.

Carrubba, Clifford J. & Gabel, Matthew & Hankla, Charles (2008). Judicial Behaviour under Political Constraints: Evidence from the European Court of Justice. *American Political Science Review*, 102(4), 435–452.

Carston, Robyn (2013). Legal Texts and Canons of Construction: A View from Current Pragmatic Theory. In Freeman & Smith (Eds.), *Law and Language* (pp. 8–33). Oxford: Oxford University Press.

Chalmers, Damian (1993). Free Movement of Goods within the European Community: An Unhealthy Addiction to Scotch Whisky? *International and Comparative Law Quarterly*, 42, 269–294.

Chalmers, Damian (2010). Looking Back at *ERT* and its Contribution to an EU Fundamental Rights Agenda. In Maduro & Azoulai (Eds.), *The Past and Future of EU Law: The Classics of EU Law Revisited on the 50th Anniversary of the Rome Treaty* (pp. 140–150). Oxford and Portland: Hart Publishing.

Chalmers, Damian, Davies, Gareth & Monti, Giorgio (2010). *European Union Law: Cases and Materials*. Cambridge, UK: Cambridge University Press.

Champollion, Lucas (2010). *Parts of a Whole: Distributivity as a Bridge between Aspect and Measurement*. A Dissertation in Linguistics (Faculties to the University of Pennsylvania). Publicly Accessible Penn Dissertations. 958. http://repository.upenn.edu/edissertations/958.

Champollion, Lucas (2017). *Parts of a Whole: Distributivity as a Bridge Between Aspect and Measurement*. New York: Oxford University Press.

Chriss, Richard (1995). Note: Keck Considered: A New Doctrinal Model for the Free Movement of Goods in the European Union. *Pace International Law Review*, 7, 149–175.

Chroma, Marta (2011). Synonymy and Polysemy in Legal Terminology and their Applications to Bilingual and Bijural Translation. *Research in Language*, 9(1), 31–50. DOI 10.2478/v10015-011-0004-2.

Conway, Gerard (2012). *The Limits of Legal Reasoning and the European Court of Justice*. Cambridge, UK: Cambridge University Press.

Conway, Gerard M. (2010). *Conflict of norms in European Union Law and the Legal Reasoning of the European Court of Justice* (A Thesis Submitted for the degree Doctor of Philosophy). Brunel University School of Law, the United Kingdom.

Craig, Paul (2011). The ECJ and Ultra Vires Action: A Conceptual Analysis. *Common Market Law Review*, 48, 395–437.

Craig, Paul & De Burca, Gráinne (2011). *EU Law: Text, Cases and Materials*. Oxford: Oxford University Press.

Cruz Villalón, Pedro (2010). 'All the Guidance', ERT and Wachauf. In Maduro & Azoulai (Eds.), *The Past and Future of EU Law: The Classics of EU Law Revisited on the 50th Anniversary of the Rome Treaty* (p.162–169). Oxford and Portland: Hart Publishing.

De Boer, Nik (2013). Addressing Rights Divergences under the Charter: *Melloni*. *Common Market Law Review*, 50, 1083–1104.

De Burca, Gráinne (2015). The Drafting of the European Union Charter of Fundamental Rights. *European Law Review*, 40(6), 799–810.

De Groot, Gerard-Rend & Luk, Ngo Chun (2014). Twenty Years of CJEU Jurisprudence on Citizenship. *German Law Journal*, 15(5), 821–834.

De la Mare, Thomas & Donnelly, Catherine (2011). Preliminary Rulings and EU legal Integration: Evolution and Stasis. In De Burca & Craig (Eds.), *The Evolution of EU Law* (pp. 363–406). Oxford: Oxford University Press.

De Sousa, Pedro Caro (2011). Catch Me If You Can? The Market Freedoms' Ever-expanding Outer Limits. *European Journal of Legal Studies*, 4(2), 149–177.

De Sousa, Pedro Caro (2012a). Negative and Positive Integration in EU Economic Law: Between Strategic Denial and Cognitive Dissonance? *German Law Journal*, 13(8), 979–1012.

De Sousa, Pedro Caro (2012b). Through Contact Lenses, Darkly: Is Identifying Restrictions to Free Movement Harder than Meets the Eye? (Comment on Ker-Optika). *European Law Review*, 37(1), 79–89.

De Witte, Bruno (2013). Tensions in the Multilevel Protection of Fundamental Rights: The Meaning of Article 53 EU Charter. In Silveira & Madeira Froufe & Canotilho (Eds.), *Citizenship and Solidarity in the European Union: From the Charter of Fundamental Rights to the Crisis, the State of the Art* (pp. 205–217). Brussels: Peter Lang.

De Witte, Floris (2011). The End of EU Citizenship and the Means of Non-Discrimination. *Maastricht Journal of European and Comparative Law*, 18(1–2), 86–108. DOI: 10.1177/1023263X1101800105.

Deemter, Kees van (2010). *Not Exactly: In Praise of Vagueness*. Oxford: Oxford University Press.

Derlén, Mattias (2009). *Multilingual Interpretation of European Union Law*. Austin, Boston, Chicago, New York, the Netherlands: Wolters Kluwer.

Derlén, Mattias (2016). A Single Text or a Single Meaning: Multilingual Interpretation of EU Legislation and CJEU Case Law in National Courts. In Šarčević (Ed.), *Language and Culture in EU Law: Multidisciplinary Perspectives* (pp. 53–72). London and New York: Routledge.

Derlén, Mattias & Lindholm, Johan (2010). Article 28 E.C. and Rules on Use: A Step Towards a Workable Doctrine of Measures Having Equivalent Effect to Quantitative Restrictions. *Columbia Journal of European Law*, 16, 191–231.

Derlén, Mattias & Lindholm, Johan (2015). Characteristics of Precedent: The Case Law of the European Court of Justice in Three Dimensions. *German Law Journal*, 16(5), 1074–1097.

Derlén, Mattias & Lindholm, Johan (2017). Is It Good Law? Network Analysis and the CJEU's Internal Market Jurisprudence. *Journal of International Economic Law*, 20, 257–277. DOI: 10.1093/jiel/jgx011.

D'Oliveira, H. U. Jessurun (2011). Court of Justice of the European Union Decision of 2 March 2010, Case C-315/08 *Janko Rottman v. Freistaat Bayern (Case Note 1)* Decoupling Nationality and Union Citizenship? *European Constitutional Law Review*, 7, 138–160. DOI:10.1017/S1574019611100073.

Dolezal, Frederic (2013). Synonymy and Sameness of Meaning: An Introductory Note. *International Journal of Lexicography*, 26(3), 255–259.

Dothan, Shai (2014). *Reputation and Judicial Tactics: A Theory of National and International Courts.* Cambridge: Cambridge University Press. https://doi.org/10.1017/CBO9781139381260.

Dothan, Shai (2019). The Three Traditional Approaches to Treaty Interpretation: A Current Application to the European Court of Human Rights, *Fordham International Law Journal*, 42(3), 765–794.

Dougan, Michael (2015). Judicial Review of Member State Action Under the General Principles and the Charter: Defining the "Scope of Union Law". *Common Market Law Review*, 52, 1201–1246.

Dowty, David R. (1987). Collective Predicates, Distributive Predicates, and 'All'. In Marshall et al. (Eds.), *Proceedings of the 1986 Eastern States Conference on Linguistics (ESCOL)* (pp. 97–116). Columbus: Ohio State University.

Duff, Andrew (2013). *Report on the Draft Protocol on the Application of the Charter of Fundamental Rights of the European Union to the Czech Republic (Article 48(3) of the Treaty on European Union).* Committee on Constitutional Affairs, European Parliament, Plenary sitting of 15.05.2013, 00091/2011 – C7-0385/2011 – 2011/0817 (NLE).

Dunahoo, Kermit L. (1970). Avoiding Inadvertent Syntactic Ambiguity in Legal Draftsmanship. *Drake Law Review*, 20(1), 137–158.

Dworkin, Ronald (1975). Hard Cases. *Harvard Law Review*, 88(6), 1057–1109.

Dyevre, Arthur (2016). Domestic Judicial Defiance in the European Union: A Systemic Threat to the Authority of EU Law? *Yearbook of European Law*, 35(1), 106–144.

Edenharter, Andrea (2018). Fundamental Rights Protection in the EU: The ECJ's Difficult Mission to Strike a Balance between Uniformity and Diversity. *Italian Journal of Public Law*, 10(2), 390–420.

Edmonds, Philip & Hirst, Graeme (2002). Near-Synonymy and Lexical Choice. *Computational Linguistics*, 28(2), 105–144.

Eeckhout, Piet (2002). The EU Charter of Fundamental Rights and the Federal Question. *Common Market Law Review*, 39, 945–994.

Eeckhout, Piet (2015). Opinion 2/13 on EU Accession to the ECHR and Judicial Dialogue: Autonomy or Autarky? *Fordham International Law Journal*, 38, 955–992.

Eijken, Hanneke van & Phoa, Pauline (2018). The Scope of Article 20 TFEU Clarified in Chavez Vilchez: Are the Fundamental Rights of Minor EU Citizens Coming of Age? *European Law Review*, 43(6), 949–970.

Eleftheriadis, Pavlos (2010). Pluralism and Integrity. *Ratio Juris*, 20(3), 365–389.

Eletheriadis, Pavlos (2014). The Content of European Citizenship. *German Law Journal*, 15(5), 777–796.

Enchelmaier, Stefan (2003). The Awkward Selling of a Good Idea, or: for a Traditionalist Interpretation of *Keck*. *Yearbook of European Law*, 22(1), 249–322.

Engberg, Jan (2016). Autonomous EU Concepts: Fact or Fiction? In Šarčević (Ed.), *Language and Culture in EU Law: Multidisciplinary Perspectiv*es (pp. 169–182). London and New York: Routledge.

Everson, Michelle (2014). A Citizenship in Movement. *German Law Journal*, 15(5), 965–983.

Fast, Jakub (2005). Structurally Underspecified Semantics for Distributive Plural Predication: Respectively Constructions in Lexical Resource Semantics. In Blaho, Schoorlemmer, & Vicente (Eds.), *Proceedings of ConSOLE XIII* (pp. 17–38). Leiden: Leiden University Centre for Linguistics.

Feiman, Roman & Snedeker, Jesse (2016). The Logic in Language. How All Quantifiers are Alike, but Each Quantifier is Different. *Cognitive psychology*, 87, 29–52. DOI: 10.1016/j.cogpsych.2016.04.002.

Fontanelli, Filippo (2014). Implementation of EU Law Through Domestic Measures After Fransson: the Court of Justice Buys Time and "Non-preclusion" Troubles Loom. *European Law Review*, 39(5), 682–700.

Friedbacher, Todd J. (1996). Motive Unmasked: The European Court of Justice, the Free Movement of Goods, and the Search for Legitimacy. *European Law Journal*, 2(3), 226–250.

Gambaro, Antonio (2012). Legislative Multilingualism and Comparative Law: A European Perspective. *Uniform Law Review: Rev. dr. unif.*, 17(3), 407–411.

Gardner, Stephen (2009). *Meaning and Interchangeability*. Thesis for PhD Degree in Philosophy. Department of Philosophy, Faculty of Arts, University of Ottawa.

Gawron, Jean Mark & Kehler, Andrew (2002). The Semantics of the Adjective Respective. In Mikkelsen & Potts (Eds.), *WCCFL 21 Proceedings* (pp. 85–98). Somerville, MA: Cascadilla Press.

Gillon, Brendan S. (1987). The Readings of Plural Noun Phrases in English. *Linguistics and Philosophy*, 10, 199–219.

Gillon, Brendan S. (1990a). Ambiguity, Generality, and Indeterminacy: Tests and Definitions. *Synthese*, 85, 391–416.

Gillon, Brendan S. (1990b). Plural Noun Phrases and Their Readings: A Reply to Lasersohn. *Linguistics and Philosophy*, 13, 477–485.

Gillon, Brendan S. (1992). Towards a Common Semantics for English Count and Mass Nouns. *Linguistics and Philosophy*, 15 (6), 597–639. DOI: 10.1007/BF00628112.

Gillon, Brendan S. (1996). Collectivity and Distributivity Internal to English Noun Phrases. *Language Sciences*, 18(1–2), 443–468.

Gormley, Laurence W. (2012). Free Movement of Goods and EU Legislation in the Court of Justice (pp. 49–61). In Syrpis (Ed.), *The Judiciary, the Legislature and the EU Internal Market*. Cambridge: Cambridge University Press.

Grimmel, Andreas (2012). Judicial Interpretation or Judicial Activism? The Legacy of Rationalism in the Studies of the European Court of Justice. *European Law Journal*, 18(4), 518–535.

Grimmel, Andreas (2014). 'This is Not Life as It is Lived Here': The Court of Justice of the EU and the Myth of Judicial Activism in the Foundational Period of Integration Through Law. *European Journal of Legal Studies*, 7(2), 61–83.

Guðmundsdóttir, Dora (2015). A Renewed Emphasis on the Charter's Distinction between Rights and Principles: Is a Doctrine of Judicial Restraint More Appropriate? *Common Market Law Review*, 52, 685–720.

Hancox, Emily (2013). The Meaning of "Implementing" EU law under Article 51(1) of the Charter: Åkerberg Fransson. *Common Market Law Review*, 50, 1411–1432.

Hanf, Dominik (2011). Reverse Discrimination in EU Law: Constitutional Aberration, Constitutional Necessity or Judicial Choice, *Maastricht Journal of European and Comparative Law*, 18, 29–61.

Hartley, Trevor C. (1996). Five Forms of Uncertainty in European Community Law. *The Cambridge Law Journal*, 55(2), 265–288.

Horsley, Thomas (2012). Unearthing Buried Treasure: Art. 34 TFEU and the Exclusionary Rules. *European Law Review*, 37(6), 734–757.

Horsley, Thomas (2013). Reflections on the Role of the Court of Justice as the "Motor" of European Integration: Legal Limits to Judicial Lawmaking. *Common Market Law Review*, 50, 931–964.

Itzcovich, Giulio (2012). Legal Order, Legal Pluralism, Fundamental Principles. Europe and Its Law in Three Concepts. *European Law Journal*, 18(3), 358–384. DOI: 10.1111/j.1468-0386.2012.00604.x.

Itzcovich, Giulio (2017). The European Court of Justice. In Jakab, A., A. Dyevre, & G. Itzcovich (Eds.), *Comparative Constitutional Reasoning* (pp. 277–322). Cambridge: Cambridge University Press. doi:10.1017/9781316084281

Jacobs, Francis G. (2010). Wachauf and the Protection of Fundamental Rights in EC Law. In Maduro & Azoulai (Eds.), *The Past and Future of EU Law: The Classics of EU Law Revisited on the 50th Anniversary of the Rome Treaty* (pp. 133–139). Oxford and Portland: Hart Publishing.

Kartalova, Sofiya (2018). The Strategic Value of Ambiguity in Divergent Terms used Interchangeably in the CJEU's Preliminary Rulings. University of Copenhagen. http://dx.doi.org/10.2139/ssrn.3214463.

Kay, Paul (1989). Contextual Operators Respective, Respectively and vice versa. In Hall, Meacham, & Shapiro (Eds.), *General Session and Parasession on Theoretical Issues in Language Reconstruction: Proceedings of the Fifteenth Annual Meeting of the Berkeley Linguistics Society* (pp. 181–193). Berkley: Berkeley Linguistics Society.

Kelemen, R. Daniel (2018). The Court of Justice of the European Union: Changing Authority in the Twenty-First Century. In Alter, Helfer & Rask Madsen (Eds.), *International Court Authority* (pp. 221–242). Oxford: Oxford University Press.

Kennedy, Christopher (2011). Ambiguity and Vagueness. In Maienborn, von Heusinger, & Portner (Eds.), *Semantics* (pp. 507–535). DeGruyter.

Kjær, Anne Lise (2007). Legal Translation in the European Union: A Research Field in Need of a New Approach. In Kredens & Gozdz- Roszkowski (Eds.), *Language and the Law: International Outlooks* (pp. 69–96). Peter Lang: Internationaler Verlag der Wissenschaften.

Kjær, Anne Lise (2010). Nonsense: The CILFIT Criteria Revisited: From the Perspective of Legal Linguistics. In Koch, Hagel-Sørensen, Haltern & Weiler (Eds.), *Europe: The New Legal Realism: Essays in Honour of Hjalte Rasmussen* (pp. 297–316). København: DjøF/Jurist –Økonomforbundet.

Kjær, Anne Lise (2016). Theoretical Aspects of Legal Translation in the EU: The Paradoxical Relationship between Language, Translation and the Autonomy of EU Law. In Šarčević (Ed.), *Language and Culture in EU Law: Multidisciplinary Perspectives* (pp.91–108). London and New York: Routledge.

Klepousniotou, Ekaterini (2002). The Processing of Lexical Ambiguity: Homonymy and Polysemy in the Mental Lexicon. *Brain and Language*, 81, 205–223.

Knape, J. & Becker, N. & Böhme (2009). Strategie. In Uedig, Gert (Ed.), *Historisches Wörterbuch der Rhetorik* (pp. 152–172). Tübingen: Max Niemeyer Verlag.

Kochenov, Dimitry (2011). A Real European Citizenship: A New Jurisdiction Test: A Novel Chapter in the Development of the Union in Europe. *Columbia Journal of European Law*, 18, 55–109.

Kochenov, Dimitry (2013a). The Right to Have *What* Rights? EU Citizenship in Need of Clarification. *European Law Journal*, 19(4), 502–516.

Kochenov, Dimitry (2013b). The Essence of EU Citizenship Emerging from the Last Ten Years of Academic Debate: Beyond the Cherry Blossoms and the Moon. *International and Comparative Law Quarterly*, 62, 97–136.

Kochenov, Dimitry & Plender, Richard (2012). EU Citizenship: From an Incipient Form to an Incipient Substance? The Discovery of the Treaty Text. *European Law Review*, 37(4), 369–396.

Korenica, Fisnik & Doli, Dren (2016). No More Unconditional "Mutual Trust" Between the Member States: an Analysis of the Landmark Decision of the CJEU in *Aranyosi and Căldăraru*. *European Human Rights Law Review*, 5, 542–555.

Koutrakos, Panos (2001). On Groceries, Alcohol and Olive Oil: More on Free Movement of Goods after *Keck*. *European Law Review*, 26(4), 391–407.

Krommendijk, Jasper (2017). Wide Open and Unguarded Stand our Gates: The CJEU and References for a Preliminary Ruling in Purely Internal Situations. *German Law Journal*, 18(6), 1359–1394.

Kühn, Zdeněk (2010). *Wachauf* and *ERT*: On the Road from the Centralised to the Decentralised System of Judicial Review. In Maduro & Azoulai (Eds.), *The Past and Future of EU Law: The Classics of EU Law Revisited on the 50th Anniversary of the Rome Treaty* (pp. 151–161). Oxford and Portland: Hart Publishing.

Kulick, Andreas (2016). From Problem to Opportunity: An Analytical Framework for Vagueness and Ambiguity in International Law, *German Yearbook of International Law*, 59, 257–288.

Kuner, Christopher B. (1991). The Interpretation of Multilingual Treaties: Comparison of Texts Versus the Presumption of Similar Meaning. *International and Comparative Law Quarterly*, 40, 953–964.

Kuo, Ming-Sung (2013). Discovering Sovereignty in Dialogue: Is Judicial Dialogue the Answer to Constitutional Conflict in the Pluralist Legal Landscape? *Canadian Journal of Law and Jurisprudence*, XXVI(2), 341–376.

Lanius, David (2019). *Strategic Indeterminacy in the Law*. New York: Oxford University Press.

Lansbergen, Anja & Miller, Nina (2011). European Citizenship Rights in Internal Situations: An Ambiguous Revolution? (Case Note on Case C-34/09 Gerardo Ruiz Zambrano v. Office national de l'emploi (ONEM)). *European Constitutional Law Review*, 7, 287–307. DOI:10.1017/S 1574019611200087.

Larsson, Olof & Naurin, Daniel (2016). Judicial Independence and Political Uncertainty: How the Risk of Override Affects the Court of Justice of the EU. *International Organization*, 70, 377–408.

Lasersohn, Peter (1989). On the Readings of Plural Noun Phrases. *Linguistic Inquiry*, 20(1), 130–134.

Lasersohn, Peter (1995). *Plurality, Conjunction and Events*. Studies in Linguistics and Philosophy (Vol. 55). Dordrecht, Boston, London: Kluwer Academic Publishers.

Leczykiewicz, Dorota (2008). Why Do the European Court of Justice Judges Need Legal Concepts? *European Law Journal*, 14(6), 773–786. DOI: 10.1111/j.1468-0386.2008.00438.x.

Lenaerts, Koen (2012). Exploring the Limits of the EU Charter of Fundamental Rights. *European Constitutional Law Review*, 8, 375–403. DOI: https://doi.org/10.1017/S1574019612000260.

Lenaerts, Koen (2015). EU Citizenship and the European Court of Justice's 'Stone-by-Stone' Approach. *International Comparative Jurisprudence*, 1, 1–10.

Lenaerts, Koen (2019). The Court of Justice of the European Union as the Guardian of the Authority of EU Law: A Networking Exercise. In Heusel, Wolfgang & Jean-Philippe Rageade (Eds.), *The Authority of EU Law: Do We Still Believe in It?* (pp. 21–32). Berlin: Springer.

Leonard, Henry S. (1967). Synonymy and Systematic Definitions. *The Monist*, 15(1), 33–68.

Lianos, Ioannis (2010). Shifting Narratives in the European Internal Market: Efficient Restrictions of Trade and the Nature of "Economic" Integration. *European Business Law Review*, 21(5), 705–759.

Lianos, Ioannis (2015). In Memoriam Keck: the Reformation of EU Law on the Free Movement of Goods. *European Law Review*, 40(2), 225–248.

Liisberg, Jonas Bering (2001). Does the EU Charter of Fundamental Rights Threaten the Supremacy of Community Law? *Common Market Law Review*, 38, 1171–1199.

Link, Goderhard (2002). The Logical Analysis of Plurals and Mass Terms: A Lattice-theoretical Framework. In: Portner, Paul & Partee, Barbara H. (Eds.), *Formal Semantics: The Essential Readings* (pp. 127–146). Blackwell Publishers. DOI:10.1002/9780470758335.

Linderfalk, Ulf (2007). *On The Interpretation of International Treaties: The Modern International Law as Expressed in the 1969 Vienna Convention on the Law of Treaties.* Dordrecht: Springer.

Lossius Falkum, Ingrid & Vicente, Agustin (2015). Polysemy: Current Perspectives and Approaches (Editorial). *Lingua*, 157, 1–16.

Maas, Willem (2014). The Origins, Evolution, and Political Objectives of EU Citizenship. *German Law Journal*, 15(5), 797–819.

MacDonald, Maryellen C., Pearlmutter, Neal J., & Seidenberg, Marc S. (1994). Lexical Nature of Syntactic Ambiguity Resolution. *Psychological Review*, 101(4), 676–703.

Maduro, Miguel P. (2007). Interpreting European Law: Judicial Adjudication in a Context of Constitutional Pluralism. *European Journal of Legal Studies*, 1(2), 137–152.

Mańko, Rafał (2016). Multilingualism, Divergent Authentic Versions of a Legal Rule and Legitimate Expectations of Individuals. *Studies in Logic, Grammar and Rhetoric*, 45(58), 141–159.

Martinico, Giuseppe (2015). The "Polemical" Spirit of European Constitutional Law: On the Importance of Conflicts in EU Law. *German Law Journal*, 16(6), 1343–1374.

Masing, Johannes (2016). Unity and Diversity of European Fundamental Rights Protection, *European Law Review*, 41(4), 490–512.

McAuliffe, Karen (2011). Hybrid Texts and Uniform Law? The Multilingual Case Law of the Court of Justice of the European Union. *International Journal for the Semiotics of Law*, 24, 97–115.

McAuliffe, Karen (2014). Translating Ambiguity. *Journal of Comparative Law*, 9(2), 65–87.

Moltmann, Friederike (1997). *Parts and Wholes in Semantics.* Oxford: Oxford University Press.

Moltmann, Friederike (2005). Part Structures in Situations: The Semantics of Individual and Whole. *Linguistics and Philosophy*, 28(5), 599–641. DOI: 10.1007/s10988-005-2142-2.

Montaldo, Stefano (2016). On a Collision Course! Mutual Recognition, Mutual Trust and the Protection of Fundamental Rights in the Recent Case-Law of the Court of Justice. *European Papers*, 1(3), 965–996.

Nerlich, Brigitte & Clarke, David D. (2003). Polysemy and flexibility: introduction and overview. In Nerlich et al. (Eds.), *Polysemy* (pp. 3–30). Trends in Linguistic Studies and Mongraphs 142. Berlin, New York: Mouton de Gruyter.

Nettesheim, Martin (2021). Rang des Unionsrechts. In Oppermann, Classen & Nettesheim (Eds.), *Europarecht* (pp. 154–169). C.H. Beck.

Nic Shuibhne, Niamh (2010). The Resilience of EU Market Citizenship. *Common Market Law Review*, 47, 1597–1628.

Nic Shuibhne, Niamh (2012). Case C-434/09, *Shirley McCarthy v. Secretary of State for the Home Department*, Judgment of the Court of Justice (Third Chamber) of 5 May 2011, Case C-256/11, *Dereci and others v. Bundesministerium für Inneres*, Judgment of the Court of Justice (Grand Chamber) of 15 November 2011: (Some of) The Kids Are All Right. *Common Market Law Review*, 49, 349–380

Nic Shuibhne, Niamh (2015). Limits Rising, Duties Ascending: The Changing Legal Shape of Union Citizenship. *Common Market Law Review*, 52(4), 889–937.

Nowak, Janek T. (2011). Case C-34/09, Gerardo Ruiz Zambrano v. Office National de L'Emploi (ONEM) & Case C-434/09, Shirley McCarthy v. Secretary of State for the Home Department (Case Note). *Columbia Journal of European Law*, 17, 673–704.

Nyikos, Stacy A. (2006). Strategic Interaction among Courts within the Preliminary Reference Process – Stage 1: National Court Preemptive Opinions. *European Journal of Political Research*, 45, 527–550.

Okada, Sadayuki (1999). On the Function and Distribution of the Modifiers *Respective* and *Respectively*. *Linguistics*, 37(5), 871–903. DOI:https://doi.org/10.1515/ling.37.5.871.

O'Leary, Siofra (2012). The Past, Present and Future of the Purely Internal Rule in EU Law. In Spaventa, Nic Shuibhne, & Dougan (Eds.), *Empowerment and Disempowerment of the European Citizen* (pp. 37–72). Oxford: Hart Publishing.

Ossa-Richardson, Anthony (2019). *A History of Ambiguity.* Princeton: Princeton University Press.

Ostropolski, Tomasz (2015). The CJEU as a Defender of Mutual Trust (Opinion). *New Journal of European Criminal Law*, 6(2), 166–178. DOI: https://doi.org/10.1177/203228441500600202.

Pagin, Peter (2001). A Quinean Definition of Synonymity. *Erkenntnis*, 55, 7–32.

Paris, Davide (2018). Limiting the Counter-Limits. National Constitutional Courts and the Scope of the Primacy of EU Law. *Italian Journal of Public Law*, 10(2), 205–225.

Paunio, Elina (2013). *Legal Certainty in Multilingual EU Law: Language, Discourse and Reasoning at the European Court of Justice.* Farnham: Ashgate.

Paunio, Elina & Lindroos-Hovinheimo, Susanna (2010). Taking Language Seriously: An Analysis of Linguistic Reasoning and Its Implications in EU Law. *European Law Journal*, 16(4), 395–416.

Peers, Steve (2012). The Opt-out that Fell to Earth: The British and Polish Protocol Concerning the EU Charter of Fundamental Rights. *Human Rights Law Review*, 12(2), 375–389.

Penot, Anastasia Iliopoulou (2012). The Transnational Character of Union Citizenship. In Spaventa, Nic Shuibhne, & Dougan (Eds.), *Empowerment and Disempowerment of the European Citizen* (pp. 15–36). Oxford: Hart Publishing.

Piantadosi, Steven T. & Tily, Harry & Gibson, Edward (2012). The Communicative Function of Ambiguity in Language. *Cognition*, 122, 280–291.

Pickering, Martin J., Garrod, Simon (2004). Towards a mechanistic psychology of dialogue. *Behavioral and Brain Sciences*, 27, 169–226.

Pliakos, Asteris & Anagnostaras, Georgios (2015). Fundamental Rights and the New Battle Over Legal and Judicial Supremacy: Lessons from *Melloni*. *Yearbook of European Law*, 34(1), 97–126.

Pollicino, Oreste (2004). Legal Reasoning of the Court of Justice in the Context of the Principle of Equality Between Judicial Activism and Self-restraint. *German Law Journal*, 5(3), 283–317.

Poscher, Ralph (2012). Ambiguity and Vagueness in Legal Interpretation. In Tiersma & Solan (Eds.), *The Oxford Handbook of Language and Law* (pp. 129–144). New York: Oxford University Press.

Poscher, Ralph (2017). The Common Error in Theories of Adjudication: An Inferentialist Argument for a Doctrinal Conception. In Giltrow & Stein (Eds.), *The Pragmatic Turn in Law: Inference and Interpretation in Legal Discourse* (pp. 307–334). Boston: De Gruyter Mouton.

Pozzo, Barbara (2016). Comparative Law and the New Frontiers of Legal Translation. In Šarčević (Ed.), *Language and Culture in EU Law: Multidisciplinary Perspectives* (pp. 73–87). London and New York: Routledge.

Raucea, Chiara (2013). Fundamental Rights: The Missing Pieces of European Citizenship? *German Law Journal*, 14(10), 2021–2040.

Rauchegger, Clara (2015). The Interplay Between the Charter and National Constitutions after *Ackerberg Fransson* and *Melloni*: Has the CJEU Embraced the Challenges of Multilevel Fundamental Rights Protection? In De Vries, Bernitz, & Weatherhill (Eds.), *The EU Charter of Fundamental Rights as a Binding Instrument: Five Years Old and Growing* (pp. 93–131). Oxford and Portland: Hart Publishing.

Rauchegger, Clara (2018). National Constitutional Rights and the Primacy of EU Law: M.A.S. *Constitutional Market Law Review*, 55, 1521–1548.

Reestman, Jan-Herman & Besselink, Leonard (2013). After *Åkerberg Fransson* and *Melloni* (Editorial). *European Constitutional Law Review*, 9, 169–175. DOI: 10.1017/S1574019612001095.

Robertson, Colin D. (2016). *Multilingual Law: A Framework for Analysis and Understanding*. London and New York: Routledge.

Rodriguez-Izquierdo Serrano, Miryam (2015). The Spanish Constitutional Court and Fundamental Rights Adjudication after the First Preliminary Reference. *German Law Journal*, 16(6), 1509–1528.

Rosas, Allen (2008). The European Court of Justice in Context: Forms and Patterns of Judicial Dialogue. *European Journal of Legal Studies*, 1(2), 121–136.

Šadl, Urška (2013). Case - Case-Law - Law: Ruiz Zambrano as an Illustration of How the Court of Justice of the European Union Constructs Its Legal Arguments. *European Constitutional Law Review*, 9, 205–229.
Šadl, Urška (2015). What is a Leading Case in EU Law? An Empirical Analysis. *European Law Review*, 40(1), 15–34.
Šadl, Urška & Hink, Sigrid (2014). Precedent in the *Sui Generis* Legal Order: A Mine Run Approach. *European Law Journal*, 20(4), 544–567.
Šadl, Urška & Panagis,Yannis (2015). What is a Leading Case in EU law? An Empirical Analysis. *European Law Review*, 40(1), 15–34.
Saka, Paul (2007). Ambiguity. In *How to Think About Meaning. Philosophical Studies Series*, 109, 155–178. Dordrecht: Springer.
Sánchez, Sara Iglesias (2013). Fundamental Rights Protection for Third Country Nationals and Citizens of the Union. Principles for Enhancing Coherence. *European Journal of Migration and Law*, 15(2), 137–153. DOI: 10.1163/15718166-12342028.
Sánchez, Sara Iglesias (2014). Fundamental Rights and Citizenship of the Union at a Crossroads. A Promising Alliance or a Dangerous Liaison? *European Law Journal*, 20 (4), 464–481. DOI: 10.1111/eulj.12094.
Sánchez, Sara Iglesias (2018). Purely Internal Situations and the Limits of EU Law. A Consolidated Case Law or a Notion to be Abandoned? In *European Constitutional Law Review* 14(1), 7–36. DOI: 10.1017/S1574019618000111.
Šarčević, Susan (1997). *New Approach to Legal Translation*. The Hague, London, Boston: Kluwer Law International.
Sarmiento, Daniel (2012). Half a Case at a Time. Dealing with Judicial Minimalism at the European Court of Justice. In Claes & De Visser et al. (Eds.) *Constitutional Conversations in Europe. Actors, Topics and Procedures* (pp. 13–40). Cambridge: Intersentia.
Sarmiento, Daniel (2013). Who's Afraid of the Charter? The Court of Justice, National Courts and the New Framework of Fundamental Rights Protection in Europe. *Common Market Law Review*, 50, 1267–1304.
Schima, Bernhard (2015). EU Fundamental Rights and Member State Action After Lisbon: Putting the ECJ's Case Law in Its Context. *Fordham International Law Journal*, 38, 1097–1133.
Schwarzschild, Roger (1993). Plurals, Presuppositions and the Sources of Distributivity. *Natural Language Semantics*, 2(3), 201–248.
Schwarzschild, Roger (1996). *Pluralities. Studies in Linguistics and Philosophy*, Vol. 61. Dodrecht: Kluwer Academic Publishers.
Scontras, Gregory & Goodman, Noah D. (2017). Resolving Uncertainty in Plural Predication. *Cognition*, 168, 294–311. DOI: 10.1016/j.cognition.2017.07.002.
Silveira, Alessandra & McKenny Engström, Claudia (2016). The Emerging Culture of EU Citizenship as "Citizenship of Rights" and the Legal Nature of the EU Polity. *UNIO: EU Law Journal*, 2(2), 140–154.
Slocum, Brian G. (2017). Pragmatics and Legal Texts: How Best to Account for the Gaps between Literal Meaning and Communicative Meaning. In Giltrow & Stein (Eds.), *The Pragmatic Turn in Law: Inference and Interpretation in Legal Discourse* (pp. 119–144). Boston: De Gruyter Mouton.
Smith, Tara (2010). Reckless Caution: The Perils of Judicial Minimalism. *New York University Journal of Law & Liberty*, 5, 347–393.

Smolka, Jennifer & Pirker, Benedikt (2016). International Law and Pragmatics: An Account of Interpretation in International Law. *International Journal of Language and Law*, 5, 1–40.

Snell, Jukka (2002). *Goods and Services in EC Law: A Study of the Relationship Between the Freedoms.* New York: Oxford University Press.

Snell, Jukka (2018). Do Fundamental Rights Determine the Scope of EU Law? (Editorial). *European Law Review*, 43(4), 475–476.

Solan, Lawrence M. (2009). The Interpretation of Multilingual Statutes by the European Court of Justice. *Brooklyn Journal of International Law*, 34(2), 277–301.

Solan, Lawrence M. (1993). *The Language of Judges.* Chicago and London: The University of Chicago Press.

Spaventa, Eleanor (2009). Leaving Keck Behind? The Free Movement of Goods after the Rulings in Commission v Italy and Mickelsson and Roos. *European Law Review*, 34(6), 914–932.

Spaventa, Eleanor (2016). *The Interpretation of Article 51 of the EU Charter of Fundamental Rights: The Dilemma of Stricter or Broader Application of the Charter to National Measures, Project Report.* Brussels: European Parliament.

Stasinopoulos, Panos (2011). EU Citizenship as a Battle of the Concepts: Travailleur v Citoyen. *European Journal of Legal Studies*, 4(2), 64–92.

Stein, Dieter (2017). *On Inferencing in Law.* In Giltrow & Stein (Eds.), *The Pragmatic Turn in Law: Inference and Interpretation in Legal Discourse* (pp. 335–368). Boston: De Gruyter Mouton.

Stone Sweet, Alec & Brunell, Thomas (2012). The European Court of Justice, State Noncompliance, and the Politics of Override. *American Political Science Review*, 106(1), 204–213.

Sunstein, Cass R. (2008). Beyond Judicial Minimalism. *Tulsa Law Review*, 43, 825–842.

Taylor, John R. (2003). Cognitive models of polysemy. In Nerlich et al. (Eds.), *Polysemy* (pp. 31–47), Trends in Linguistic Studies and Mongraphs 142. Berlin, New York: Mouton de Gruyter.

Teuber, Marianne L. (1974). Sources of Ambiguity in the Prints of Maurits C. Escher. *Scientific American*, 231(1), 90–105.

Thomas, Jenny A. (2014). *Meaning in Interaction: An Introduction to Pragmatics.* London and New York: Routledge, Taylor & Francis.

Thym, Daniel (2013). Separation versus Fusion – or: How to Accommodate National Autonomy and the Charter? Diverging Versions of the German Constitutional Court and the European Court of Justice. *European Constitutional Law Review*, 9, 391–419.

Torres Perez, Aida (2014). *Melloni* in Three Acts: From Dialogue to Monologue. *European Constitutional Law Review*, 10(2), 308–331. DOI: 10.1017/S1574019614001199.

Torres Perez, Aida (2017). The Federalizing Force of the EU Charter of Fundamental Rights. *I•CON*, 15(4), 1080–1097. DOI: 10.1093/icon/mox075.

Tridimas, Takis (2011). Constitutional review of member state action: The virtues and vices of an incomplete jurisdiction. *ICON*, 9(3–4), 737–756. DOI: 10.1093/icon/mor052.

Tridimas, Takis (2015). The ECJ and the National Courts: Dialogue, Cooperation and Instability. In Arnull & Chalmers (Eds.), *The Oxford Handbook of European Union Law.* Oxford: Oxford University Press.

Tryfonidou, Alina (2007). Was *Keck* a Half-Baked Solution After All? *Legal Issues of Economic Integration*, 34(2), 167–182.
Tuggy, David (1993). Ambiguity, Polysemy and Vagueness. *Cognitive Linguistics*, 4(3), 273–290.
Van Bockel, Bas & Wattel, Peter (2013). New Wine into Old Wineskins: The Scope of the Charter of Fundamental Rights of the EU after Åkerberg Fransson. *European Law Review*, 38, 866–883.
Van der Woude, Marc (1990). The Limits of Free Circulation: The Torfaen Borough Council Case. *Leiden Journal of International Law*, 3(2), 57–63.
Van Elsuwege, Peter & Kochenov, Dimitry (2011). On the Limits of Judicial Intervention: EU Citizenship and Family Reunification Rights. *European Journal of Migration and Law*, 13, 443–466.
Vismara, Fabrizio (2006). The Role of the Court of Justice of the European Communities in the Interpretation of Multilingual Texts. In Pozzo & Jacometti (Eds.), *Multilingualism and the Harmonisation of European Law* (pp. 61–77). The Netherlands: Kluwer Law International.
Von Danwitz, Thomas & Paraschas, Katherina (2012). Fresh Start for the Charter: Fundamental Questions on the Application of the European Charter of Fundamental Rights. *Fordham International Law Journal*, 35, 1396–1425.
Von Papp, Konstanze (2018). A Federal Question Doctrine for EU Fundamental Rights Law: Making Sense of Articles 51 and 53 of the Charter of Fundamental Rights. *European Law Review*, 43(4), 511–533.
Voßkuhle, Andreas (2010). Multilevel Cooperation of the European Constitutional Courts Der Europäische Verfassungsgerichtsverbund. *European Constitutional Law Review*, 6, 175–198.
Walker, Neil (2005). Legal Theory and the European Union: A 25th Anniversary Essay. *Oxford Journal of Legal Studies*, 25(4), 581–601.
Wasow, Thomas (2015). Ambiguity Avoidance is Overrated. In Winkler (Ed.), *Ambiguity: Language and Communication* (pp. 29–47). Berlin/Boston: De Gruyter Mouton.
Weatherill, Stephen (1996). After *Keck*: Some Thoughts on How to Clarify the Clarification. *Common Market Law Review*, 33, 885–906.
Weatherill, Stephen (2017). The Several Internal Markets. *Yearbook of European Law*, 36(1), 125–178. doi:10.1093/yel/yex007.
Weiler, Joseph H. H. (2019). The Authority of EU Law: Do We Still Believe in It? In Heusel, Wolfgang & Jean-Philippe Rageade (Eds.), *The Authority of EU Law: Do We Still Believe in It?* (pp. 3–20). Berlin: Springer.
Weiler, Paul (2010). *Legal Values and Judicial Decision-making. Canadian Bar Review*, 48(1), 1–46.
Wenneras, Pal & Moen, Ketil Boe (2010). Selling Arrangements, Keeping Keck. *European Law Review*, 35(3), 387–400.
Widmann, Anne-Marieke (2002). Article 53: Undermining the Impact of the Charter of Fundamental Rights. *Columbia Journal of European Law*, 8, 342–358.
Wiesbrock, Anja (2012). Granting Citizenship-related Rights to Third-Country Nationals. An Alternative to the Full Extension of European Union Citizenship? *European Journal of Migration and Law*, 14(1), 63–94. DOI: 10.1163/157181612X628282.
Winkler, Susanne (2015). Exploring Ambiguity and the Ambiguity Model from a Transdisciplinary Perspective. In Winkler (Ed.), *Ambiguity: Language and Communication* (pp. 1–25). Berlin/Boston: De Gruyter Mouton.

Winter, Yoad (2002). Atoms and Sets: A Characterization of Semantic Number. *Linguistic Inquiry*, 33(3), 493–505.

Winter-Froemel, Esme & Zirker, Angelika (2015). Ambiguity in Speaker-Hearer Interaction: A Parameter-Based Model of Analysis. In Winkler (Ed.), *Ambiguity: Language and Communication* (pp. 283–339). Berlin/Boston: De Gruyter Mouton.

Xanthopoulou, Ermioni (2018). Mutual Trust and Rights in EU Criminal and Asylum Law: Three Phases of Evolution and the Unchartered Territory Beyond Blind Trust. *Common Market Law Review*, 55, 489–510.

Preliminary rulings of the CJEU: chronological order

Judgment of 15 July 1964, *Flaminio Costa v E.N.E.L.*, Case 6/64, ECLI:EU:C:1964:66.

Judgment of 12 November 1969, *Erich Stauder v City of Ulm*, Case 29–69, ECLI:EU:C:1969:57.

Judgment of the Court of 17 December 1970, *Internationale Handelsgesellschaft mbH v Einfuhr- und Vorratsstelle für Getreide und Futtermitte*, Case 11–70, ECLI:EU:C:1970:114.

Judgment of the Court of 11 July 1974, *Procureur du Roi v Benoît and Gustave Dassonville*, Case 8–74. ECLI:EU:C:1974:82.

Judgment of the Court of 20 February 1979, *Rewe-Zentral AG v Bundesmonopolverwaltung für Branntwein* („Cassis de Dijon“), Case 120/78. ECLI:EU:C:1979:42.

Judgment of 28 March 1979, *The Queen v Vera Ann Saunders*, Case 175/78, ECLI:EU:C:1979:88.

Judgment of 14 July 1981, *Summary proceedings agains Sergius Oebel.* Case 155/80, ECLI:EU:C:1981:177.

Judgment of 6 October 1982, *Srl CILFIT and Lanificio di Gavardo SpA v Ministry of Health*, Case 283/81, ECLI:EU:C:1982:335.

Judgment of 15 December 1982, *Criminal proceedings against Oosthoek's Uitgeversmaatschappij BV*, Case 286/81, ECLI:EU:C:1982:438.

Judgment of 7 February 1984, *Duphar BV and others v The Netherlands State*, Case 238/82, ECLI:EU:C:1984:45.

Judgment of 22 March 1984, *Michael Paterson and others v W. Weddel & Company Limited and others*, Case 90/83, ECLI:EU:C:1984:123.

Judgment of 18 June 1984, *Hans Moser v Land Baden-Württemberg*, Case 180/83, ECLI:EU:C:1984:233.

Judgment of 11 July 1985, *Cinéthèque SA and others v Fédération nationale des cinémas français*, Joined cases 60 and 61/84. ECLI:EU:C:1985:329.

Judgment of 23 April 1986, Parti *écologiste "Les Verts" v European Parliament*, Case 294/83, ECLI:EU:C:1986:166.

Judgment of 18 November 1989, *Torfaen Borough Council v B & Q plc.*, Case C-145/88, ECLI:EU:C:1989:593.

Judgment of 23 November 1989, *Hubert Wachauf v Bundesamt für Ernährung und Forstwirtschaft*, Case 5/88, ECLI:EU:C:1989:321.

Judgment of 27 March 1990, *Milk Marketing Board of England and Wales v Cricket St. Thomas Estate*, Case C-372/88, ECLI:EU:C:1990:140.

Judgment of 28 February 1991, *Criminal proceedings against André Marchandise & Others*, Case C-332/89, ECLI:EU:C:1991:94.

Judgment of 28 February 1991, *Union départementale des syndicats CGT de l'Aisne v SIDEF Conforama, Société Arts et Meubles and Société Jima*, Case C-312/89, ECLI:EU:C:1991:93.

Judgment of 18 June 1991, *Elliniki Radiophonia Tiléorassi AE and Panellinia Omospondia Syllogon Prossopikou v Dimotiki Etairia Pliroforissis and Sotirios Kouvelas and Nicolaos Avdellas and others*, Case C-260/89, ECLI:EU:C:1991:254.

Judgment of 7 July 1992, *Mario Vicente Micheletti and others v Delegación del Gobierno en Cantabria*, Case C-369/90, ECLI:EU:C:1992:295.

Judgment of 16 December 1992, *Council of the City of Stoke-on-Trent and Norwich City Council v B & Q plc.*, Case C-169/91, ECLI:EU:C:1992:519.

Judgment of 24 November 1993, *Criminal proceedings against Bernard Keck and Daniel Mithouard*, Joined cases C-267/91 and C-268/91. ECLI:EU:C:1993:905.

Judgment of 15 December 1993, *Ruth Hünermund and others v Landesapothekerkammer Baden-Württemberg*, Case C-292/92, ECLI:EU:C:1993:863.

Judgment of 9 February 1995, *Société d'Importation Edouard Leclerc-Siplec v TF1 Publicité SA and M6 Publicité SA*, Case C-412/93, ECLI:EU:C:1995:26.

Judgment of 15 December 1995, *Union royale belge des sociétés de football association ASBL v Jean-Marc Bosman, Royal club liégeois SA v Jean-Marc Bosman and others and Union des associations européennes de football (UEFA) v Jean-Marc Bosman*, Case C-415/93, ECLI:EU:C:1995:463.

Judgment of 27 May 1997, *Friedrich Kremzow v Republik Österreich*, Case C-299/95, ECLI:EU:C:1997:254.

Judgment of 9 July 1997, *Konsumentombudsmannen (KO) v De Agostini (Svenska) Förlag AB (C-34/95) and TV-Shop i Sverige AB (C-35/95 and C-36/95)*, Joined cases C-34/95, C-35/95 and C-36/95, ECLI:EU:C:1997:344.

Judgment of 13 October 1997, *Criminal proceedings against Harry Franzén*, Case C-189/95, ECLI:EU:C:1997:504.

Judgment of 18 December 1997, *Daniele Annibaldi v Sindaco del Comune di Guidonia and Presidente Regione Lazio*, Case C-309/96, ECLI:EU:C:1997:631.

Judgment of 2 April 1998, *The Queen v Commissioners of Customs & Excise, ex parte EMU Tabac*, Case C-296/95, ECLI:EU:C:1998:152.

Judgment of 13 January 2000, *Schutzverband gegen unlauteren Wettbewerb v TK-Heimdienst Sass GmbH*, Case C-254/98, ECLI:EU:C:2000:12.

Judgment of 27 January 2000, *Volker Graf v Filzmoser Maschinenbau GmbH*, Case C-190/98, ECLI:EU:C:2000:49.

Judgment of 13 April 2000, *Jyri Lehtonen and Castors Canada Dry Namur-Braine ASBL v Fédération royale belge des sociétés de basket-ball ASBL (FRBSB)*, Case C-176/96, ECLI:EU:C:2000:201.

Judgment of 8 March 2001, *Konsumentombudsmannen (KO) v Gourmet International Products AB (GIP)*, Case C-405/98, ECLI:EU:C:2001:135.

Judgment of 20 September 2001, *Rudy Grzelczyk v Centre public d'aide sociale d'Ottignies-Louvain-la-Neuve*, Case C-184/99, ECLI:EU:C:2001:458.

Judgment of 11 July 2002, *Mary Carpenter v Secretary of State for the Home Department*, Case C-60/00, ECLI:EU:C:2002:434.

Judgment of 17 September 2002, *Baumbast and R v Secretary of State for the Home Department*, Case C-413/99, ECLI:EU:C:2002:493.

Judgment of 2 October 2003, *Carlos Garcia Avello v Belgian State*, Case C-148/02, ECLI:EU:C:2003:539.
Judgment of 11 December 2003, *Deutscher Apothekerverband eV and 0800 DocMorris NV, Jacques Waterval*, Case C-322/01, ECLI:EU:C:2003:664.
Judgment of 25 March 2004, *Herbert Karner Industrie-Auktionen GmbH v Troostwijk GmbH*, Case C-71/02, ECLI:EU:C:2004:181.
Judgment of the Court (Full Court) of 19 October 2004, *Kunqian Catherine Zhu and Man Lavette Chen v Secretary of State for the Home Department*, Case C-200/02, ECLI:EU:C:2004:639.
Judgment of the Court (Grand Chamber) of 15 March 2005, *The Queen, on the application of Dany Bidar v London Borough of Ealing and Secretary of State for Education and Skills*, Case C-209/03, ECLI:EU:C:2005:169.
Judgment of the Court (Grand Chamber) of 25 July 2008, *Blaise Baheten Metock and Others v Minister for Justice, Equality and Law Reform*, Case C-127/08, ECLI:EU:C:2008:449.
Judgment of 4 June 2009, *Åklagaren v Percy Mickelsson and Joakim Roos*, Case C-142/05, ECLI:EU:C:2009:336.
Judgment of the Court (Grand Chamber) of 10 February 2009, *Commission of the European Communities v Italian Republic*, Case C-110/05, ECLI:EU:C:2009:66.
Judgment of the Court (Grand Chamber) of 2 March 2010, *Janko Rottmann v Freistaat Bayern*, Case C-135/08, ECLI:EU:C:2010:104.
Judgment of the Court (Grand Chamber) of 8 September 2010, *Winner Wetten GmBH v Mayor of Bergheim*, Case C-409/06, ECLI:EU:C:2010:503.
Judgment of 2 December 2010, *Ker-Optika bt v ÀNTSZ Dél-dunántúli Regionális Intézete*, Case C-108/09, ECLI:EU:C:2010:725.
Judgment of the Court (Grand Chamber) of 8 March 2011, *Gerardo Ruiz Zambrano v Office national de l'emploi (ONEm)*, Case C-34/09, ECLI:EU:C:2011:124.
Judgment of 5 May 2011, *Shirley McCarthy v Secretary of State for the Home Department* Case C-434/09, ECLI:EU:C:2011:277.
Judgment of the Court (Grand Chamber) of 15 November 2011, *Murat Dereci and Others v Bundesministerium für Inneres* Case C-256/11, ECLI:EU:C:2011:734.
Judgment of the Court (Grand Chamber) of 21 December 2011, *N. S. (C-411/10) v Secretary of State for the Home Department and M. E. and Others (C-493/10) v Refugee Applications Commissioner and Minister for Justice, Equality and Law Reform*, Joined Cases C-411/10 and C-493/10, ECLI:EU:C:2011:865.
Judgment of the Court (Grand Chamber) of 29 January 2013, *Proceedings relating to the execution of European arrest warrants issued agains Ciprian Vasile Radu*, Case C-396/11ECLI:EU:C:2013:39.
Judgment of the Court (Grand Chamber) of 26 February 2013, *Åklagaren v Hans Åkerberg Fransson*, Case C-617/10, ECLI:EU:C:2013:105.
Judgment of the Court (Grand Chamber) of 26 February 2013, *Stefano Melloni v. Ministerio Fiscal*, Case C-399/11, ECLI:EU:C:2013:107.
Judgment of 30 May 2013, *Jeremy F. v Premier minister, Case C168/13 PPU*, ECLI:EU:C:2013:358.
Judgment of 6 March 2014, *Cruciano Siragusa v Regione Sicilia – Soprintendenza Beni Culturali e Ambientali di Palerm*, Case C206/13, ECLI:EU:C:2014:126.
Judgment of 27 March 2014, *Emiliano Torralbo Marcos v Korota SA and Fondo de Garantía Salarial*, Case C265/13, ECLI:EU:C:2014:187.

Judgment of 30 April 2014, Case C390/12, *Robert Pfleger and Others*, ECLI:EU:C:2014:281.

Judgment of 8 May 2014, *Pelckmans Turnhout NV v Walter Van Gastel Balen NV and Others*, Case C483/12, ECLI:EU:C:2014:304.

Judgment of 10 July 2014, *Víctor Manuel Julian Hernández and Others v Reino de España (Subdelegación del Gobierno de España en Alicante) and Others*, Case C –198/13, ECLI:EU:C:2014:2055.

Judgment of the Court (Grand Chamber) of 8 September 2015, *Criminal proceedings against Ivo Taricco and Others*, Case C-105/14, ECLI:EU:C:2015:555.

Judgment of the Court (Grand Chamber) of 5 April 2016, *Pál Aranyosi and Robert Căldăraru v Generalstaatsanwaltschaft Bremen*, Joined Cases C-404/15 and C-659/15 PPU, ECLI:EU:C:2016:198.

Judgment of the Court (Grand Chamber) of 13 September 2016, *Alfredo Rendón Marín v Administración del Estado*, Case C-165/14, ECLI:EU:C:2016:675.

Judgment of the Court (Grand Chamber) of 10 May 2017, *H.C. Chavez-Vilchez and Others v Raad van bestuur van de Sociale verzekeringsbank and Others*, Case C133/15, ECLI:EU:C:2017:354.

Judgment of the Court (Grand Chamber) of 5 December 2017, *Criminal proceedings against M.A.S. and M.B*, Case C-42/17, ECLI:EU:C:2017:936.

Advocate General Opinions: chronological order

Opinion 1/91, *Opinion delivered pursuant to the second subparagraph of Article 228 (1) of the Treaty*, delivered on 14 December 1991. ECR I-6079. ECLI:EU:C:1991:490.

Opinion of Advocate General Van Gerven, *Criminal proceedings against Bernard Keck and Daniel Mithouard* (Joined Cases C-267/91 and C-268/91), *delivered on* 18 November 1992. ECLI:EU:C:1992:448.

Opinion of Advocate General Tesauro, *Ruth Hünermund* and others *v Landesapothekerkammer Baden-Württemberg* (Case C-292/92), delivered on 27 October 1993. ECLI:EU:C:1993:863.

Opinion of Advocate General Jacobs, *Société d'Importation Edouard Leclerc-Siplec v TF1 Publicité SA and M6 Publicité SA* (Case C-412/93), delivered on 24 November 1994. ECLI:EU:C:1994:393.

Opinion of Advocate General Stix-Hackl, *Igor Simutenkov v Ministerio de Educación y Cultura and Real Federación Española de Fútbol* (Case C-265/03), delivered on 11 January 2005. ECLI:EU:C:2005:6.

Opinion of Advocate General Sharpston, Gerardo Ruiz Zambrano v Office national de l'emploi (ONEm) (Case C-34/09), delivered on 30 September 2010. ECLI:EU:C:2010:560.

Opinion 1/09, *Opinion delivered pursuant to Article 218(11) TFEU*, delivered on 8 March 2011. ECR I-1137. ECLI:EU:C:2011:123.

Opinion of AG Cruz Villalón, Åklagaren v Hans Åkerberg Fransson (Case C-617/10), delivered on 12 June 2012. ECLI:EU:C:2012:340.

Opinion of Advocate General Bot, Criminal proceedings against Stefano Melloni (Case C-399/11), delivered on 2 October 2012. ECLI:EU:C:2012:600.

Opinion 2/13, Opinion pursuant to Article 218(11) TFEU, delivered on 18 December 2014. ECLI:EU:C:2014:2454.

Judgments by the German Constitutional Court (Bundesverfassungsgericht): chronological order

BVerfGE 133, 277–377: the *Antiterrordatei* judgment.
BVerfGE 140, 317–376: the *Identitätskontrolle* judgment.

Other documents: chronological order

Explanations Relating to the Charter of Fundamental Rights of 14.12.2007, 2007/C 303/02.

Protocol No. 30 (Protocol on the Application of the Charter of Fundamental Rights of the European Union to Poland and to the United Kingdom) of 17.12.2007, C 306/157.

Joint Practical Guide of the European Parliament, the Council and the Commission for Persons Involved in the Drafting of European Union Legislation (2015). Luxembourg: Publications Office of the European Union. European Parliament/ Council of the European Union/European Commission. doi: 10.2880/5575.

Declaration No. 61 (Declaration by the Republic of Poland on the Charter of Fundamental Rights of the European Union) of 07.06.2016, C 202/358.

Declaration No. 62 (Declaration by the Republic of Poland concerning the Protocol on the application of the Charter of Fundamental Rights of the European Union in relation to Poland and the United Kingdom) of 07.06.2016, C 202/358.

Other sources:

IATE (Interactive Terminology for Europe) database, available at: https://iate .europa.eu/home last accessed: 11.02.2022.

Index

For Product Safety Concerns and Information please contact our EU
representative GPSR@taylorandfrancis.com
Taylor & Francis Verlag GmbH, Kaufingerstraße 24, 80331 München, Germany

www.ingramcontent.com/pod-product-compliance
Ingram Content Group UK Ltd.
Pitfield, Milton Keynes, MK11 3LW, UK
UKHW021308260926
475702UK00048B/863
* 9 7 8 1 0 3 2 2 7 9 9 0 9 *